Jackie Kud

MW01114078

CAMBRIDGE STUDIES IN LINGUISTICS

General Editors: B. COMRIE, C. J. FILLMORE, R. LASS,
D. LIGHTFOOT, J. LYONS, P. H. MATTHEWS, R. POSNER,
S. ROMAINE, N. V. SMITH, N. VINCENT

Relevance relations in discourse

In this series

Supplementary volumes

Earlier titles not listed are also available
* Issued in hard covers and as a paperback

Relevance relations in discourse

A study with special reference to Sissala

REGINA BLASS
Summer Institute of Linguistics

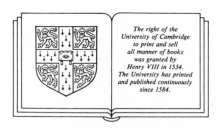

The right of the University of Cambridge to print and sell all manner of books was granted by Henry VIII in 1534. The University has printed and published continuously since 1584.

CAMBRIDGE UNIVERSITY PRESS

CAMBRIDGE

NEW YORK   PORT CHESTER

MELBOURNE   SYDNEY

Published by the Press Syndicate of the University of Cambridge
The Pitt Building, Trumpington Street, Cambridge CB2 1RP
40 West 20th Street, New York, NY 10011, USA
10 Stamford Road, Oakleigh, Melbourne 3166, Australia

© Cambridge University Press 1990

First published 1990

Printed in Great Britain at the University Press, Cambridge

British Library cataloguing in publication data

Blass, Regina
Relevance relations in discourse: a study with special
reference to Sissala. – (Cambridge studies in linguistics, 55)
1. Language. Discourse Analysis
I. Title
415

Library of Congress cataloguing in publication data

Blass, Regina.
Relevance relations in discourse: a study with special reference
to Sissala/Regina Blass.
    p.   cm. – (Cambridge studies in linguistics: 55)
ISBN 0-521-38515-6
1. Discourse analysis.   2. Semantics.   3. Pragmatics.
4. Sissala language – Discourse analysis.
5. Sissala language – Semantics.
I. Title.   II. Series.
P302.B55   1990
401'.41 – dc20   90-1452 CIP

ISBN 0 521 38515 6

CE

To Sara, Abraham, Antie and all the others who shared
with me tô, stories and the stars

Contents

Acknowledgements

Numerous people have contributed in some way to this book. It is not possible to mention them all by name, but I am indebted to all of them.

I would like to thank the Summer Institute of Linguistics (SIL) for making this research possible and I am indebted to my colleagues who have given me my initial training in linguistics, especially in methods of conducting fieldwork.

I am grateful to the staff at University College London, who first introduced me to modern linguistic theories while I was preparing for my MA. I would like to mention especially Geoff Pullum, who first pointed out to me that linguistic fieldwork can be highly relevant to theory development.

During my Ph.D studies it was a special challenge and privilege to work with Deirdre Wilson, whose own theory I have taken as the basis for my research. I would like to express my gratitude for her encouragement, dedication to my field of interest and the many insights I have gained through contact with her. She has given me a completely new understanding of what communication is about and the role natural language plays in it. This new understanding has sparked numerous ideas for further research. I am also grateful for her comments at the manuscript stage of the book.

I would like to thank Neil Smith for advice on various parts of the analysis and his help in preparing my work for publication.

While I was writing the book, some linguists especially influenced my ideas through their own published or unpublished work, through personal communication or through comments on my dissertation. I would like to thank Dora Bieri, Gillian Brown, Kathleen Callow, Annabel Cormack, Joseph Grimes, Austin Hale, Monika Höhlig, Steven Levinsohn, Steven Levinson, Robert Longacre, Tony Naden, Mary Steele, Ursula Wiesemann, Betsy Wrisley and George Yule. I owe special gratitude to Diane Blakemore, Keith Brown, Robyn Carston, Ernst-August Gutt, Ruth Kempson and Dan Sperber.

However, my interest in linguistics as a profession was born not in a classroom but through fascination with natural-language data in Africa itself. My very special thanks go to the Sissala people whose kindness, patience and sense of humour have made linguistic fieldwork easy and enjoyable.

I am indebted to my four informants, Nicolas Tandia, Marc Zalvé, Timotheé Zalvé and Luc Zogdia, who not only answered hundreds of my questions, but who composed a number of the texts used for the thesis and who transcribed and translated a body of 2,000 pages of text.

My gratitude goes to all those who have contributed to the spoken texts – too numerous to mention by name. However, I would like to mention Antie Nadie, who provided many folk stories, riddles and accounts of the history of the Sissala people.

I would also like to mention a few of my colleagues and friends, whose care and encouragement meant a lot to me during the work on the book. I would like to thank John Bendor-Samuel, Leoma Gilley, Eugene Loos, Liz Olsen, Janice Ratcliffe and Joan Rennie.

I would also like to thank Yayaa Bikubi, who freed me from much worry over the practical duties of life in Africa, so that I could keep my nose to the grindstone.

More than anyone else I have to thank God, who gave me the strength, endurance and ability to achieve the goal.

Abbreviations and symbols

Aj	adjective
AH	attention holder
ATR	advanced tongue-root
COMP	complementiser
DEF	definite marker
F	focus
IM	interpretive-use marker
IMP	imperative
INT	intensifier
IPF	imperfective
NEG	negative
Num	numeral
NP	noun phrase
NVC	non-verbal constituent
P	particle
PAST	past
PF	perfective
PL	plural
PP	postpositional phrase
Q	question
S	sentence
SDM	specific discourse marker
SOV	subject–object–verb
SPEC	specific
SVC	serial-verb construction
SVO	subject–verb–object
TDM	typicality discourse marker
VP	verb phrase
∀	universal quantifier
∃	existential quantifier

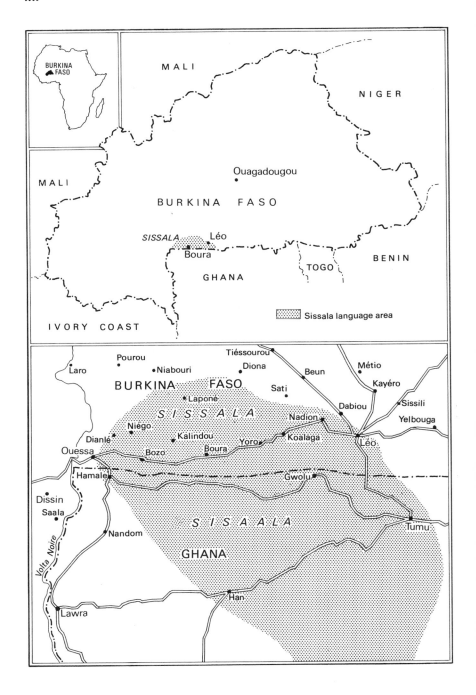

Introduction

The main aim of this book, which developed out of my Ph.D thesis (Blass 1988), is to show how relevance governs discourse.

Although the book makes a contribution to the semantic and pragmatic analysis of a particular unstudied language – Sissala – this is not the only or most important aim of my study. My main intention is to show, using Sperber and Wilson's relevance theory (1986a), that connectivity in discourse is a pragmatic rather than a semantic matter: it results from relevance relations between text and context rather than from relations linguistically encoded in the text.

In the first two chapters, I discuss a variety of approaches to the analysis of discourse, and argue that in the current state of knowledge, relevance theory offers the only possibility of a genuinely explanatory account. In the remainder of the book, I look at a variety of semantic and pragmatic phenomena, and try to show not only that they can be analysed perceptively in terms of relevance theory, but also that their analysis has interesting implications for the theory I have used.

If it is not my main aim to provide a study of some phenomena in Sissala, why did I choose a so-called 'exotic', unanalysed, language rather than English or German (my mother tongue) to make my point? The importance of the book lies primarily in what it has to say about pragmatic theory, and in particular in its demonstration that although there may be enormous variation in cultural backgrounds, the principles by which hearers use contextual information in interpreting utterances in discourse are universally the same. In focusing on an unanalysed, 'exotic' language of a quite different culture this point can be demonstrated very clearly, more clearly than by using English or German examples alone; although in many cases I have given English or German examples too.

My position is in a way idiosyncratic, in that ethnographically minded discourse analysts have not focused on what is universal, but on the diversities of language and discourse arising out of different cultural backgrounds and language-specific idiosyncrasies, while those from the fields of philosophy and psychology have tried to find culture-independent explanations for the way communication works and the part natural language plays in it. It almost seemed that the two approaches to discourse would for ever have to stay apart, disregarding each other's views because of the special nature of the evidence that they took as their domain. I hope that this book provides a step towards a new 'friendship' between ethnographers and others interested in discourse, and will spark fruitful research in the area of semantics and pragmatics by investigating attested data from natural language within a philosophically and psychologically well-grounded framework – the framework of relevance theory.

The Sissala language and culture, and a note on field methods

Sissala, which is spoken in Burkina Faso and Ghana, is a Niger–Congo, Gur (Voltaic) language, of the subgroup Gurunsi. 'Sissala' is the French name, used by governmental offices and the linguists at the University of Ouagadougou. The Sissala people call their language 'Sɪsaalɪ'.

Sissala is spoken by around 10,000 people in the south of Burkina Faso, who live in twenty-six villages near the Ghanaian border and the bigger town Léo (see map, p. xii). A further, and in fact larger, group – around 90,000 – of Sissala speakers is located across the border in Ghana (here the name is usually spelt Sisaala). There are three very diverse dialect groups (as perceived by the Sissala people). The data on which this book is based come exclusively from the village of Boura, the political centre of the Sissala area in Burkina Faso. The dialect is called 'Buuni'.

The first published linguistic notes about the Sissala language which I was able to find – an eighteen-page grammatical outline – were written in 1928 by the German missionary linguist Funke, in German (Funke 1928). Funke apparently did not elicit the data in the Sissala area itself, but states that he obtained his data from Sissalas who were living in Togo. Although the data are definitely from a dialect of Sissala, they are not traceable to any particular dialect spoken there today.

The first linguistic work done in the area itself, in the Tumu dialect of Ghana, was conducted by members of SIL: in 1965 Ron Rowland published field reports on the phonology; research mainly on grammatical aspects was done by Gertrud Sopp, Margrit and Justin Frempong; and on lexicography by myself. Most of this work, except for Rowland's phonology reports and a Sisaala–English, English–Sisaala dictionary, which I edited and published in 1975, is unpublished and can be found in the SIL library in Tamale, Ghana. (Some information about Gur languages, including Sissala/Sisaala, is also to be found in Naden (1989) and in Manessy (1969, vols. 1 and 2; 1979).)

No linguistic work at all had been done on Sissala in Burkina Faso before I started my fieldwork there in 1981. The dialect in Ghana has a cognate similarity of only 50 per cent to the dialect in Burkina Faso, and has major phonological, lexical and grammatical differences from that dialect. Accordingly I had to start the linguistic analysis from scratch. From 1981 to 1983 I wrote a phonological outline in French, on which the orthography used in this book is based, I also analysed the morphology and the syntax to some extent, and computerised a Sissala–French, French–Sissala dictionary.

Most of the data for this book were collected during that time; the rest were obtained during a further field trip from January to October 1985.

My main informants and helpers in collecting and transcribing the data were Nicolas Tandia, Marc Zalvé, Timotheé Zalvé and Luc Zogdia. All text directly written without prior recording was composed by them. Most of the recorded texts had been planned, i.e. a particular person or group of people was asked to tell stories or make conversation. However, cultural habits were adhered to as closely as possible. Thus many texts were collected in the evening in a local compound with a sizable audience, very much as is the custom amongst the Sissala people for evening entertainment. A few texts were also recorded in unplanned situations, where it was known that the speakers were willing to be recorded.

The main problem in collecting the texts, which made staging to some extent necessary, was the great variety of dialects in the community. Because of the patrilinear system and a taboo which does not allow the men to marry women from their own home area, the married women in the village usually speak quite different dialects. It was therefore necessary to ensure that the speakers of the texts were born in Boura, and for this reason the main contributors of the data are men, except for two women who had returned to their village after marriage, and who were willing to make a contribution to the texts.

The texts I have drawn on in this book reflect a great deal of the Sissala situation and culture. Let me therefore briefly give some background information.

The landscape of the Sissala area is dry savanna, with only one rainy season, during the months of May to September. The area is not densely populated, and the stretches of uninhabited bushland are the home of all kinds of animals: antelopes, monkeys, elephants, warthogs, snakes, lizards, crocodiles.

The Sissala people are mainly engaged in farming. They grow millet, corn, rice, beans and yams; to a lesser degree they are involved in keeping cattle, hunting, fishing and craftwork. They live in square mud huts which are connected by walls into sizable compounds, in which up to 200 people may live.

They are deeply rooted in their traditions, as is especially manifest in their elaborate funeral celebrations and the mastery of their numerous musical instruments: xylophones, drums, horns and flutes.

There is also a variety of oral literature: folk stories, legends, riddles and proverbs, which until recently were transmitted to the younger generation by oral means alone. The masters of this literature are the praise singers (griots), who can not only sing creatively about the history of particular individuals in the area, alive or dead, but also know the history of the Sissala people, dating back a few hundred years. For instance, they can reproduce details of the slave trade, which affected the Sissala people badly.

Most of the people follow their traditional animistic religion; however, some are Muslims and some are Christians.

The greatest problems, according to the Sissala people themselves, are extreme poverty, worsened in recent years by recurring spells of drought, and an illiteracy rate of 95 per cent. To make ends meet, the men often have to work for long periods in the Ivory Coast.

The data on which the book is based comprise 2,000 pages of natural text. The individual examples are extracts from different types of text: for instance, narrations of personal experience, folk stories, legends, historical accounts; others are expository, e.g. descriptions of animals or places; others are procedural, e.g. about farming, fishing, building methods and cookery recipes; others are hortatory, e.g. sermons. Most of my examples, however, are taken from discussion or conversation, in which particles, one of my main objects of analysis, are frequently used.

The large body of texts made it possible not only to find adequate support for my claims, but to see them illustrated in different ways in the different types of text. One of the conclusions of my research is that quite wrong predictions can be made about linguistic phenomena such as particles when they are only examined in one particular type of text. For instance, what might be analysed in narrative as a 'paragraph marker' turns out to be freely used in conversation, and its primary function, when both conversation and narrative are taken into account, is something other than paragraph marking.

As regards word order, Sissala is an SVO language, with SOV in the negative. However, many structural phenomena in the language do not accord with Greenberg's (1966) universals for SVO languages; they are more typical of SOV languages. Thus Sissala has postpositions and the order genitive–noun. In addition to postpositions, serial-verb constructions, co-ordinate constructions and the co-ordinate marker *arí* may convey the information typically expressed by prepositions in European languages. Adjectival roots, determiners and quantifiers follow the head noun, as does the relative-clause marker. There is derivational as well as inflectional morphology, preceding as well as following the root. Aspect is marked by tone and suffixes and by partial reduplication of the verbal root, while tense is indicated by adverbials or tense particles.

Especially interesting structural phenomena are the dominant occurrence of co-ordination of S, VP and non-verbal constituents, and parataxis (see chapter 8). In fact discourses of considerable size can consist of one complex sentence made up of numerous co-ordinate sentences or parataxis. Of further interest is the fact that Sissala has no passive and therefore has to use topicalisation as a means of providing the most important information for the hearer in sentence-final position. Topicalisation may occur over a number of co-ordinate structures and optional resumptive pronouns represent the element topicalised. Another interesting phenomenon, the one I have exploited most in this book, is the rich variety of particles in the language. Some have purely grammatical function, while others have pragmatic functions. Many of these particles either have a use that does not exist at all in many languages, or replace the functions that intonation and stress have in many languages of the world.

Most of the texts were transcribed by the mentioned helpers and translated word for word, as well as more freely, into French. I have used abbreviated grammatical notations – explained on page xi – for most particles and for some morphological indication. For ease of readability I have refrained from marking grammatical facts not relevant to the arguments in question; rather, I have given lexical translations. As all discourse analysts know, it is impossible to focus one's attention simultaneously on every aspect of linguistic analysis. Thus in transcribing the data I have refrained from marking wrong starts, pauses, intonation, etc., which may give valuable insights into aspects of discourse analysis which have not been my primary concern. Sissala is a tone language, and tone, as it is marked, presupposes a two-tonal system of high and low, of which only high is marked. Since not all aspects of tone have been analysed yet, tone is written in citation form. However, where tone is crucial to the analysis, it is pointed out.

1   *What is discourse?*

1.1   Discourse and discourse analysis

We all know that hearers have intuitions about the grammaticality of sentences. It is also true that they have intuitions about the well-formedness of discourses. However, are we talking about the same kind of well-formedness judgement? Some seem to think this is the case. I quote Werth (1984:17): 'We will argue that connectivity at both levels – that is, both between and within sentences – is crucially semantic, and that the obvious formal links which exist are in fact the overt manifestations of semantic connections.' Those who propose discourse and text grammars, such as Harris (1952), Longacre (1983) and proponents of discourse-production models, think along similar lines.

However, the fact that utterances of single grammatical sentences can themselves constitute acceptable or unacceptable, well-formed or ill-formed discourses, can be used to show that there is a fundamental difference between judgements of grammaticality and judgements about the acceptability or well-formedness of discourses.[1]

Consider examples (1)–(4):

(1)   A dog is for life.
(2)   Trespassers will be prosecuted.
(3)   She can't.
(4)   Every chair has a nose.

All four are grammatical sentences of English: but which of them constitute complete and well-formed discourses? This question cannot be answered without taking background or contextual assumptions into account. Although it may be hard to understand in isolation, we realise that (1) is a complete and acceptable discourse when, for instance, we see it on a sticker on the back of somebody's car. We can all, in these circumstances, recall that some people are cruel to animals or abandon them, and the above message makes us draw conclusions to the effect that keeping a dog means taking over responsibility for it for its entire life. In other words, what is conveyed by an utterance of (1) – what we need to recover in order to understand it – is not merely its semantic representation, or the proposition it expresses, but the implications which it carries in a context to which we have access.

Example (2) is readily perceived as conveying a complete message because we have all had the experience of seeing signs with this content, which are designed to warn people not to enter a property, or at least we have intuitions about the type of situation in which such signs may appear. Example (2), like (1), connects up with common assumptions to yield common conclusions. However, (2) is different from (1) in that although we can think of situations in which the message would be appropriate, it will not be perceived as fully appropriate unless actually encountered in an appropriate situation.

What about (3)? In the absence of more specific information, (3) would not be perceived as conveying a complete message at all. We do not have assumptions readily available which would make it clear to us who *she* is and what she is unable (or not permitted) to do. The sentence as it stands cannot be assigned a unique propositional content, and as a result its utterance conveys no unique set of implications. Hence the intuition that it is not a well-formed discourse as it stands – though it would become one if uttered in a situation in which appropriate assumptions were accessible.

Example (4) seems to contradict a common assumption, one we are not prepared to abandon since we do not believe that chairs could conceivably have noses. As a result, it is perceived as bizarre. Here it might be argued that there is an internal semantic contradiction with no appeal to context being necessary. But is it really its semantic content alone which makes (4) unacceptable? Obviously, we have processed the utterance in a particular context, in which it is assumed that chairs do not, and cannot, have noses. In certain imaginative situations this assumption, and the oddness of (4), may disappear. Imagine that (4) is uttered at a children's party, where every child is dressed up as a clown and wears a clown's nose. During an interval of playing on the lawn every child takes off its nose and hangs it on its chair. At that time another child arrives late. One of the hostesses asks whether there is a seat free for the child. The answer is (4) 'Every chair has a nose.' Not only does the oddness we formerly perceived disappear, but the utterance, in this new situation, has acceptable implications, one of which, the intended one, is (5):

(5)   There is no seat free.

Therefore, although sentences clearly have semantic content, and we have subconscious knowledge of it, as we do of all aspects of linguistic structure, sentence (4) is not contradictory in virtue of its semantic content alone.

It seems then, that the well-formedness of discourses, those composed of single utterances as well as the longer kind (see 1.2), is highly dependent on context, while the grammaticality of sentences is not dependent on context at all.

Notice, too, that even utterances of ungrammatical sentences can be understood. Consider the following, which is a literal translation from German as far as tense and word order is concerned, but with *bekommen* wrongly translated as 'become' instead of 'get' or 'receive':

(A German talks to a waiter in a restaurant)
(6)   I wait now already twenty minutes and when become I a sausage?

This utterance, in these circumstances, might well be correctly understood by an English hearer. Since the semantic content of 'become a sausage' is incompatible with normal assumptions about human beings, the hearer may well reject this interpretation and find a more appropriate alternative which he assumes his German-speaking customer intended. This shows that context and the speaker's intentions play as important a role in communication as the linguistic stimulus itself, and even a defective stimulus may serve its communicative purpose.

By 'context' here I do not mean the real world or the co-text (the preceding or following text of a discourse); rather it is a set of assumptions retrieved or derived from memory or acquired by perception, and used in the interpretation process. It is easy to see that the same utterance may have different implications in different contexts: that is, when different background assumptions are used. Consider (7):

(7)   It's half past three.

To someone who is running towards the station hoping to catch the 3.25 train, (7) will suggest that he has missed his train; to someone whose tea-break starts at half-past three it will imply that the tea-break has just begun, and so on. The process of utterance interpretation, and the role of context in this process, will be discussed in detail below (see pp. 53ff.).

Discourse analysis can therefore not be a purely linguistic matter; it necessarily involves an analysis of the role of context in the interpretation process. It thus falls within the domain of pragmatics – the field concerned not with how sentences are structured but with how utterances are understood. In chapter 2 I will outline in detail the particular pragmatic framework I will adopt. In the remainder of this section, I will make some remarks about the nature of text and discourse, and approaches to their analysis.

Some English speakers have an intuition that there is a difference between 'discourse' and 'text'. However, as technical terms they very often turn out to be synonyms: for example, Lyons (1981) calls everything that is uttered 'text', others would probably use the term 'discourse' here. We all feel that if we talk about something deliberately constructed as a unit, the term 'text' is more appropriate. However, intuitions about textual well-formedness generally coincide with those about discourse well-formedness and both crucially involve and appeal to contextual assumptions. Beyond that, it seems to depend largely on broader interests whether one talks about discourse or text analysis. Those interested in literature usually see themselves as text linguists, whereas those coming from the field of ethnography, oral communication and cognitive science talk about 'discourse analysis'.

I intend to use 'discourse' as a general term to refer to all acts of verbal communication, and to reserve the term 'text' (following Brown and Yule 1983:6) for the 'explicit', or 'recorded part' of discourse. Thus text is a purely linguistic, formal object, whereas discourse has both linguistic and non-linguistic properties.

Discourse analysis has been done with various goals in mind. Some analysts are primarily interested in the working of the mind in delivering, processing and storing information (e.g. Clark and Clark 1977; Johnson-Laird 1983; Sperber and Wilson 1986a). They provide a limited range of linguistic examples to illustrate their points, but it is not always part of their aim to work out the full implications of their hypotheses by considering data from a variety of languages.

Others (e.g. Longacre 1983; Pike 1977, 1983) have mainly worked on corpuses of text in a variety of languages, and have done their analysis by searching for regularities and frequencies in the occurrence of certain phenomena. Most of them have been little or not at all concerned with the psychological relevance of their findings or the psychological mechanisms which underlie them.

A third group, the formal semanticists (e.g. Dowty, Wall and Peters 1981; Seuren 1985), have seen discourse as falling within the domain of truth-conditional semantics. They do make reference to context in describing the mapping between sentences and their truth-conditions. However, it does not take much to show that this approach has difficulty dealing with the complexity of real language use, nor does the approach make any serious claims about psychological reality.

How, then, do I view discourse analysis? As a field linguist and ethnographer, I am naturally concerned with real language data and the investigation of phenomena from a particular language – Sissala. As I have demonstrated, sentence structure determines only a fraction of what is communicated, and context plays a crucial role in the interpretation of discourse. Therefore I am centrally concerned with how the Sissala hearer processes the particular parts of discourse. I do not share Brown and Yule's view that data-based discourse analysis is something quite different from the investigation of the hearer's task in processing; I quote Brown and Yule (1983:254) which is taken from an evaluation of Johnson-Laird's *Mental models*: 'Possibly for this reason, the practical details of mental models remain elusive. They seem to represent a way of thinking about how we understand discourse rather than a way of doing analysis of discourse.' Although Brown and Yule criticise analyses which look only at texts, they seem to assume that there is a way of analysing discourse without reference to what the hearer does in understanding it:

If the representation of a piece of text can be made in terms of propositions which are to be treated as concepts in the reader's mind, then it follows that the discourse analyst must be capable of providing, not just an analysis of a piece of text, but an analysis of the mental representation of that text. That is, the discourse analyst may claim that the product of his analysis is not simply a good account of the facts ('good' in analytic terms such as economy and exhaustiveness), but can go on to claim that the product of his analysis is psychologically 'real'. (Brown and Yule 1983:110–11)

I am not suggesting that the linguistic structure of the text should be ignored, nor that all the conclusions an ethnographer draws have to be psychologically real. However, to me, discourse analysis is nothing else *but* tracing the hearer's part in understanding utterances, and I claim that any other approach either yields uninteresting statements of statistical frequency, or is like going on a journey without a destination in mind. The latter impression is particularly strong in those approaches which, while talking of speakers' and hearers' goals, 'topic of discourse', 'topic of speaker', 'topic of sentence', say little about the nature of topics and goals, except that they are partly determined by content and partly by context, though it is not clear exactly what context is and how it is chosen. I believe we will make little progress in the analysis of discourse unless we set ourselves a different goal. This goal to me seems obvious – tracing the hearer's route in the interpretation of the speaker's intention, and finding out how a piece of text can modify the hearer's assumptions about the world.

My research has been conducted with three main goals in mind. First, I want to explain certain aspects of discourse connectivity in a particular, hitherto unanalysed language – Sissala. Secondly, and more importantly, I want to demonstrate, using Sperber and Wilson's relevance theory, which principles underlie discourse connectivity. This involves proposing a framework for data-based discourse analysis, as well as providing data which shed light on various aspects of the theory. Thirdly, I would like to draw conclusions from my research for universals and language typology.

Thus, I do not see myself as in a different boat from those who are concerned with psychological mechanisms and psychological reality. In fact, my technique will invariably be to suggest how the hearer goes about interpreting the data. In this approach, statistical analysis will play, if any, a very minor role.

Why is the role of the hearer so important? Following Sperber and Wilson (1986a), I take the view that speakers are constrained by the hearer's expectation of relevance, and in particular, optimal relevance. I shall elaborate on this in chapter 2. A speaker who makes no effort to conform to this expectation risks being misunderstood. Therefore it is the hearer's expectation of relevance which has to be the basis for discourse analysis.

Contrary to Brown and Yule's view (1983:110–11), I see the most interesting issues in discourse analysis as issues not about *how* text is structured but about *why* it is structured in a particular way. The interesting issues, in other words, are not descriptive but explanatory.

I would like to go even a step further and claim that it is an illusion to speak about textual 'facts', as Brown and Yule do in the above quote, unless it is recognised that background assumptions can alter 'facts'. For example, a discourse that is incoherent or uncohesive in one context may be cohesive and coherent in another. Moreover, it is now well known that pragmatic (i.e. non-linguistic, psychological) considerations, can simplify analyses on the purely linguistic level (see, for example, Grice 1975). Finally, as I have already shown, a concern with mental factors is necessary in discourse analysis because discourse itself is not a purely linguistic notion, and cannot therefore be dealt with in a purely linguistic way.

I am not claiming that in every instance I shall trace the actual background assumptions that the hearer brought to bear while processing the utterances I analyse. I may suggest assumptions that are logically similar to those actually used, or assumptions that might possibly have been used. My analysis, therefore, is not necessarily a representation of what was *actually thought* when the recorded data were produced. What I am proposing is an analysis of how the interpretation process might have gone.

To some, this may seem very subjective. However, constructing assumptions is far less subjective than one might think. As we saw with (1) and (2), we have very good intuitions about possible or probable contexts. Some may say, 'This is nothing new. We always knew that ultimately the context plays a role.' Longacre (1983) and Pike (1967), for instance, mention the non-linguistic context as playing some role, and Firth (1957) makes frequent reference to the 'context of situation'. Others (e.g. Hobbs 1979; van Dijk 1977) make some provision for non-linguistic context in their theories. However, as I shall show, unless context and the psychological mechanisms underlying it are at the *base* of our theory, no adequate explanation of the interpretation process, and more generally of the structuring of discourse, can result.

Some may say that a speaker from one culture operating with data from a very different culture will meet insuperable problems.

Leaving aside the question of whether it is even possible to understand another language, cultural relativists have argued that it is never possible to share the background assumptions of another culture; and logical relativists have argued that even the inference systems used in thinking and speaking may vary considerably from culture to culture.[2]

Communication occurs in a social and cultural context, which strongly influences people's assumptions about the world. The discourse analyst has to know some of the hearer's assumptions, no matter in what culture the analysis is done. It is necessary, therefore, for a discourse analyst in a quite different culture to live in that culture and work closely with native speakers. In the case of the Sissala data, this was the situation. Also, the natural data were translated and transcribed by native speakers into French, which helped to preserve the native view in the translation from a non-Western to a Western language.

It will become clear, moreover, that the emphasis of my research is not on social and cultural influences on language use. I shall be less interested in the way that Sissala assumptions (their world view) differ from ours, than in how Sissalas use these assumptions in utterance interpretation. In fact, those who expect my research in a so-called 'exotic language' to show up all sorts of *cultural* linguistic idiosyncrasies will be disappointed.

The cultural differences are mostly reflected in the lexical content of nouns and verbs (e.g. Sissala has seven terms for 'to carry'); however, I will argue that the content of many 'discourse' particles, for instance, is cognitively rather than culturally determined. I hope to show that there are striking similarities in linguistic/pragmatic phenomena among quite unrelated languages, which can only be explained on the assumption that the way language is interpreted is largely universal. On the other hand, many structural idiosyncrasies can be fruitfully analysed as resulting from grammaticalisation of processing strategies, rather than in cultural or interactional terms.

As far as logic is concerned, cultural relativism is not the only view possible. My assumption has been that people from all cultures operate with the same logic.[3] By applying the logic of relevance theory I hope to show that the discourse data make sense in a way we would rationally expect them to, given the assumptions of speakers and hearers: that, though background assumptions may vary, inferential strategies remain the same.

The main claim of this section has been that discourse analysis involves tracing the hearer's path in utterance interpretation: that the linguistic structure of the utterance is only one of many factors which determine the intended message. It is, of course, an important part, and this book is about how Sissala linguistic structure and contextual assumptions interact to achieve certain effects in the hearer's mind.

In the next section I investigate in more detail and provide further arguments against the claim introduced at the beginning of this section, that textual connectivity is semantic.

1.2   Discourse and grammar

As the above quotation from Werth (1984) showed, some linguists assume that discourse well-formedness has its roots in grammar. The most obvious proof of this is taken to be the fact that discourses exhibit cohesion and coherence relations, and that these are felt to be part of linguistic structure. In this section I shall look more closely at these claims.

Practically everybody concerned with text analysis considers the study of cohesion and coherence relations as central. On the one hand, it is felt that the possession of these relations is what distinguishes a well-formed text or discourse from an arbitrary sequence of utterances; on the other, that the recognition of these relations is crucial to comprehension. In this approach, the main role of background assumptions in the processing of texts should be to supply information required for judgements of cohesion and coherence.

Consider (8):

(8)　　The river had been dry for a long time.
　　　Everybody attended the funeral.

In order to see this as a well-formed and comprehensible text, one would need to know not only which river and whose funeral were being referred to, but what attendance at a funeral has to do with rivers being dry. On a coherence-based account, these background assumptions would be used to establish the cohesion and coherence relations, whose recognition is crucial to the comprehension of (8). I quote Thavenius (1983:44–5), who sums up the coherence-based research tradition: 'text is distinguished from non-text by displaying unity of meaning. This unity is to a large extent achieved through cohesion and coherence.'

Unfortunately, the concepts of cohesion and coherence sometimes seem to be almost as vague as the notions of text (discussed section 1.1) and unity of meaning themselves. The basic feature of cohesion and coherence relations is said to be connectivity: cohesion is formal connectivity, and coherence is connectivity at a deeper, semantic level. Here I will look briefly at some of the ways these notions have been developed and used.

1.2.1　Cohesion

Cohesion is described by Halliday and Hasan (1976:5) as follows: 'Cohesion is part of the system of language. The potential for cohesion lies in the systematic resources of reference, ellipsis and so on that are built into the language itself.' Cohesion therefore involves the form of language rather than the content. Thus in (9)

(9)　　John isn't tall, nor is Susan,

the contraction of *is not*, the use of *nor* and the ellipsis (*tall*) are cohesive devices. In (10) the pronoun *he* and the ellipsis in the final clause are cohesive devices.

(10)   Somebody came yesterday. The man wanted to sell me a vacuum cleaner. He almost succeeded.

More generally, all anaphoric devices, or constructions involving inter-dependency among elements of a text, e.g. *so, therefore*, are seen as contributing to cohesiveness. Where such devices are involved, order is important: cohesion may be destroyed if the order of the utterances is changed, as can be seen in (11):

(11)   ?The man wanted to sell me a vacuum cleaner. Somebody came yesterday. He almost succeeded.

Cohesion, then, is essentially a formal relationship between elements of a text.[4]

There are a number of reasons for thinking that cohesion alone is neither necessary nor sufficient for textuality, and is thus inadequate to account for discourse well-formedness. As Hobbs (1979:78) points out, the pronoun *he* in (12) could in principle be interpreted as referring to either John or Bill:

(12)   John can open Bill's safe. He knows the combination.

He adds that although both interpretations would be cohesive, only on the assumption that *he* refers to John will the result be a coherent text. Hence cohesion is not sufficient for textuality.

Nor is it necessary. As we have seen with (1) and (2), a single sentence may be a well-formed text, though it contains no obvious cohesive devices. The same is true of (13), which is easily recognisable as an appropriate exchange:

(13)   A: Where can I get a good meal around here?
        B: I'm afraid I'm in a bit of a hurry.

Moreover, as Blakemore (1987:106 and 1982b:232) shows, even if the text contains so-called cohesive devices, these do not always link explicit elements of the text. Consider (14) with *so* and (15) with *too*.

(A leaves the house with a parcel and flowers. B says:)
(14)   So you **are** going to the birthday party.
(15)   The government has promised to provide funds for famine-stricken areas this year too.

Here, the use of *so* and *too* encourages the hearer to access certain implicit assumptions from the context (not the co-text), and use them in processing the utterance. It seems, therefore, that, although Halliday and Hasan may be right that cohesive devices are rooted in language, what these devices connect are not always explicit elements of the text.

The above examples strongly suggest that cohesion is merely a surface symptom of some deeper relation which can exist independently of it, and that it is in terms of this deeper relation that the distinction between texts and non-texts should be drawn, and the notion of discourse well-formedness defined. The obvious relation to consider here is that of coherence.

1.2.2   Coherence

The notion of coherence plays two separate roles in the literature on pragmatics and discourse. On the one hand, it is said to be a semantic/ pragmatic notion and to underlie textuality (Werth 1984:89–104); on the other hand, it is said to be a kind of mental principle which guarantees the correct filling in of linguistic gaps in order to achieve comprehension (Bellert 1974; Charolles 1983; Hobbs 1979; van de Velde 1984). I shall therefore deal with coherence in relation to textuality separately from coherence in relation to comprehension.

1.2.2.1   Coherence and textuality
Coherence is connectivity of semantic or pragmatic content. For example, two utterances, or parts of the same utterance, may be connected by expressing similar or identical concepts. Thus the two clauses of example (9) are connected by cohesive devices on the one hand, and on the other by the fact that the second clause is semantically similar to the first. The two clauses of (16) are connected by relations of antonymy or semantic opposition:

(16)   The wise master makes his servants respect him. The unwise master makes his servants despise him.

Coherence is widely taken to be at the heart of all textuality, of loose conversational utterances as well as deliberately composed text. In this section I will argue that that view is incorrect.

Different analysts define coherence in different ways. Here, I will look at a proposal by Hobbs (1978, 1979), to define coherence relations among elements of a text, and use them in turn to account for judgements of textual well-formedness. Hobbs assumes that there is a finite set of specifiable coherence relations between propositions. The idea is that to be well formed and appropriate, a text must exhibit some such coherence relations.

To take just one example, repetition is a frequently encountered device, both in literature and ordinary conversation. Hobbs (1979:73) treats it as an instance of a coherence relation called 'elaboration', defined as follows:

Elaboration: S1 is an Elaboration of S0 if a proposition P follows from the assertions of both S0 and S1 (but S1 contains a property of one of the elements of P that is not in S0).
At a sufficiently deep level the two sentences say the same thing. In the typical case, new information is conveyed by the second sentence, since there must be some reason for saying it again. This is why I have called the relation 'Elaboration' rather than 'Paraphrase'. However, I also mean to include under this heading such trivial moves as pure repetitions, repairs, tag questions, and the like.

Thus this relation would subsume both identical repetitions such as (17) and elaborative repetitions such as (18):

(17)   Help. Help.
(18)   Go down Washington Street. Just follow Washington Street three blocks to Adams Street.

But not every repetition is appropriate. If the only constraint on texts is that they exhibit coherence, what is to distinguish the well-formed (17) and (18) from (19) and (20), which in normal circumstances would be ill-formed?

(19)   A box of cornflakes. A box of cornflakes, please. A box of cornflakes, please. . .
(20)   I'd like a box of cornflakes. I'd like a box with cornflakes in it. Just take some cornflakes off the shelf and bring them to me, please.

It is possible, of course, to think of circumstances in which both (19) and (20) would be appropriate: for example, if the hearer is either very deaf or very stupid. However, there has to be a reason for a repetition, and this reason may be apparent not in the text itself but only in the circumstances in which it is produced. Similarly, other types of elaboration cannot be explained on grounds of coherence alone. Example (21), as an answer on an immigration form where I was asked to state where I had spent the last two years, would not only be superfluous but also very inappropriate:

(21)   I have spent the last two years in the Ivory Coast, which is very pleasant. It has plenty of exotic fruits and the people have been very kind.

However, in a letter to a friend (21) might be appropriate. Hence, coherence relations are not sufficient for textuality.

That coherence relations are not necessary for textuality can also be shown by the following example:

(22)   A: Is he an atheist?
         B: He is and he isn't.

Semantically, (22B) is contradictory and the text should be necessarily incoherent. However, in context it would often be interpreted as both coherent and true. Again it is impossible to explain this interpretation without reference to the context, and more generally to pragmatic considerations. Thus the study of coherence relations within the text is not enough to establish textuality or non-textuality; for that, we need to look at the relation between text and context: that is, at pragmatics.

By the same token, coherence relations are not necessary for textuality. A notice saying *Trespassers will be prosecuted* exhibits no obvious internal coherence relations. Again, despite this lack of coherence relations it will be an appropriate message in some circumstances but not others. Again for an adequate account of appropriateness and inappropriateness we must turn to something outside the text.

To sum up, neither cohesion nor coherence alone yields an adequate account of textuality. In fact, it is possible to provide a text which exhibits both cohesion and coherence relations but which is nevertheless nonsense:

(23)   Amos, a blue-eyed Friesian, who has a sister in Kenya, went there on safari. One of the elephants was just about to give birth and stepped on a blade of grass when Amos decided to eat a mango. There are onions, mangoes and bowls from China in the markets of Kenya. Enamel bowls have pretty patterns but are more expensive than clay pots. Amos enjoys watching Kenyan women carry clay pots on their heads.

Just as cohesion is merely a superficial symptom of coherence relations, it seems that coherence relations themselves are merely a superficial symptom of something deeper, which itself is the key to textuality. These examples are enough to suggest that what is lacking in approaches based on cohesion and coherence is an adequate notion of context, and of the relation between text and context.

1.2.2.2   Coherence and comprehension

According to Hobbs (1979:79–82), coherence relations in text and discourse are *motivated ultimately by the speaker's or writer's need to be understood*. Van de Velde (1984:43) claims that 'If coherence *cannot* be constructed for a sequence of utterances ... then their complete and successful comprehension *cannot* be achieved' (my italics). The idea has been widely accepted that comprehension depends on, or even consists in, the recognition or imposition of coherence relations. It in turn implies a particular conception of the role of background or contextual assumptions in comprehension: they are those assumptions necessary for the recognition of the coherence relations in terms of which the text is to be understood.

For instance, Johnson-Laird (1981, 1983) argues that there are two levels of representation for discourse: 'a superficial propositional format close to linguistic form, and a mental model that is close to the structure of the events or states of affairs that are described in the discourse' (1983:377). Coherence is established in terms of the latter rather than the former. On Johnson-Laird's view, words in a sentence help the hearer to construct a mental model. This mental model is only partially based on the linguistic text, and has to be enriched with contextual assumptions: so the hearer uses context in order to establish coherence.

Others (e.g. Charolles 1983; Lundquist 1986a) have stipulated a maxim of coherence. According to Charolles (1983) (in Lundquist 1986a:3–4), 'in case of problems in coherence-creating, a general heuristic principle intervenes, according to which humans tend to consider all acts, and among these verbal acts, as coherent because they are goal directed'. This general principle, or 'maxim of coherence', is seen as comparable to the Gricean co-operative principle and maxims.

Brown and Yule (1983:66) advocate a similar approach: 'human beings do not require formal textual markers before they are prepared to interpret a text. They naturally assume coherence, and interpret the text in the light of that assumption.'

However, there are a number of reasons for rejecting coherence-based approaches to comprehension. Again, isolated utterances such as (24) would pose a problem for somebody who takes coherence as essential for comprehension:

(24)   Parking prohibited for non-customers.

These utterances do not exhibit obvious internal coherence relations and there is no other text with which they could cohere. Yet it is unrealistic to think that isolated utterances are interpreted by entirely different principles from longer text.

It is also hard to see how the first utterances in a text would be accounted for on a coherence-based approach. But discourse-initial utterances such as (25), and beginnings of books, such as (26), are expected to be understood:

(25)   Hello, you look well.
(26)   It is a truth universally acknowledged that a single man in possession of a good fortune must be in want of a wife. (Austen: *Pride and prejudice*)

Although later utterances might be interpreted by recognising their coherence relations with previous text, it is unrealistic to imagine the hearer of discourse-initial utterances delaying interpretation until coherence relations can be established with the following text. Indeed such a process would probably be circular. It is more realistic to assume that discourse-initial utterances are interpreted by whatever principles apply to isolated utterances. We have thus two clear types of case in which a coherence-based approach could not in principle apply.

Hobbs (1979:83–7) makes the suggestion that referential ambivalences are resolved by an appeal to coherence relations. Thus, in example (12) above, he argues that the hearer interprets the pronoun *he* as referring to John because on this interpretation the text exhibits the coherence relation of elaboration (described on p. 18, above). More generally, the claim behind this approach is that wherever an utterance has a range of possible interpretations, the actual interpretation chosen will always be the one that maintains coherence with preceding text. However, this can be shown not to be the case. Consider the following utterance:

(27)   The man who has made a bomb may use it.

The utterance is ambiguous: it may refer to a particular known man or any man of the set of men who have made bombs. It is possible that a speaker actually knows about a particular person who has made a bomb, and may have just spoken about him, but utter the above utterance as a word of wisdom and warning, not referring to the particular man he knows but to *any* man who has made a bomb. This example shows that the coherence-based approach cannot account for the disambiguation of (27).

Another counter-example to Hobbs' claim is given by Sperber and Wilson (personal communication). Consider (28):[5]

(28)   A: What did Susan say?
        B: You've dropped your purse.

Example (28B) has two possible interpretations: it could be either a report of Susan's assertion that the speaker of (28A) has dropped her purse, or an assertion by the speaker of (28B) that the speaker of (28A) has dropped her purse. Only on the first interpretation does it maintain coherence relations by providing an answer to the preceding question. It is clear, however, that such an utterance would often be both intended and successfully understood as conveying the alternative, non-coherent interpretation which, in the circumstances, might be seen as conveying information that is more urgent. Again the conclusion must be that something deeper than coherence is involved.

It has often been assumed that larger units of discourse, such as a paragraph or a whole text, are distinguished by the use of special particles (Longacre 1976:468–75). However, in many cases these particles take not only these larger discourse units but also smaller units such as noun or verb phrases within their scope. It is then up to the hearer to find out what the scope of one of these particles is. Let us look at an example from Sissala.

There is a particle *dé* in Sissala, which marks important utterances in narrative leading up to the peak of a story, thus apparently contributing to the coherence of the text. However, in conversation this particle may also intensify noun or verb phrases. The following extract from a recorded natural conversation illustrates both types of use. The conversation is about a woman who expresses her anger about another woman taking dawa dawa pods from her tree. The background to the conversation is that the woman who has taken the fruits has claimed (as an excuse) that she had thought the fruits had already been harvested and the ones left were for general use. However, the tree owner explains that the tree gives fruit well but a little at a time. In (29) only the tree owner is speaking:[6]

(29)   a. Ná ŋné má ha há   wɪ ɛ   tenni í   sísényɛ́
           there that also yet which NEG make finish you now
           sɪɛ́ ko kʋɔrɛ a   dé zɛ́ a-á   bɔnnɛ.
           then come secretly and INT climb and-IPF pluck
           'There, that which is also not yet ripe you now come secretly and climb in order to pluck them.'

b. ʅ dé a̋ ŋ kiso má.
you INT make my totem even
'You have even acted against my totem.'

c. ʋ nɔné né dé-é ɛ.
its production SDM INT-IPF that
'That is how it always produces fruit.'

d. ʋ dé fɛ fʉla a a weri.
it INT flowers flowers and does well
'It has lots of flowers and produces well.'

e. Wíbʉ́lé né ní sɪé rí-í dé ká-á li miŋ
speech this SDM then COMP-you INT take-IPF leave in
zɔ́péké mɛɛ?
houses in
'Is it this speech then that you are taking to town?'
(Did you come to cause quarrels in town?)

While in (29a), (29b) and (29e) the scope of the particle *dé* is meant to be the whole sentence, marking this sentence as especially important, in (29c) and (29d) it modifies the interpretation of sentence-internal constituents. Thus in (29c) the interpretation of the utterance without *dé* would be (29'c):

(29')   c. That is how it produces fruit.

With *dé* the imperfective aspect, marked with length, is intensified, yielding the interpretation (29c):

(29)   c. That is how it always produces fruit.

Dé in (29d) has the same function that reduplication would have, yielding the interpretation 'lots of'. Without *dé* the interpretation would be (29'd):

(29')   d. It has flowers and produces well.

The difference in the function of *dé* in (29d) and (29a) can be seen from the fact that it would be possible to reduplicate the verb for emphasis in (29d) as an alternative to *dé*, but this is not possible in this context with the verb in (29a), as is shown by (29'd) and (29'a) below:

(29')   d. ʋ fɛ fɛ fʉla
'It has lots of flowers.'

(29')   a. ʔa zɛ́ zɛ́ a-á ɓɔnnɛ
'and climb in order to pluck them.'

What these examples show is that just as the reference of anaphoric pronouns as in (12) is not sitting there waiting to be discovered, but has to be imposed by the hearer, so the chunking of a text and a scope of particles is not sitting there waiting to be discovered, but has to be imposed as part of the comprehension process. Moreover, different scope assignments yield different interpretations, in only some of which – those involving sentence scope – can the particle *dé* be seen as contribut- ing to coherence relations among different elements of the text: in others, it merely adds further semantic content to one particular element of the text.

By concentrating only on the role of particles in maintaining coher- ence, a linguist could make serious mistakes. At the very least, he would be likely to assign different functions or, worse, too many different senses to these particles, thus missing an important generalisation. Just as *even* and *also* have different scopes within the clause but only a single sense, so *dé* has different scopes but only a single intensifying function.

As we have seen, what is important for comprehension is to establish the scope of the particles. There seems to be no way of using consider- ations of cohesion and coherence alone to perform this task. However, hearers are able to interpret the particles rightly. If they are asked how they are able to do this they say 'it makes sense'. The question is what 'making sense' involves, if it is not the establishing of cohesion and coherence relations.

Lundquist (1986b:2), discussing a paper of mine (Blass 1986), suggests a modified approach:

Between the two extremes which characterise the study of coherence at the moment, on the one hand the syntactic perspective of anaphoric cohesion between two sentences, and on the other hand the concept of coherence, not as a linguistic fact, but as a general principle of relevance (Blass 1986), we adopt a position in between; for us, the (re)construction of coherence is based on the linguistic markers which a speaker employs in order to facilitate the work for the addressee, who himself seeks to (re)establish this intended coherence due to a general principle of relevance. (Translation from French my own.)

This, however, mistakes the point of my argument. As I have tried to show in this section, the existence of coherence relations is neither necessary nor sufficient for comprehension. The appeal to coherence is superfluous: coherence relations, like cohesion relations, are merely a superficial symptom of something deeper, which is itself the key to comprehension. In this book I shall adopt the suggestion of Sperber and Wilson (1986a) that what is crucial to discourse comprehension is the recognition of relevance relations, which are relations between the content of an utterance and its context. In the next chapter I will give an outline of this approach, but first I would like to look at another notion which is believed by many to play a key role in textuality and comprehension: the notion of topic.

1.2.3 Topic

The notion of topic is widely used by those concerned with discourse analysis, and is seen as of particular importance in the description of content, the establishment of coherence and the identification of participants and units of discourse. Usually (e.g. van Dijk 1977) a distinction is made between discourse and conversational topic on the one hand, and sentence topic on the other. Brown and Yule (1983) also introduce the notion of speaker topic.

Considering the importance given to topic as a theoretical notion, it is surprising to find that no proper definition of it exists. Brown and Yule (1983:68) are quite open about this:

we shall explore some recent attempts to construct a theoretical notion of 'topic', a notion which seems to be essential to concepts such as 'relevance' and 'coherence', but which itself is very difficult to pin down. We shall suggest that formal attempts to identify topics are doomed to failure, but that the discourse analyst may usefully make appeal to notions like 'speaking topically' and 'the speaker's topic' within a 'topic framework' . . . we shall insist on the principle that speakers and writers have topics, not texts.

Here I shall discuss, as a representative example, the work on topics of van Dijk (1977).

Although van Dijk nowhere gives a definition of 'topic', it is clear that he regards topics as propositions, and that they bear some relation to what he calls 'frames' (1977:99). 'Frames' are units of encyclopaedic information in long-term memory. This idea is not idiosyncratic to van Dijk; it has its origin in artificial intelligence: objects of this type have been described by Minsky (1975) as 'frames', Rumelhart and Norman (1978) as 'schemata' and Schank and Abelson (1977) as 'scripts'. Samet and Schank (1984) account for textual coherence in terms of scripts, i.e. networks of conceptual dependencies, of 'topics', and de Beaugrande (1980) sees topics as arising from a network of conceptual representations.

Van Dijk defines a frame more specifically as 'a set of propositions' which make up our conventional knowledge of some more or less autonomous situation (activity, course of events, state). According to him, frames also impose possible *orderings* on facts, e.g. along cause–consequence, general–particular or whole–part lines: thus the frame predicts whether a certain order of events is plausible or not. Whenever the frame changes, it is said that there is 'a change in the topic of the discourse' (1977:100).

'Topic' in van Dijk's view is a semantic notion, and judgements about whether propositions belong to the same or different topics are based on the semantic content of the propositions. The topic of a discourse can be expressed as a complex proposition which is entailed by the set of propositions expressed by the sequence of sentences in the text.

To illustrate what he considers to be identity and diversity in topic, he examines co-ordinate sentences, of which he considers (30) to express one topic and (31) two topics (1977:48):

(30)   We went to the beach and played football.
(31)   We went to the beach and Peter was born in Manchester.

He argues that one criterion for topic unity would be to ask whether the two clauses in (30) and (31) can be seen as answering the same question. Thus both clauses of (30) could be answers to the question 'What did you do yesterday?', but for (31) no such question exists. Van Dijk adds that relations between facts are established with respect to some common basis, and as he notes (1977:51), this common basis has to do with knowledge of the world. He admits that pragmatics is involved here, but nowhere does he show where he draws the borderline between semantics and pragmatics, or whether 'common basis' and 'knowledge of the world' are part of his definition of 'frame' and therefore semantic, or part of 'context' and therefore pragmatic.

As far as the criterion of asking questions is concerned, it does not take long to create a suitable question for (31). Consider (32):

(32)   A: Why do you remember 10 August 1980 so well?
        B: We went to the beach and Peter was born in Manchester.

The relevance of the first conjunct could be to indicate that the date is especially memorable not only because Peter was born, but because B was not aware of it and went to the beach with the other children, which he still finds annoying.

Surely there could be a 'common basis' for interpreting the two conjuncts in (31) as answering a single question. However, the relationship of the two conjuncts still does not match van Dijk's notion of topic as involving 'one frame'. Would van Dijk therefore have seen (31) as involving 'one topic' had he thought of exchanges like (32)? The answer is not clear.

Although van Dijk does not admit it, his notion of topic is undefined. Brown and Yule (1983:110) are right in claiming that he says no more than any child would be able to say when asked what a story was about: that is, to produce a single-sentence summary of the text under consideration.

Brown and Yule claim that although 'topic' cannot be defined formally, we do have intuitions about it. Thus they provide text material from thought-disordered and schizophrenic speakers, whose discourses are connected somehow but are incoherent. They claim that what is lacking is a common topic.

Brown and Yule also quote a sizable text from Bransford and Johnson (1973:400) which, although all the sentences are grammatical and coherence is obvious, can only be interpreted with a 'topic title' given. This topic is not recoverable from the text itself. This shows, according to Brown and Yule, that topics are central to comprehension, but cannot be established on the basis of the text alone.

Brown and Yule reinforce their point by considering the following example, in which a text from Anderson (1977:372) was presented to different groups with different titles:

(33)   Rocky slowly got up from the mat, planning his escape. He hesitated a moment and thought. Things were not going well. What bothered him most was being held, especially since the charge against him had been weak. He considered his present situation. The lock that held him was strong but he thought he could break it.

This text was provided with the two titles (33′a) and (33′b):

(33′)   a. A prisoner plans his escape.
         b. A wrestler in a tight corner.

Anderson *et al.* (1977) show that these different starting points constrain the interpretation of the text in terms of the knowledge structures or schemata which were activated and used in their interpretation. Thus the title (33′a) caused such impressions in the reader as that Rocky was alone, that he had been arrested by the police, and that he disliked being in prison.

What these texts show is that context plays a crucial role in the interpretation of a discourse, and that a text may be interpreted quite differently in different contexts. Contexts are therefore not determined by particular text structures, they have to be *chosen*. Choosing the right or intended context then becomes another problem.

In the light of example (33) it is perhaps surprising that Brown and Yule (1983:75) propose procedures for identifying the right context without claiming any great interest in the overall pragmatic standards which speakers are trying to meet, or which hearers assume that speakers are trying to meet:

In chapter 2, we discussed the problem for the discourse analyst of deciding just what features of context were relevant in the interpretation of a particular fragment of discourse. We suggested there that the strategy available to him would be, on the one hand, to work predictively in terms of his previous experience (similar speakers, similar genres, etc.) and on the other hand to examine the content of the text. From the content of the text the analyst can, in principle, determine what aspects of the context are explicitly reflected in the text as the formal record of the utterance. Those aspects of the context which are directly reflected in the text, and which need to be called upon to interpret the text, we shall refer to as *activated features of context* and suggest that they constitute the contextual framework within which the topic is constituted, that is *the topic framework*.

Brown and Yule seem to see discourse analysis like a jigsaw puzzle. An incomplete number of pieces constitute the text structure. There are some clues from somewhere, as to what the complete picture is like, and the individual pieces give clues to be used in the search for the right connecting pieces. However, Brown and Yule seem to forget that in the case of text there are two 'pictures' involved. One is in the mind of the speaker, the other will be in the mind of the hearer, and they are not necessarily the same. In processing a text, the speaker is concerned about which picture the hearer will construct, and takes his assumptions into account. It cannot be assumed that every text provides enough content for anyone who reads it to activate the right context, so that a discourse analyst will be able to complete the puzzle. Neither picture nor context is fixed in advance, and there is no reason to think that the text itself provides all the necessary clues. There is no one-to-one relation between the content of the text and the intended context, and as Brown and Yule point out themselves, the identification of a topic depends on context as well as on content.

Brown and Yule nowhere explain by which criteria contexts or topics are chosen; after all, as we have seen, there may be a choice. In fact, I will argue that nothing would be lost if the notion of topic was not employed at all. The fact that this term belongs to our everyday language does not mean it is necessarily a useful theoretical term. I shall show in chapter 2 how Sperber and Wilson account for the intuitions we have about 'aboutness' and 'topic' in contextual terms. I shall also show that there are many conversations which are well-formed and are not usefully approachable in terms of topic. In other words, the notion of topic, like the notion of cohesion and coherence, is neither necessary nor sufficient for textuality or comprehension.

1.3   Discourse and context

Throughout this chapter I have argued that context plays a central role in the interpretation of utterances. Few people would disagree. However, exactly what context is and how it affects interpretation has been viewed quite differently. Below I shall introduce and evaluate a number of proposals.

1.3.1   Context, situation and culture

The importance of non-linguistic context in the interpretation of utterances was first noticed by the anthropologist Malinowski (cited in Halliday 1984:8), who created the terms 'context of situation' and 'context of culture', which some linguists (e.g. Halliday 1984:8) still use. Malinowski saw the need for these notions when he realised that he had enormous problems in translating ethnographic notes in the language of the Trobriand Islanders. By referring to aspects of the situational context the translation task became easier.

Malinowski assumed that it was due to the 'primitive nature' of the languages of 'primitive man' that context played such a great role, and made context-free comprehension such a difficult task. He believed that these languages were more closely associated with the practical needs of 'primitive societies' than languages of more 'civilised cultures'. However, he never proposed a model of how context is determined, nor of what role it plays in utterance interpretation.

Malinowski's ideas were taken up by Firth (1957) who placed great emphasis on the 'social context'. Firth held the view that words and sentences do not have meaning in themselves, i.e. apart from their use in contexts of situation. That is, he denied the existence of sentence meaning in the modern sense.

He saw contexts of situation as crucial determinants of utterance meaning. However, like Malinowski, Firth never provided a theoretical account of the effect of contexts on utterance meaning: in fact he believed that we could never capture the whole of meaning.

Some have criticised this work, claiming that Firth's notion of 'context of situation' does not get us very far. However, Palmer (1976:51) does not see this objection as decisive: 'This does not prove that Firth was wrong. If we cannot get very far with context of situation this is perhaps no more than a reflection of the difficulty of saying anything about semantics.'

In my view, though, there is a decisive objection, to do with the psychology of hearers. Speakers and hearers do succeed in communicating by means of utterances. They do not do this by magic. They must, therefore, have some principled procedures for utterance interpretation, which are a legitimate object of theoretical interest. If hearers can succeed, describing how they do it seems a reasonable theoretical aim.

Considering Palmer's bleak statement, it is perhaps surprising that some linguists continued to work with the notion of 'context of situation'. To Bloomfield (1933), the meaning of a linguistic form *is* 'the situation in which the speaker utters it and the response it calls forth in the hearer'. Bloomfield therefore defined meaning *as* 'situation', i.e. as a physical object.

Lately some linguists with sociological interests (e.g. Halliday, Labov and others) have again taken up Malinowski's and Firth's notion of context. A further advocate of analyses based on 'context of situation' is Hymes (1964), who proposes a list of ethnographic features which are meant to offer a characterisation of context to which form can be related. Such features include knowledge of the communicator, addressee and audience on the one hand, and 'topic' and 'setting' on the other hand. He also considers 'channel', 'code', 'message-form', 'event', 'key' and 'purpose' as important elements of context. Hymes intends these contextual features to be very much like phonetic features such as 'bilabial stop', 'lateral', etc., which would, according to Brown and Yule (1983:39) 'enable a visiting ethnographer to arrive by helicopter in a location where a communicative event is in process and to check off the detail of the nature of the communicative event.' For this to be possible, though, each one of these notions would have to be defined.

The defect of all these proposals based on 'situational context' is that context is largely seen as something given in the real world. However, physical context never affects language directly, but only via the speaker's and hearer's knowledge of it. Not everything that could potentially be perceived attracts attention. Moreover, people perceiving the same physical environment do not necessarily represent it to themselves in the same way.

It is also clear that not all contextual assumptions which play a role in utterance interpretation are available by visual or auditory perception; perhaps the majority of contextual assumptions are retrieved or derived from memory. In other words, the context for comprehension is drawn not only from the physical environment, but from what Sperber and Wilson (1986a) call the speaker's and hearer's *cognitive environment*: the set of assumptions that are manifest to them.

Notice that I am not rejecting the view that physical, social and cultural factors play a major role in utterance interpretation. Of course they do. I am claiming, however, that they affect interpretation by affecting the individual's assumptions about the world. Physical, social and cultural assumptions are just some of the many types of assumptions of which the context for utterance interpretation is composed.

Brown and Yule feel that Hymes' proposals are especially helpful for discourse analysis. Although they may be right that the discourse analyst is more dependent on situational clues than the hearer or reader for whom the message was intended in the first place, the discourse analyst has to bring these clues together with other assumptions and make hypotheses similar to those of the hearer or reader for whom the message was intended. Such factors as knowledge of the communicator and addressee, the topic, setting, etc. are not necessarily the most important here. I want to suggest that the most important question is, do I know enough about the contextual assumptions of the hearer(s) or reader(s) for whom the message was intended? If I do not know enough about particular contexts (i.e. particular sets of assumptions) my research may still be of interest if I can construct hypothetical contexts which the particular hearer might have used. In other words the notion of 'context of situation' is inadequate for utterance interpretation and for discourse analysis alike: what is needed is a psychological account.

1.3.2   Choice of context

A context, then, is a set of assumptions brought to bear in the interpretation of an utterance. How are contexts chosen? That is, how does the hearer decide which set of assumptions to use?

Most discourse analysts agree that assumptions drawn from the 'co-text' play a major role in utterance interpretation; it is claimed that the interpretation of later utterances in discourse is highly influenced by earlier ones.

Consider (34) from Sacks (1972):

(34)   a. The baby cried.
        b. The mommy picked it up.

Sacks claims that it would be normal to interpret *it* as referring to *the baby*. However, as Brown and Yule (1983:80) point out, one could imagine contexts in which *it* might refer to another object: for instance, a toy which the baby has dropped. Similarly, there might be contexts in which *the mommy* does not refer to the mother of the baby but to somebody else's mother. It is not enough to say that there is 'a normal interpretation', i.e. one which comes immediately to our mind, while others are somehow more 'unlikely'. Some general account of both 'normal' and 'less likely' interpretations is needed.

Brown and Yule (1983) are aware of this problem, and introduce two principles, which they say should take care of choosing the right context: the principle of 'local interpretation' and the principle of 'analogy'.

The principle of 'local interpretation', according to Brown and Yule (1983:59), will 'instruct the hearer not to construct a context any larger than he needs to arrive at an interpretation. Thus if he hears someone say "Shut the door" he will look towards the nearest door available for being shut.'

This raises the immediate question: nearest to whom? To the speaker? To the hearer? To someone mentioned in the utterance? Moreover, what is meant by 'context needed to arrive at an interpretation'? At any interpretation? At a plausible interpretation? At a coherent interpretation, or what? Without these clarifications it seems unlikely that this principle can provide an adequate criterion for reference assignment.

Can it really be assumed that it is always the nearest object which is the appropriate referent of a pronoun? As mentioned above, Brown and Yule suggest that in the case of an utterance like *Shut the door*, the hearer would look for the nearest door and if that door was shut he would look no further and just say *The door is shut*. Is that really what one would do? Suppose a room has three doors, and the furthest from the speaker and hearer is open. On hearing *Shut the door*, would the natural reaction not be to assume that it referred to the door that is open, even though this is not the nearest door? Or imagine that a man says to his wife outside his house, *Let's take the car*. Surely he does not have in mind to take the nearest car parked in the street, but his own car. The very fact that people can talk in this way shows that nothing so simple as a principle of locality is operative; otherwise they would indeed assume that the nearest object was intended.

In temporal interpretation, too, it is not necessarily the most local interpretation which is the right one. As we have seen, an utterance like *Come at noon* may not refer to noon of the same day, but to noon on some other day. The principle of local interpretation would make the wrong prediction in such a case.

Brown and Yule (1983:65) propose a second principle, the principle of analogy, to explain how contexts and interpretations are chosen. Though they do not provide a clear statement of this principle, they claim that 'the principle of analogy is one of the fundamental heuristics which hearers and analysts adopt in determining interpretations in context. They assume that everything will remain as it was before unless they are given specific notice that some aspect has changed.'

Brown and Yule claim that in example (34) the interpretation of *it* is guaranteed by the principle of analogy. Picking up a crying baby is something we expect; it is conventional behaviour. So, in the absence of any other linguistic cues, Brown and Yule claim that by analogy to what we know about the world the baby will be the referent of *it*.

Now consider a slightly more complex example:

(35)   The baby dropped the toy and cried.
         The mother picked it up.

Here there are two possible analogies to be drawn. It is just as 'conventional' to pick up a toy as it is to pick up a baby. The principle of analogy will not help assign a reference to *it*. The principle of 'local interpretation' does not seem to help much either, since presumably both the baby and the toy are near to the mother; and it is unlikely that the mother will simply pick up the one that is nearer. Now it is true that in some circumstances the hearer may be unable to decide between the possible interpretations of (35). In others, however, he may have additional contextual assumptions which help him decide. It therefore seems that co-text alone is not enough to help with interpretation, and that principles of locality and analogy are not adequate to deal with every case.

1.4   Discourse and pragmatics

1.4.1   Pragmatics and the code model

My argument so far has been that we will not achieve adequate accounts of text or discourse until we have an adequate theory of pragmatics: that is, an empirical psychological theory of how utterances are understood. I have said very little as yet about what pragmatics is. Rather than discussing a number of individual views, which are more or less based on the same theoretical notions, I will outline one basic idea which underlies most current theories, and examine its adequacy. In the next chapter I will propose an alternative account.

Approaches to communication in the past have assumed that communication in general, and verbal communication in particular, is achieved by encoding and decoding messages. This code-based, or 'semiotic' approach, assumes that communication involves a set of unobservable messages, a set of observable signals and a code; that is, a method of pairing signals with messages. In verbal communication, the signals would be the phonetic (or graphemic) representations of utterances, and the message would be the thoughts that the speaker wanted to convey. The task of pragmatics would be to discover the code that hearers use to recover the intended message from the observable signal. A typical approach of this kind was the Saussurian idea of the transmission of a 'signified' by use of a 'signifier'. A more recent example would be the work in formal pragmatics of Gazdar (1979).

Sperber and Wilson (1986a:36–7) have severely criticised this semiotic approach. An adequate pragmatic theory, they point out, must go well beyond recovery of the semantic representation of the sentence uttered. It must deal, at least, with disambiguation, reference assignment, resolution of semantic indeterminacies, recovery of implicit import, figurative interpretation, illocutionary force and a variety of stylistic effects. While it is reasonable to talk of the grammar of a language as a code, and hence of sentences as encoding their semantic representations, there is no reason to think that the remaining aspects of utterance interpretation, those that lie outside the scope of the grammar, can be satisfactorily dealt with in terms of a code.

Let us consider a few examples designed to illustrate their point:

(36)   I like C. S. Lewis' books.

Does the speaker of (36) intend to refer to the books C. S. Lewis wrote, the books he owns, the ones he ordered, or the ones situated near him? To understand this utterance within the code model, the hearer must decide what code he could use to help him.

Or consider (37):

(37)   Kate: Are you going to play chess with me on Sunday?
        Jane: The Spring Harvest Festival is on Sunday.

In order to be able to recover the implicit import of Jane's answer, Kate needs to have the particular knowledge that the Spring Harvest Festival is a special Christian praise meeting and to decide whether Jane wants to go there herself, whether she wants to remind Kate of the fact that Kate wanted to go there, or whether she wanted to remind Kate that playing chess is a trivial occupation for a Christian on a Sunday and that she should spend her time worshipping God. What code could the hearer use to decide which of these possible interpretations is the intended one?

A second problem with the code model of communication is that it is based on the assumption that communication involves the exact reproduction in the hearer of the thoughts the speaker wanted to convey. But as Sperber and Wilson (1986a:231–7) point out, communication often involves indeterminacies, the thoughts recovered by the hearer are merely intended to resemble those of the speaker. Poetic metaphors are an obvious example. Consider (38):

(38)   He was a plant destroyed by morning frost.

We can all see roughly what this metaphor is intended to convey, but we all arrive at slightly different interpretations, most of which would be acceptable to the speaker. How would this be possible if utterance interpretation was ruled by a code?

Or consider how the hearer decides whether an utterance such as (39B) is ironical or not?

(39)   A: If we get up early we'll make it to the Swiss border by noon.
        B: Nothing could be more pleasing to me.

A must have special knowledge of B's getting-up habits or of how important it is to B to arrive at the Swiss border at noon, in order to know whether B's utterance was meant to be ironical or not. The claim that the ironical intention can be *decoded* has never been satisfactorily spelled out.

Moreover, as Sperber and Wilson (1986a:200–1) show, irony does not merely communicate the opposite of what is said: it expresses a whole attitude, it covers a whole range of indeterminate effects, different in each hearer, which cannot be described by means of a code.

Sperber and Wilson (1986a:21–54) show further that communication is possible without a code. Consider (40):

(40)   Janice: How is your chapter coming along?
       Jane: (Lifts up a bulky envelope and shows it to Janice.)

Jane communicates, in the appropriate situation, that the chapter is finished and ready to be sent to her supervisor. Yet it could not be said that lifting up a bulky envelope 'means' that a chapter has been finished, or that Janice understands Jane by use of a code. Janice is able to interpret Jane correctly because of her knowledge of the world and her reasoning ability: she needs no code because she can work out what Jane means.

Code theorists assume that the pragmatic interpretation process is very similar to processing of grammatical information – I started this chapter by mentioning some such claims. Pragmatists in the Chomskyan tradition tend to assume without argument that pragmatics, like grammar, is a special-purpose modular system which associates the semantic representation of sentences to full utterance interpretation. But if pragmatics is not a code – if, as I have suggested, following Sperber and Wilson, pragmatic interpretation involves working out the intended message – then there can be no pragmatic module either. According to Fodor (1983:101–19) and Sperber and Wilson (1986a:65–7), whereas the processing of grammatical information is an automatic decoding process, not affected by contextual information, pragmatic interpretation is a non-demonstrative inference process with free access to contextual information. An adequate pragmatic theory must therefore contain an account of what such non-demonstrative inference processes are like.

Fodor (1983:105–8), who takes scientific theorising as the typical example of a non-demonstrative inference process, claims that these processes are not amenable to investigation: nothing is known, he argues, about either the logic or the psychology of scientific hypothesis formation and confirmation. Sperber and Wilson (1986a:65–117) are less pessimistic. They propose an inferential theory of utterance interpretation which, they suggest, might well shed light on non-demonstrative inference processes in general, thus quieting Fodor's scepticism. Given that pragmatic interpretation – for the reason given above – cannot be handled in terms of a code, an inferential approach along these lines seems to be the only available alternative.

I hope to show that the issue of whether pragmatics involves decoding or inference is not just a theoretical one, of no real value to those concerned with the description of natural language and communication. It seems to me that many of the views discussed in sections 1.1, 1.2 and 1.3 above have their roots in the idea that communication is a decoding process. The idea that there is a finite set of coherence relations, or contextual co-ordinates or features, which are 'signalled' in the text, has an obvious relation to the idea that comprehension is a matter of decoding. Thus discourse analysis will never have a sound foundation if the code model is inadequate. The idea of the code has been so deeply established that some (e.g. Gazdar 1979) have even taken Grice's ideas (see Grice 1975, 1978) – the first explicitly inferential approach to pragmatics – and unconsciously added to them some of the assumptions of the code model. In the next section I will look at Grice's proposals, and show how they can lay the foundation for an inferential pragmatic theory.

1.4.2 Grice's theory of 'meaning' and conversation

Grice (1957:58) made a distinction between what he calls 'natural meaning' (as in *Those black clouds mean rain*) and non-natural meaning, or 'meaning-nn'. His characterisation of meaning-nn is as follows:

(41) 'S meant-nn something by x' is (roughly) equivalent to 'S intended the utterance of x to produce some effect in an audience by means of the recognition of this intention.'

Grice's analysis indicates what it is for an individual S to mean something by an utterance x (where 'utterance' is to be understood as referring not just to linguistic utterances but to any form of communicative behaviour).[7]

The distinction between natural and non-natural meaning is roughly that between accidental information-transmission (e.g. I see Jane's car in the car park with a dent in the boot and draw the conclusion that she must have had an accident) and intentional communication (e.g. Jane herself points to the dent in the boot, intending to inform me that she has had an accident). Thus, Grice shows how intentional communication can take place in the absence of a code – as long as the hearer has some way of recognising the speaker's intentions.

According to Grice, communication is achieved by the communicator providing *evidence* for her intentions and the audience inferring her intentions from the evidence. As already indicated, the evidence can be a variety of phenomena: pointing to a dent in the boot of a car, lifting up a bulky envelope or producing an utterance. On this view, an utterance is nothing else but a piece of evidence about the communicator's intention. Sentences encode their meanings. However, as Sperber and Wilson (1986a:23) point out: 'Hearers are interested in the meaning of the sentence uttered only insofar as it provides evidence about what the speaker means. Communication is successful not when hearers recognise the linguistic meaning of the utterance, but when they infer the speaker's "meaning" from it.' In other words, the pragmatic interpretation process begins once the grammatical decoding process ends.

How are the speaker's intentions recognised? Here too Grice makes an important suggestion – Grice's idea in his William James Lectures (Grice 1975) was that hearers assume that communicators try to meet certain general standards. From knowledge of these standards, observation of the communicator's behaviour and the context, Grice claims, the communicator's specific intention can be inferred. The standards he suggested were a co-operative principle and maxims of quantity, quality, relation and manner:

(42)   *Co-operative principle*
       Make your conversational contribution such as is required, at the stage at which it occurs, by the accepted purpose or direction of the talk exchange in which you are engaged. (Grice 1975:45)

(43)   *Maxims of quantity*:
       1. Make your contribution as informative as is required.
       2. Do not make your contribution more informative than is required.

       Maxims of quality: try to tell the truth.
       1. Do not say what you believe to be false.
       2. Do not say that for which you lack adequate evidence.

       Maxim of relation: be relevant.

       Maxims of manner: be perspicuous.
       1. Avoid obscurity of expression.
       2. Avoid ambiguity.
       3. Be brief.
       4. Be orderly. (Grice 1975:45)

The suggestion was that these general standards provide a means of explaining how an utterance which may be an ambiguous and fragmentary representation of a thought can none the less communicate that thought.

Grice's account suggests a general solution to the set of specific pragmatic problems, such as disambiguation, reference assignment, recovery of implicature, etc. that the hearer of an utterance encounters. Consider (44):

(44)   Janice: Do you like African food?
        Jane: It is always very hot.

The word 'hot' is ambiguous. How does Janice know which sense was intended? Suppose she knows, for example, that African food is always spicy, and that Jane likes spicy food. Then, by assuming that Jane observed the co-operative principle, that she did not say what is false (maxim of quality) and gave the required information (maxim of quantity) the intended interpretation of 'hot' can be inferred. By the same token, Janice can infer the implicit information in (45):

(45)   Jane likes African food.

Grice calls such implicit information, recovered by reference to the co-operative principle and maxims, 'conversational implicatures'.

As Sperber and Wilson (1986a:21–38) point out, Grice's proposals, though suggestive and important, do not amount to a theory. They contain undefined terms: e.g. 'relevance', 'brevity', 'required information', 'adequate evidence', 'accepted purpose or direction of the talk exchange'. They contain no account of context selection or of inference. They are not restrictive enough to exclude all but a single interpretation: there could be many interpretations, all compatible with the maxims. Thus, though Grice's ideas provided a starting point for an adequate model of communication, they do not in themselves provide one.

Grice draws a fundamental distinction between 'showing' and speaker meaning. Sperber and Wilson (1986a:53) show that there is a continuum from 'showing' to 'saying that', where 'saying that' is a paradigm case of speaker meaning. Thus I can hold a hand behind my ear to draw attention to the fact that there is a car coming, or I can open the curtains to make somebody see that it is coming. I can also say *There is a car coming*. In the former cases there is no Gricean speaker meaning. However, those three acts are clearly related. In each case information is intentionally communicated, though in the first two something more than a single, determinate proposition is conveyed. Sperber and Wilson argue that by ignoring cases of 'showing', Grice deprives himself of the means to deal with vagueness or indeterminacy of communication, where something more than a single, determinate proposition is conveyed. Thus Grice still retains one of the basic assumptions of the code model: that what is conveyed is a determinate message analysable in finite propositional terms.

Here is an example of indeterminacy in communication that has obvious relations to the case of 'showing' rather than 'saying that': Jane ostentatiously puffs out some air during her first three minutes off the plane in the tropics, to draw Janice's attention to an indefinite range of assumptions; that it is hot, sticky and humid, that she feels frustrated, that the queue is long, etc. In other words, Janice communicates not a speaker meaning but an impression.

It is easy to think that this is just a minor aspect of communication, and that we mostly communicate clearly determinate messages. However, this is a fallacy, a legacy of the code model. For instance in commercials, where it is important to make an audience want to buy a certain product, attitudes and impressions are all-important. Thus a recent commercial on TV showed a Peugeot 405 driving through the flames of a bush fire. The only thing that was explicitly said at the end was: 'The Peugeot 405 takes your breath away.' It is clear that the power of the commercial lies in the impression it creates in the viewer of the usefulness and quality of the car, for *his* situation, and the favourable attitude that is supposed to result. Such cases are entirely ignored by those who concentrate on Gricean speaker meanings.

I have tried to show in this section that Grice provides the basis for a valid alternative to the code model of communication. Communication can be achieved by providing evidence of the communicator's intentions, evidence which can be correctly interpreted on the assumption that certain standards have been aimed at, if not achieved. This basic insight was Grice's major contribution to the theory of communication.

1.5   Conclusion

The purpose of this chapter has been to examine proposals that have been made in the area of discourse analysis, text analysis and pragmatic theory.

The main point of section 1.1 was that discourse is not a purely linguistic notion, and can therefore not be investigated in purely formal linguistic terms.

In section 1.2 I pointed out that the notions of cohesion, coherence and topicality are neither necessary nor sufficient for textuality and comprehension. I suggested that cohesion and coherence are only superficial symptoms of a deeper type of relation, which I will argue is a relevance relation, a relation between utterances and context. I pointed out that the notion of topic has no adequate theoretical definition and should therefore be dispensed with in theoretical accounts of textuality and comprehension.

In section 1.3 I investigated various views on the notion of context. I argued that it is a mistake to assume that context is something given in advance, automatically determined by co-text or physical environment. I pointed out that no theory so far has succeeded in making adequate proposals as to how the right context is chosen in any given situation.

In section 1.4 I introduced some views on pragmatic theory, and argued that many of the problems discussed in sections 1.1–1.3 arose from the mistaken assumption of the semiotic approach to communication. I suggested, following Sperber and Wilson (1986a) that verbal communication involves a combination of coding and inference. I discussed the view of Grice and others on how inferential communication might work. I pointed out some inadequacies in these views, and suggested that many of these inadequacies are remedied in the relevance theory developed by Sperber and Wilson. This is the theory which I propose to adopt for my own analysis of the Sissala data in the rest of this book.

I mentioned in 1.1 that I propose a 'framework' for discourse analysis, and the main point of this chapter has been to show what this framework should *not* be based on. A fundamental assumption of many text analysts is that texts are hierarchical structures which can be analysed using the techniques of formal linguistics. As many of my examples will show, spontaneous conversation provides a wealth of counter-examples to this assumption. The reaction of text analysts tends to be that although there may be discourses which do not exhibit hierarchical structure, there are many discourses which do, and the rest should be dealt with under a different category and with different goals. Relevance theory, by contrast, when construed as a pragmatic theory, takes the whole of communicative discourse, planned and unplanned, formal and informal, connected or unconnected, as its domain, and shows that the principles involved in understanding it are essentially the same. From this point of view, it is both arbitrary and misleading to restrict one's attention to hierarchically structured discourses: misleading because one may mistake what are merely the formal properties of a certain type of discourse for essential features of textuality and comprehension.

Behind this rejection of the formal linguistic approach to text is something very fundamental. The semiotic approach which underlies it is inadequate as an account of verbal communication. The grammars of natural languages fall far short of relating utterances to the thoughts they were designed to convey.

Does the fact that discourse analysis is not a purely linguistic matter mean that the importance of natural-language phenomena – i.e. utterances – is being disregarded? Does it mean that we could just as well do discourse analysis of photographs, as Brown and Yule (1983:113) fear? Indeed photographs could be used in inferential communication; however, this book is not about photographs but about natural-language utterances. My special concern is to show how speakers use particular linguistic phenomena to achieve pragmatic effects. The linguistic form of utterances plays a vital role in this. Before turning to the data, though, I will introduce relevance theory, the framework I will use throughout this work.

2 *Relevance theory and discourse*

2.1 Introduction

Sperber and Wilson (1986a) point out that, as a general tendency or in given situations, humans pay attention to some phenomena rather than others; they represent these phenomena to themselves in one way rather than another; they process these representations in one context rather than another. What determines which phenomena they attend to, and what representations and contexts they construct? Sperber and Wilson suggest that there is a single general answer to these questions. Humans tend to pay attention to what is *relevant* to them; they form the most relevant possible representations of these phenomena, and process them in a context that maximises their relevance. They claim that relevance, and the maximisation of relevance, is the key to human cognition. This has consequences for the communicator: by demanding attention from the audience she suggests that the information she is offering is relevant enough to be worth the audience's attention. Thus relevance is the key to communication too. In this chapter, I hope to explain and justify these claims.

By showing why speakers might be expected to aim at a certain standard of relevance if they want to keep their audience's attention, Sperber and Wilson remedy one of the main inadequacies of Grice's pragmatic approach: Grice provides little justification or explanation of his own pragmatic maxims. I will show later on in this chapter that their criterion for utterance interpretation is strict enough to eliminate all but a single interpretation, thus remedying another of the main weaknesses of Grice's approach.

In a later section, I will show how relevance theory provides a better theoretical foundation for comprehension and textuality than coherence models. Towards the end of the chapter I will show how aspects of the theory discussed can be applied to actual Sissala texts.

2.2   Relevance theory and comprehension

2.2.1   Relevance and contextual effects

Relevance is often seen exclusively as a property of utterances or a relation between an utterance and a text or discourse. Sperber and Wilson show that relevant information may be derived not only from utterances and other acts of communication, but also from observation, memory and inference. They therefore define relevance, in the first instance, for propositions or assumptions (information units, units of sense and reference) rather than for utterances. They see a proposition, moreover, as relevant in the first instance not to discourse but to a context: that is, a stock of propositions or assumptions derived not only from preceding discourse, but also from memory, perception of the environment and inference. Context selection is subject to a variety of psychological constraints, in particular the search for relevance. I will elaborate on this later in the chapter.

According to Sperber and Wilson, people pay attention only to information that seems relevant. A communicator, by claiming an audience's attention, suggests that the information she is offering is relevant enough to be worth the audience's attention. But how exactly can information be relevant? Sperber and Wilson claim that information is relevant to somebody if it interacts in a certain way with his existing assumptions about the world: as they put it, if it has *contextual effects* in some context that he has accessible. They claim that contextual effects are of three types: contextual implication; strengthening an existing assumption; and contradicting and eliminating an existing assumption. I will consider each type in turn.

Suppose I see an African in a coat going to a conference party. I form the following hypothesis:

(1)   a. If he is wearing a Kente cloth, then he may be Ghanaian.

Later, I see him without his coat and discover:

(1)   b. He is wearing a Kente cloth.

Then from the existing assumption (1a) and the new information (1b) I can deduce the conclusion in (1c):

(1)   c. He may be Ghanaian.

According to Sperber and Wilson, (1c) is a contextual implication of (1b) in the context (1a): that is, it is deducible from (1a) and (1b) together, but from neither (1a) nor (1b) alone. Intuitively, the information in (1b) would be relevant in a context containing assumption (1a). According to Sperber and Wilson (1986a:107–8) it is relevant precisely because it combines with the context to yield a contextual implication. More generally, new information is relevant in a context if it has contextual implications in that context, and the more contextual implications it has, the more relevant it is.[1]

Contextual implications are one important type of contextual effect. There are, however, two more. Suppose that, as described above, I have formed hypothesis (1a), acquired the new information (1b), and derived the contextual implication (1c). In other words, the fact that the African is wearing a Kente cloth gives me some reason to think he is Ghanaian. However, I cannot be absolutely certain about this: although Kente cloth is made in Ghana and mainly worn by Ghanaians, one can buy Kente cloths in London, and other people than Ghanaians could wear them. Suppose now I see him confirming a flight ticket to Accra/Ghana. Then my suspicion that he is a Ghanaian is strengthened. Intuitively, this new information would be relevant in the context just described. According to Sperber and Wilson (1986a:112–14), it is relevant because it provides further evidence for an assumption.

In Sperber and Wilson's terms, assumptions may vary in their *strength*: we treat some as more likely to be true than others. How much confidence we have in the information we obtain depends partly on how we acquired it: thus assumptions gained by perception tend to be very strong, the strength of assumptions gained from somebody's report depends on how much we trust the speaker. The strength of an existing assumption may also be modified by the acquisition of new information, as in the above example, where my suspicion that the African is a Ghanaian is strengthened by seeing him book a plane ticket to Ghana. According to Sperber and Wilson, new information may achieve relevance by strengthening an existing assumption; and the more assumptions it strengthens, and the more it strengthens them, the greater the relevance. *Strengthening* is thus a second type of contextual effect.

The third way in which new information can be relevant is by *contradicting* and eliminating an existing assumption. Suppose, for example, that I go to the immigration office and see the African who I had seen before on two occasions, about whom I had formed the hypothesis (2a):

(2)   a. He is a Ghanaian.

Then I see him showing his Nigerian passport and I discover that my past hypothesis was wrong. I know now:

(2)   b. He is not a Ghanaian.

While it is, after all, possible for anyone to acquire a Kente cloth and to fly to Ghana, it is less possible for just anyone to have a Nigerian passport. My current conviction that he is not a Ghanaian overturns my previous, less well-supported assumption. According to Sperber and Wilson, when a contradiction is discovered – that is, when the individual discovers that he is entertaining both a proposition P and its negation −P, the weaker of the two assumptions is abandoned.

Intuitively, in the case just described, the new information (2b) would be relevant. According to Sperber and Wilson, it would be relevant precisely because it contradicts and eliminates an existing assumption; and the more assumptions it eliminates, and the stronger they were, the more relevant it is. This is the third type of contextual effect.

So far we have established that assumptions may have contextual effects, and that there are three different types of contextual effect. However, we have not yet examined under which conditions these effects arise; that is, exactly how an assumption may have contextual effect in relation to other assumptions.

Let us assume you are sitting in a hotel room in the Canaries writing a letter to your favourite aunt describing your holiday experiences. With those assumptions about your aunt and your holiday experiences as a readily accessible context, you switch on the TV and on the first channel you hear (3), you switch to the second channel and you hear (4), you switch to the third channel and you hear (5).

(3)   Mary's lover died in a Scottish castle.
(4)   J.R. I've learned all your dirty tricks.
(5)   The temperature in London is 35 degrees Celsius.

The proposition expressed by the utterance in (3) is not likely to have any contextual effects in a context consisting of the assumptions about your aunt and your holiday experiences that you had in mind when you switched on the TV. The reason is that it is completely unrelated to any of these assumptions: it does not strengthen them, or contradict them, or combine with them to yield any sort of contextual implication. Hence, according to Sperber and Wilson, it would be irrelevant in the context described. Nor does (4) have any relation to the immediate context, described above; however, if you are a regular watcher of *Dallas* then it will not be as irrelevant to you as (3). You will be able to retrieve a number of assumptions about the person J.R. and his devious character and you will know that the woman speaking is Sue Ellen, his wife. These assumptions then should make it possible for you to achieve a certain number of contextual effects. How willing you are to engage in extended processing depends on how pressing the letter to your aunt is, and how confident you are that your effort in looking for further contextual effects of this information rather than any other will be well spent.

If you are an English person, (5) will probably be the most relevant to you, and it may connect up with your immediate context, the planned letter to your aunt. You may, for example, draw contextual implications to the effect that it is as hot in England as in the Canaries, and that this may be of relevance to your aunt.

Let us assume that you switch back to channel 1, on which there is a documentary about Scotland, and hear the following:

(6)   The Palace of Holyroodhouse is the home of the Queen of England in Scotland.

The proposition expressed by the utterance in (6) will be irrelevant to you if you are already certain of the fact that this palace is the home of the Queen. It is irrelevant because it has no contextual effects: it neither strengthens an existing assumption, nor contradicts an existing assumption, nor combines with an existing assumption to yield a contextual implication.

Now let us assume further that a chambermaid enters your room at the moment when you hear (6), and she points to your TV and says (7):

(7)   This is François Mitterrand's residence.

Example (7) contradicts your firmly held assumptions that the palace in question does not belong to F. Mitterrand. As we saw with example (2) above, when a contradiction arises, the weaker of the two contradictory assumptions is rejected. In this case, the assumption to be rejected is the new information in (7). Hence, unlike example (2), nothing in the context is modified. Therefore the chambermaid's remark is irrelevant; it has no contextual effects.

Thus, as Sperber and Wilson (1986a:121) indicate, there are three types of cases in which an assumption will have no contextual effect, and therefore be irrelevant, in a context: first, if it is entirely unrelated to the context; second, if it is already in the context and unable to be strengthened; and third, if it is inconsistent with existing assumptions, and is not strong enough to overturn them.

However, as Sperber and Wilson also point out, an utterance which expresses an irrelevant proposition may achieve relevance in other ways. For example, the fact that you have chosen to express a certain proposition may be relevant even though the proposition itself is irrelevant: it may give me the information that you hold a certain false belief, or have made a mistake in deciding what I already know, it may have contextual effects which are highly relevant and so on. An utterance makes manifest a variety of propositions, only one of which is the proposition explicitly expressed. Hence, it can achieve relevance in a variety of ways.

Sperber and Wilson claim that having contextual effects in a context is a necessary condition for relevance. They suggest that it is also sufficient. Consider the following example:

(8)   A: How did you hurt your finger?
         B: We had 'Reibekuchen' for lunch.

In order to understand B's utterance, A must be able to supply the following assumptions:

(8′)   a.   Reibekuchen is a dish made of raw grated potatoes.
         b.   If grating by hand, it is easy to 'grate' one's fingers too.
         c.   B had cooked the lunch.

Processed in this context, (8b) carries the contextual implication (8′d), which directly answers the question in (8A):

(8′)   d.   B hurt her finger when grating the potatoes.

It is clear that someone who is unable to supply the contextual assumptions (8′a) – (8′c) is unable to derive the contextual implication (8′d), and so is unable to see the intended relevance of B's answer. Thus there is a close interconnection between relevance and contextual effect, and one could reasonably claim that an assumption is relevant in a context if and only if it has some contextual effect in that context. This, then, explains the intuition that an utterance is relevant if and only if it connects up with a context in some way.

It is useful here to distinguish between intended and unintended contextual effects. Generally, the process of utterance interpretation yields a combination of both. For instance, my sole intention with example (8) was to achieve the contextual effect in you that you understand the interconnection between relevance and contextual effects. However, it may well be that the nature of the example, and especially the German word *Reibekuchen*, motivated you to engage in further processing, and to draw the conclusion 'the author could be German' or strengthened an assumption to this effect that you had already acquired. The distinction between intended and unintended contextual effects is crucial to the Sperber and Wilson account of implicature, as I will show in section 2.3.2.

2.2.2   Degrees of relevance

So far I have introduced the notion of contextual effect, illustrated the three types of effect, and shown how contextual effects contribute to relevance: the greater the contextual effect, the greater the relevance. However, there is a second, equally important factor in the definition of relevance, as the following case will show: I see an African and think:

(9)   a. If he is wearing a Kente cloth then he may be Ghanaian.

When he has taken off his coat, I might think either

(9)   b. He is wearing a Kente cloth.

or

(9)   c. He is wearing a Kente cloth and black shoes.

Now (9b) is more relevant in a context consisting solely of assumption (9a). Our account of relevance so far is unable to explain this, since both (9b) and (9c) have the same contextual effects in this context. Both yield the contextual implication (9d):

(9)   d. He may be Ghanaian.

This shows that contextual effects cannot be the only factor which contributes to relevance. According to Sperber and Wilson, the other crucial factor is processing effort.

Sperber and Wilson see the search for relevance as a 'cost–benefit' system. Let us compare it with athletics. A runner not only has to reach a certain goal, but to reach it in the least time possible. Reaching, say, a 1,000-metre goal is nothing very special: many runners can achieve that, but to achieve it with the least expenditure of time is what determines the champion. And in ranking champions, one might propose the following cost–benefit criterion: the greatest champion is the one who can reach the furthest goal with the least expenditure of time.

Assessing relevance is like assessing athletic achievements: contextual effects are balanced with processing effort, and just as there are degrees of excellency in athletic performance, so there are degrees of relevance in communication. Just as a runner who takes three times as long as everybody else to reach the goal is not qualified to enter a race, so information which makes it necessary to check through all one's existing assumptions to see if it interacts with them, can lead the hearer to give up the endeavour when he realises that the effect to be achieved is not great enough to offset the processing effort. According to Sperber and Wilson, then, relevance increases with contextual effects, but decreases with every increase in the amount of processing effort needed to achieve those effects.

To return to examples (9b) and (9c): if contextual effects alone were taken into account, (9c) would be indistinguishable from (9b); however, when processing effort is taken into account, (9b) is more relevant than (9c), because its contextual effects are achieved with less effort. In the case of (9c), there is more information to be processed than is the case in (9b), which detracts from the relevance of the information in (9c).

What exactly determines the amount of processing effort needed to derive a set of contextual effects? In the case of (9c), the hearer has to process an additional phrase *and black shoes*, which costs him some additional purely linguistic effort. Thus linguistic complexity is one factor affecting processing effort. As Sperber and Wilson show, however, it is not the only one. They note that processing effort may vary because not all contextual assumptions are equally accessible. By definition, the most accessible contexts are those that require least effort to retrieve or construct, and therefore will be investigated first. Thus a speaker who wants to make sure that a certain context or contextual assumption is used must make sure that it is easily accessible: otherwise the hearer may fail to retrieve it, and may misunderstand the utterance or judge it to be irrelevant. The following example will illustrate:

(10)   a. Jane: Do I look strange in my cover cloth?
        b. Janice: Everybody wears them around here.

Here, in order to see the relevance of (10b), the hearer would have to supply a contextual assumption such as (10c):

(10)   c. People do not look strange wearing what everybody else is wearing.

In this context, (10b) will have the contextual implication (10d), thus answering the question in (10a):

(10)   d. She does not look strange in her cover cloth.

By comparison the alternative response in (11b) would require more effort to understand:

(11)   a. Jane: Do I look strange in my cover cloth?
        b. Janice: We are in Africa.

Here, in order to see the relevance of (11b), the hearer would have to supply background assumptions such as (11c–d):

(11)   c. Many women in Africa wear cover cloths.
        d. Jane does not look strange wearing what many other women are wearing.

In this context, (11b) will have the contextual implication (11e), which will take more effort to derive since it requires the hearer to supply two assumptions, (11c) and (11d), both of which will take some effort to retrieve:

(11)   e. Jane does not look strange in her cover cloth.

Finally, consider an even more indirect answer, (12b):

(12)   a. Jane: Do I look strange in my cover cloth?
        b. Janice: We are in a hot continent.

Here, in order to see the relevance of (12b) the hearer would have to supply something like the assumptions in (12c–e):

(12)   c. Africa is the continent in question.
        d. Many women in Africa wear cover cloths.
        e. Jane does not look strange wearing what many other women are wearing.

Given these assumptions, she will be able to derive the contextual implication (12f):

(12)   f. Jane does not look strange in her cover cloth.

However, the answer in (12b) will cost considerably more effort to understand than those in (10b) and (11b), since the context needed to establish its relevance consists of three assumptions, each of which will require some effort to retrieve or infer.

This example illustrates how processing effort can determine degrees of relevance. Thus, of (10b), (11b) and (12b), understood as carrying the single contextual implication described above, (10b) will be the most relevant, since it enables this implication to be derived with the least effort. On the other hand, of two assumptions which involve the same amount of effort to process, it will be the one that has the greatest contextual effects that will be most relevant. Hence relevance increases with contextual effects and decreases as amount of processing effort increases.

As these examples also suggest, processing effort and therefore degrees of relevance depend not only on the accessibility of the context used, but on its size. For example, if the exchange (12a,b) is processed in a wider context, the degree of relevance of (12b) as an answer to (12a) may change drastically. Suppose the context contains the assumption that cover cloths leave the shoulders bare and putting them on could look inappropriate, then the question in (12a) will have the contextual implication (12g):

(12)   a. Do I look strange in my cover cloth?
        g. Do I look too bare?

And in this situation, the answer (12b) might be processed in a context containing (12h), yielding the contextual implications (12i) and (12j):

(12)   b. We are in a hot continent.
        h. It is appropriate to leave the shoulders bare when it is hot.
        i. It is appropriate for Jane to leave her shoulders bare.
        j. Jane does not look strange in her cover cloth.

This example shows that questions as well as answers can have contextual effects. It also shows that the linguistic properties of an utterance cannot uniquely determine its contextual effects, and therefore its interpretation. Utterance (12b) has the contextual implication (12f) in one context and (12i) and (12j) in another context. The contextual implications (12i) and (12j) are more easily derived than the contextual implication (12f). This is because fewer contextual assumptions have to be taken into account in deriving the latter than the former. Therefore the answer (12b) is more relevant in a situation in which the speaker thinks she might be too bare than in a context in which she thinks she might just look strange.

The notions of contextual effect and processing effort are very important for discourse analysis. As a discourse proceeds, the hearer works out the contextual effect of the newly presented information in a context retrieved or derived from memory and perception. These contextual effects and new assumptions then become part of the context in which later stretches of the discourse are processed. Selection of a context will be affected by the twin aims of minimising processing effort and maximising contextual effect. Thus relevance theory suggests an answer, not only to the traditional pragmatic problems for which Grice's maxims have been used, but also for the problem of context selection, which, as I pointed out in the last chapter, has defeated so many pragmatic theories.

2.2.3   Context and context selection

In chapter 1, I discussed a variety of views on context and context selection. It became clear that an adequate account of context and context selection is vital for a theory of comprehension and discourse. Comprehension involves recovering a speaker's intended message, and therefore also identification of an intended context and an intended set of contextual effects.

Before discussing the identification of intended contexts, let us consider first how an individual goes about accessing and selecting contexts in general.

According to Sperber and Wilson, people invariably try to maximise the relevance of any new information they acquire. Thus, if I discover by accident that I have lost my purse, I will try to retrieve from memory, or access via perception or inference, those beliefs and assumptions which will interact with this discovery to yield as many contextual effects as possible for the least possible processing effort.

According to Sperber and Wilson (1986a:138) the actual context used in interpreting an utterance is constrained by the organisation of the individual's encyclopaedic memory, his perceptual and other cognitive abilities, and the mental activity in which he is engaged. Each individual has an enormous amount of information potentially available, but only a small part will be accessible at any given moment. The initial or immediately given context consists of the most recently processed information and is therefore easily accessible. In discourse, this is usually the information used in the interpretation of the immediately preceding utterance, together with the information derived from it.

However the immediately given context is generally extended by the addition of further accessible information, in particular information in the encyclopaedic memory. This raises the question of how information is accessed from memory. Sperber and Wilson see the role of *concepts*, the constituents of assumptions or propositions, as crucial here. Concepts are psychological objects, which consist of a label or address in memory, under which certain information is stored. This information is stored in three different types of entry: *logical*, *encyclopaedic* and *lexical*.

The logical entry for a concept consists of a set of inference rules. The logical entry for *and*, for instance, contains a rule of *and*-elimination, governing the inference from (13a) to (13b):

(13)   a. Lizards are reptiles and mice are mammals.
        b. Lizards are reptiles.

The encyclopaedic entry for a concept contains information about the objects, properties or events that instantiate it. For instance, the encyclopaedic entry for 'Black Forest' in (14) may include the following information:

(14)   a. The Black Forest is in the South of Germany.
        b. The Black Forest has mainly fir trees.
        c. A famous cake comes from the Black Forest area – Black Forest gateau.

There is a crucial distinction between logical and encyclopaedic entries. While encyclopaedic entries are representational, the logical entry of a concept is computational: i.e. it consists of a set of deductive rules which apply to propositions in which that concept appears. Thus, if the mind contains a rich system of representations, this is largely in virtue of encyclopaedic entries. As Sperber and Wilson point out, computational approaches to the mind are only possible if there is a distinction made between representation and computation. Their distinction between logical and encyclopaedic entries is a special case of this more general distinction.[2]

The lexical entry for a concept contains information about its natural-language counterpart, i.e. the word or phrase that expresses it. This is the sort of syntactic and phonological information normally seen as belonging in a linguistic lexicon.

Concepts may also appear as constituents of logical forms. Logical forms may be semantically complete or incomplete: complete if they have a fully determinate set of truth-conditions, and indeterminate otherwise. Sperber and Wilson call a logical form which is semantically complete a 'fully propositional form'. The sense of a sentence is a logical form but not a fully propositional form. It requires enrichment to be capable of being true or false. Sperber and Wilson claim that incomplete logical forms may be stored in conceptual memory as assumption schemas, to be completed by contextual information in a particular comprehension process.

Logical forms are not just constructed and stored by the individual, they are entertained in the mind in different ways. Some may be stored as basic factual assumptions: that is, as true descriptions of the actual world; others may be stored embedded under terms of belief and desire (see chapter 3). Thus a stock of factual assumption schemas, some basic and others embedded, make up the individual's total representation of the world.

A lot of work has been done on the structure and organisation of encyclopaedic entries. Many theories share the view that humans have stereotypical assumptions about frequently encountered objects and events. Thus I have an idea of what is a typical chair or stool. It is generally believed that these stereotypical assumptions, also referred to as 'frames', 'prototypes', or 'scripts', are stored and accessed as a unit or 'chunk'; these chunks are seen as being part of larger chunks and containing smaller chunks.

Sperber and Wilson make one basic assumption about the accessibility of information in encyclopaedic memory. They claim that encyclopaedic information about 'cats', say, becomes accessible only when the concept 'cat' is present in the individual's working memory: that is, in the information being processed, or in the context that has already been accessed. In other words, you gain access to your encyclopaedic entry for cats only when an assumption containing the concept 'cat' is being processed. This encyclopaedic entry will in turn contain other concepts, to whose encyclopaedic entries you will therefore gain access, and so on indefinitely.

Because encyclopaedic memory is organised in this way, the initial context may easily be extended by the addition of the encyclopaedic entries for concepts already present; these will in turn contain concepts which give access to further encyclopaedic entries, which in turn contain concepts which are addresses for further entries and so on. Thus someone processing assumption (15) may have access to the information in (16) and (17):

(15)   I come from near Cologne.
(16)   Cologne has a cathedral.
(17)   Cathedrals in Germany belong to the Catholic Church.

The encyclopaedic entry for 'Cologne' may contain (16), which gives access to the encyclopaedic entry for 'cathedral', which may in turn contain (17) and give access to the encyclopaedic entry for 'Catholic Church'.

In principle, a person could continue to access further encyclopaedic entries indefinitely, gaining more contextual effects each time. However, every addition means an increase in processing effort, and on the assumption of relevance theory he will not spend this effort unless it is adequately offset with contextual effects. Trains of thought are governed by the search for maximal relevance, and may be diverted at any moment by hopes of relevance elsewhere.

In processing any new item of information, Sperber and Wilson claim that contextual selection is guided by the search for relevance. To see how the process of context selection might go, let us suppose that the individual has access to four possible contexts: an initial context C1, and three possible extensions resulting from the addition of C2, C3 and C4, in that order:

(18)   C1. The government determines the price of fuel.
         C2. If fuel goes up by more than 5p then air fares go up.
         C3. If air fares go up, then holidays are more expensive.
         C4. If holidays are more expensive, then we will have to economise.

Let us consider now what would happen if we processed two alternative new items of information, (19) and (20), in this set of potential contexts:

(19)   Fuel has gone up by 6p.
(20)   Fuel has gone up by 4p.

Example (19) gains an extra contextual implication with each possible extension of the context. The contextual implication which is derived from the union of C1 and (19) is (19'):

(19')   The government has raised the price of fuel by 6p.

This implication itself combines with C2 to yield the further contextual implication that air fares will go up, which in turn combines with C3 to yield a contextual implication, and so on for C4. Thus, given the information in (19), it might be worthwhile to extend the initial context by adding C2, C3 and C4. In each case the extra effort is offset by extra effect.

In the case of (20), things are different. In the initial context C1, this assumption carries the following contextual implication:

(20′)   The government has raised the price of fuel by 4p.

However, the addition of C2–C4 would incur extra processing effort, but would yield no additional contextual effect. Thus the extension of the initial context would in this case lead to a decrease in relevance. An individual aiming to maximise relevance might be well advised to extend the context along these lines in the case of (19), but not in the case of (20).

According to Sperber and Wilson, the individual should aim to access the context which involves the best possible balance of effort against effect. When this balance is achieved, Sperber and Wilson (1986a:144) say that the assumption has been '*optimally processed*'. They then define the relevance of an assumption to an individual as follows:

(21)   *Relevance to an individual (comparative)*
         Extent condition 1: an assumption is relevant to an individual to the extent that the contextual effects achieved when it is optimally processed are large.
         Extent condition 2: an assumption is relevant to an individual to the extent that the effort required to process it optimally is small.
         (1986a:145)

Behind this definition lies the assumption that the individual will develop strategies for optimal processing, and for optimal context selection in particular. It is these strategies that account for the decision to extend the context in one direction rather than another, as in examples (19)–(20) above.

Sperber and Wilson (1986a:151–3) then extend the definition of relevance to apply not only to propositions or assumptions, but also to phenomena in general, and to utterances in particular. A phenomenon may make many assumptions manifest; however, this does not guarantee that an individual will actually construct all of them, or indeed any of them. Suppose that I hear Big Ben strike once. Using my encyclopaedic entries for striking clocks, and in particular for Big Ben, I may access the following assumptions:

(22)   Big Ben has struck once.
(23)   If Big Ben strikes once, then it is one o'clock.

From (22) and (23) I can draw the contextual implication:

(23′)   It is one o'clock.

And there may be circumstances in which that is what I will do. It would also be possible for me to access assumptions (24) and (25):

(24)   Big Ben has struck.
(25)   If Big Ben strikes then it is not broken.

However, in normal circumstances this is a route one is much less likely to take. Which assumptions will actually be constructed on presentation of a given phenomenon? According to Sperber and Wilson, this will, as always, be determined by considerations of relevance.

A phenomenon can be more or less efficiently processed, depending on which and how many assumptions are constructed. Some phenomena may be most efficiently processed by not being conceptually represented at all, being filtered out at the perceptual level; others will be most efficiently dealt with by being conceptually represented and processed in a rich encyclopaedic context.

According to Sperber and Wilson, a phenomenon is relevant to an individual if and only if one or more of the assumptions it makes manifest is relevant to him. In comparing the relevance of different phenomena, as always, both effect and effort must be taken into account. On the effort side, this will involve not only the effort needed to access a context and process a given assumption in that context, but also the cost of constructing the assumption itself. Thus Sperber and Wilson define the relevance of a phenomenon as follows:

(26)   *Relevance of a phenomenon (comparative)*
        Extent condition 1: a phenomenon is relevant to an individual to the extent that the contextual effects achieved when it is optimally processed are large.
        Extent condition 2: a phenomenon is relevant to an individual to the extent that the effort required to process it optimally is small.
        (1986a:153)

This definition makes it possible to talk of utterances and other acts of communication being relevant, and lies at the heart of Sperber and Wilson's account of communication in general and pragmatics in particular. This account will be discussed in more detail in a later section. For the moment, let us return to the nature of contexts, and the process of context selection.

Most approaches to context assume that a context is already given, uniquely determined and fixed in advance of when an utterance is processed. For Sperber and Wilson, by contrast, the context is chosen as part of the interpretation process, or, more generally, as part of the process of maximising the relevance of *all* newly presented information.

I discussed above how the hearer may be motivated to extend the initial context by adding chunks from encyclopaedic entries which are accessible to him through the presence in working memory of a particular concept. There are further ways in which a hearer may extend his initial context, for instance by adding information derived via perception of the environment. Consider (27):

(27)   Those daffodils are really early.

We do not always pay attention to everything in our physical environment, and it is quite possible that the hearer of (27) was not aware of the daffodils until the speaker mentioned them. Sperber and Wilson point out that in the appropriate situation a hearer may access new information from his environment and add it to the context. This again shows that the context cannot be given in advance.

I have argued that the initial context consists of the assumptions most recently processed: e.g. in discourse, the proposition expressed by the immediately preceding utterance, and the assumptions used in processing it, together with its contextual effects. However, there are more easily accessible assumptions than just those present in the immediate context. One reason for thinking this is that we can easily refer back with pronouns to something mentioned earlier in the discourse. Compare (28a–c):

(28)   a. A: The car needs to be washed before we leave tomorrow.
         b. B: I have to go to London tomorrow, to get my visa.
         c. A: Don't worry, I will do it alone.

The initial context in which B will process (28c) has to do with London and visas. However, B is expected to have (28a) still highly accessible, and to use it in determining the reference of the proform *do it* in (28c). Sperber and Wilson therefore suggest that there may be a variety of short-term memory stores, to which different types of proform might direct the hearer's attention.

However, it is not to be assumed that all information accessed during a discourse remains in short-term memory. Sperber and Wilson assume that most assumptions will be dismantled and stored at their respective conceptual addresses. Thus if a speaker wants to refer back to something he discussed much earlier on in the discourse, these assumptions may have to be reassembled. This may provide less incentive to use proforms, and greater incentive to use context-reintroducing phrases such as *as I said before, as far as x is concerned*, etc. These phrases increase the accessibility of assumptions which have passed out of short-term memory and are therefore too costly to use directly in establishing the reference of proforms.

Thus the choice of the context for comprehension is constrained by the initial context, a general-purpose short-term memory store and the organisation of encyclopaedic memory and perceptual systems, and which context is chosen is determined by the search for relevance.

On this account, comprehension does not proceed in the order sometimes assumed in the pragmatic literature, with the context being determined first, then the interpretation process taking place, then relevance being assessed. Sperber and Wilson do not share the view that relevance is a variable to be assessed as a function of a predetermined context. They claim instead (1986a:141) that

on the contrary people hope that the assumption being processed is relevant (or else they would not bother to process it at all), and they try to select a context which will justify that hope: a context which will maximise relevance. In verbal communication in particular, it is relevance which is treated as given, and context which is treated as a variable.

2.2.4   The principle of relevance

In the last section it was suggested that people invariably try to maximise the relevance of any new information they acquire. How much attention I pay to any new information will depend on how relevant it proves to be. Thus I am likely to spend more time pondering the implications of the fact that I have lost my purse than the implications of the fact that a train has just passed by: one fact is rich in implications, and the other is not.

However, there is an important difference between information which we gain by observing the environment around us or which we overhear accidentally, and information which is deliberately addressed to us. If somebody deliberately attracts my attention in order to offer me information, then, according to Sperber and Wilson, he suggests that the information he has to offer will be relevant enough – that is, rich enough in contextual effects and economical enough in processing terms – to be worthy of my attention. In other words, deliberately communicated information creates a presumption that it will be relevant enough to be worth the audience's attention.

But how relevant is that? According to Sperber and Wilson, to be relevant enough, deliberately communicated information must have 'adequate' contextual effects. What counts as adequate depends on what you are doing or thinking at the time. For example, if you are watching a fascinating film, your attention will be fully occupied, and you would be unlikely to find the information that I have just bought a stunning outfit in the sales relevant enough. After the film, though, if there is nothing immediately demanding your attention, the same information might be relevant enough. The presumption of adequate contextual effects, then, varies from situation to situation, and would normally be defeated only by a blatantly false or patently true assertion, which, at the level of the proposition expressed, would yield no contextual effects at all.

On the processing-effort side, however, the presumption of relevance is more substantive. A speaker who deliberately wastes her hearer's processing effort is either irrational or not genuinely attempting to communicate. Thus, deliberate communication creates a presumption that the speaker has tried to achieve adequate contextual effects, and has put the hearer to no unjustifiable effort in achieving them.

According to Sperber and Wilson, an utterance or other act of communication is *optimally relevant* when it achieves an adequate range of contextual effects for the minimum justifiable processing effort. The key to their theory of inferential communication is the following *principle of relevance*:

(29)   *Principle of relevance*
         Every act of ostensive communication communicates the presumption
         of its own optimal relevance. (1986a:158)

As Sperber and Wilson point out, the presumption of optimal relevance may or may not be borne out. For example, I may tell my neighbour that the roof is going to be repaired, and discover that she already knows it, so that the information is irrelevant to her. The utterance is thus inconsistent with the presumption of optimal relevance: it is not optimally relevant. None the less, according to Sperber and Wilson, it will be *consistent with the principle of relevance* as long as the speaker might rationally have thought it would be optimally relevant to the hearer. It is the criterion of consistency with the principle of relevance that, according to Sperber and Wilson, is the single criterion governing every aspect of utterance interpretation: in testing possible interpretations of an utterance, the hearer should be looking for an interpretation consistent with the principle of relevance – that is, an interpretation that a rational speaker aiming at optimal relevance might have intended to convey.

This criterion raises an obvious question: could there be more than one interpretation consistent with the principle of relevance? Sperber and Wilson (1986a:167) argue that the criterion of consistency with the principle of relevance warrants the selection of at most a single interpretation for any given utterance, and that this interpretation is the first one found to be consistent with the principle. Their argument goes as follows: a hearer who has been addressed with a certain utterance and who takes it that the presumption of relevance has been communicated, will be in a position to construct hypotheses about the communicator's intention: that is, about the proposition the speaker intended to express, about the intended context and contextual effects. We have already seen that there is a variety of possible hypotheses about the intended context and contextual effects. The fact that the linguistically encoded semantic representation of a sentence is merely an incomplete 'assumption schema' which must be completed in various ways to yield a fully propositional form, means that there is a variety of possible hypotheses, too, about the proposition the speaker intended to express. Let us call a particular combination of context, content and contextual effects a possible *interpretation* of an utterance. Then every utterance has a variety of possible interpretations.

Sperber and Wilson draw our attention to the fact that not all possible interpretations of an utterance will be equally accessible in a given situation. We have already seen that the members of the set of potential contexts are ordered by their accessibility. In the same way, the set of potential contextual effects will be more or less accessible, depending, on the one hand, on the accessibility of contexts, and on the other hand on the fact that one contextual implication may be derivable only by using another contextual implication as premise. Finally, the various possible propositions that an utterance may be taken to express will not all be equally accessible, if only because of ordering in the accessibility of the various potential referents of its referring expressions.

The fact that the various possible interpretations of an utterance are not equally accessible means that they will be tested for consistency with the principle of relevance not all at once, but in a fixed order. This means that in the case of disambiguation, for instance, it is not necessary to consider all the possible interpretations before making a choice. One interpretation will invariably be more accessible than the others, and this first accessible interpretation will be the first to be tested for consistency with the principle of relevance. Consider the ambiguous utterance (30), with the possible interpretations (31) and (32):

(30)   Bob went to the bank.
(31)   Bob went to the river bank.
(32)   Bob went to the financial institution.

In a situation where the hearer has assumptions immediately accessible about Bob rowing on the river, she should have immediate access, via the encyclopaedic entry for 'river', to a context in which interpretation (31) would have adequate contextual effects. In a situation where it is known that Bob wants to deposit a cheque, the hearer should have immediate access, via the encyclopaedic entry for 'cheque', to a context in which (32) would have adequate contextual effects.

Suppose that the first accessible interpretation of (30), on a given occasion, is (31), and that this interpretation yields adequate contextual effects for the minimum justifiable processing effort, in a way the speaker could manifestly have foreseen. In these circumstances, a speaker who intended to convey (32) would have caused the hearer the considerable unnecessary processing effort of first accessing and processing (31), and finding this interpretation acceptable, and then engaging in some further form of inference to choose between the two interpretations. The result could never be consistent with the principle of relevance. Hence, according to Sperber and Wilson, the first accessible interpretation consistent with the principle of relevance is the *only* interpretation consistent with the principle of relevance, and is the one the hearer should choose.

It is worth emphasising here just what is being claimed, and what is not. As already noted, it is not being claimed that the hearer should choose the first accessible interpretation or the first adequately relevant interpretation: he should choose the first interpretation consistent with the principle of relevance – that is, which a rational speaker might have thought would achieve adequate contextual effects for the minimum justifiable processing effort. It is not being claimed that an utterance which expresses an irrelevant proposition cannot be understood: on the one hand, the speaker may have thought the proposition it expressed would be relevant; on the other hand, the speaker may have intended to make manifest some other proposition than the one explicitly expressed, on the basis of which the utterance might still achieve optimal relevance. It is not being claimed that all the possible interpretations of an utterance must be compared before comprehension is achieved: on the contrary, if the speaker has done his job correctly, the interpretation that is selected may have been the only one considered. In short, the criterion of consistency with the principle of relevance is both rigorous and easily incorporated into a plausible psychological model.

Having outlined the main tenets of relevance theory, I want to look more closely in the next section at how it deals with some specific aspects of utterance interpretation.

2.3   Relevance theory and pragmatics

In this section I will show how relevance theory, and in particular the criterion of consistency with the principle of relevance, applies to solve the traditional pragmatic problems of disambiguation, reference assignment, recovery of implicatures, etc. The discussion will be divided into two parts: relevance and propositional form; and relevance and implicature.

2.3.1   Relevance and propositional form

As we have seen, the semantic representation of an utterance, which is recovered by linguistic decoding, does not normally determine a unique proposition. The sentence itself may be ambiguous – i.e. there may be more than one possible semantic representation. The sentence may contain referential expressions, which need to be assigned a unique reference. It may contain vague expressions, whose interpretation needs further specification. And it may be semantically incomplete in various ways, and need to be completed before it can be understood as representing a determinate state of affairs.

According to Sperber and Wilson (1986a:176–93) in deciding on the propositional form of an utterance – that is, in deciding which proposition the speaker intends to express – the criterion of consistency with the principle of relevance plays a vital role. The criterion, as I have already shown, is strong enough to select at most a single proposition from the range of propositions that the utterance could in principle express.

In order to identify the propositional form of an utterance, two mental mechanisms are involved: the linguistic input module and the central inferential ability. The input module decodes the semantic representation of the sentence uttered, which is then passed on to the central systems, where, for instance, disambiguation and reference assignment are carried out.

Let us consider a case of disambiguation:

(33)   The meal at the Taj Mahal last night was too hot.

It is generally assumed that both senses of an ambiguous word are automatically recovered by the linguistic input system, which will thus assign two interpretations to (33): one in which the meal was boiling hot and the other in which the meal was too spicy. How would the hearer decide which interpretation was intended?

In the absence of any special context, it is the interpretation that the meal was spicy which is the one the hearer is likely to choose. This is because the encyclopaedic entry for 'Taj Mahal restaurant' should make the information available that it is an Indian restaurant, which in turn gives access to the information that Indian food is normally hot (spicy). It is easy to think of a context in which the information that last night's meal was too spicy would have adequate contextual effects. If the speaker did *not* intend this interpretation, then, he should have reformulated his utterance to eliminate it, thus avoiding the risk of misunderstanding, and sparing his hearer some unnecessary processing cost. In other words, the first interpretation tested and found consistent with the principle of relevance is the only interpretation consistent with the principle of relevance, and is the one the hearer should choose.

As far as reference assignment is concerned, the hearer should first search the immediate context for possible referents, extending the context only if that initial search fails. Consider the following Biblical passage:

(34)   a. Then the whole company of *them* arose,
         b. and brought *him* before Pilate.
         c. And they began to accuse *him*, saying,
         d. 'We found *this man* perverting our nation.' (Luke 23:1–2)

In processing the proposition expressed in (34a) the hearer must be able to identify the members of 'the company' in order to assign a reference to *them*. In processing (34b), he will not find a referent for *him* in the immediately preceding clause, but should be able to identify the referent of *him* as Jesus, who was mentioned only a few utterances before. In (34c) and (34d) the question is, who is the referent of *him* and who is the referent of *this man*? From a grammatical point of view, the referent could be either Jesus or Pilate, or any other man. However, the assumption that Pilate was in a position to be accused of perverting the nation would not only be less accessible in the circumstances than the assumption that Jesus was in such a position, but would also contradict manifest assumptions about the status of Pilate, the purpose of bringing Jesus before Pilate, and so on. Hence the criterion of consistency with the principle of relevance selects Jesus as the intended referent of *him* and *this man*.

Most pragmatists note that disambiguation and reference assignment must be performed by pragmatic means. However, they often do not consider a whole range of other factors affecting the identification of the proposition expressed. For instance, consider (35):

(35)   This cat is small.

Is (35) true or false? It is impossible to tell without specifying some standard of comparison: for example, small for a cat, small for a Siamese cat, small for an adult cat, small for a young cat, small for a prize cat and so on. The appropriate standard must be identified by pragmatic means. As always, the criterion involved is consistency with the principle of relevance. That is, the hearer should select the first accessible standard which yields an interpretation that a speaker aiming at optimal relevance might have wanted to convey – an interpretation yielding adequate contextual effects for the minimum justifiable processing effort.

In this section my aim was to show how the propositional form of an utterance is identified in context. I have argued that the semantic representation of a sentence is an incomplete logical form; i.e. an assumption schema, which is recovered by an automatic process of decoding and enriched with contextually accessible information into a fully propositional form. The enrichment process is inferential, and is constrained by the criterion of consistency with the principle of relevance. The enrichment of logical forms will be discussed further in chapters 5, 7 and 8.

Sperber and Wilson (1986a:183–93) draw a distinction between the *explicatures* and *implicatures* of an utterance. The explicatures of an utterance are explicitly communicated: where the speaker asserts, for example, *I am happy*, they will include the proposition that the speaker is happy, the speaker says she is happy, and the speaker believes she is happy. The implicatures of an utterance are implicitly communicated. For Sperber and Wilson, they are intended contextual assumptions and contextual effects. In the next section, I will describe how they are recovered.

2.3.2   Implicatures

In the last section I showed how the propositional form and explicatures of an utterance are identified. Explicatures, I suggested, are part of what the speaker said and not of what he implicated. In this section I would like to take a closer look at the way Sperber and Wilson (1986a:193–202) define 'implicature'.

It was mentioned that the purpose of communication is to achieve contextual effects, but does an utterance always have the effects the speaker intended? Sperber and Wilson emphasise that it has to be the concern of a pragmatic theory to provide an explanation of how the hearer recovers not just any interpretation, but the one the speaker intended. There has to be a distinction made between the information which the speaker intended the hearer to recover and the processes by which hearers recover unintended effects, and which are undertaken on the hearer's own initiative rather than through his desire to identify the intended interpretation. According to Sperber and Wilson implicatures are contextual assumptions and implications that are part of the *intended* interpretation of an utterance, and are thus recovered by the criterion of consistency with the principle of relevance.

Sometimes a speaker provides information without knowing or caring what its contextual effect will be. Thus I may have the following conversation with the conductor at the underground station in Highbury:

(36)   R: Where do I have to change for Heathrow?
        C: At King's Cross.

This answer need have no implicit import or implicatures. By asking a question, R guarantees that a direct answer will be relevant to her. C simply provides the information requested, and leaves it to R to decide what context to access, and what effect to achieve. Sperber and Wilson claim that C's utterance has no implicatures precisely because there is no reason to think that the speaker expected his utterance to be interpreted one way rather than another, in one context rather than another, achieving one set of effects rather than another. In other words, this utterance will have contextual implications, but no implicatures, i.e. no specifically intended contextual effect; it will be processed in a context, but not one that is specifically implicated or intended.

Now consider example (37), where it is obvious how the second speaker expects his utterance to be relevant.

(37)   a. Jane: Did you watch the figure-skating last night?
        b. Michael: I don't watch TV.

The utterance in (37b) is not a direct answer to Jane's question. However, the proposition expressed will give Jane access to encyclopaedic information about TV programmes, and more specifically to the information:

(37)   c. Figure-skating is shown on TV.

The only way Michael could have seen the figure-skating is by watching it on TV. By processing (37b) in a context containing (37c), Jane can derive the contextual implication (37d):

(37)   d. Michael did not watch the figure-skating.

Moreover, it is hard to see how the first speaker could have expected her utterance to be optimally relevant to the hearer if she did *not* expect the hearer to supply assumption (37c) and derive conclusion (37d). Examples (37c) and (37d) are needed if the utterance itself is to be seen as consistent with the principle of relevance. For Sperber and Wilson, this is the necessary feature of implicatures. They are assumptions and conclusions a rational speaker aiming at optimal relevance must have expected her audience to supply.

Sperber and Wilson distinguish between two types of implicature: *implicated premises* and *implicated conclusions*. Example (37c) is an implicated premise of (37b) and (37d) is an implicated conclusion. All standardly discussed implicatures fall into one of these two categories.

Example (37b) is an indirect answer to the question in (37a). Consider now another question: why would a speaker answer indirectly, when answering directly would have saved the hearer processing effort? Here relevance theory suggests an interesting answer. If Michael had intended simply to communicate the information that he did not watch the figure-skating, together with any effects derivable from this, then his utterance in (37b) would not be consistent with the principle of relevance, because he could have achieved these effects more economically by saying simply *No*. It follows, then, that if he was aiming at optimal relevance, he must have intended to convey more than this.

Thus, to find an interpretation consistent with the principle of relevance, Jane must access further assumptions and derive further conclusions, which, by the above definition, will also be implicatures. For example, Jane could access assumptions along the lines of (38a) and (39a) and derive conclusions along the lines of (38b) and (39b):

(38)   a. The news is a TV programme.
(39)   a. *Dallas* is a TV programme.
(38)   b. Michael does not watch the news.
(39)   b. Michael does not watch *Dallas*.

But these are probably not the only contextual implications she will or could draw. She might construct assumptions along the lines of (40a) and derive conclusions along the lines of (40b):

(40)   a. People who do not watch TV think they would be wasting their time if they did.
(40)   b. Michael thinks he would be wasting his time if he watched TV.

Thus the indirect answer in (37b) encourages Jane to derive a further set of conclusions, beyond those needed to understand the first answer, in order to achieve an interpretation consistent with the principle of relevance. The indirect answer in (37b) could not be optimally relevant unless some additional conclusions were derived. They are needed to offset the extra processing effort incurred by the indirectness of the answer.

Sperber and Wilson distinguish strong and weak implicatures. Example (37b) above very strongly implicates (37d), since it is hard to see how the utterance could achieve optimal relevance if this contextual implication were not recovered. By contrast, (37b) much less strongly implicates (38b) – (40b): some such implicatures must be recovered if the utterance is to achieve optimal relevance, but there is no one implicature in this range which the hearer is specifically intended to recover.

Now let us assume the hearer continues processing (37b), and that the encyclopaedic entry for TV gives her access to assumptions (41) – (43):

(41)   Video is similar to TV.
(42)   Cinema is similar to TV.
(43)   Radio is similar to TV.

and let us assume that she is further prepared to make the assumption that Michael would not engage in any activity similar to watching TV. Then she would be able to derive contextual implications such as

(44)   Michael would not watch video, cinema, etc.

It does not seem reasonable to assume that Michael was encouraging Jane to construct assumptions and derive conclusions such as these. If Jane does so, she must take most of the responsibility herself. In other words, they are not intended contextual assumptions and implications: they are not implicatures. In Sperber and Wilson's terms, they do not have to be recovered in order to see the utterance as optimally relevant. They are *not* part of the first accessible interpretation consistent with the principle of relevance.

Sperber and Wilson assume that there is no clear cut-off point between implicated and non-implicated assumptions and conclusions. The strongest possible implicatures are the fully determinate premises and conclusions, such as (37c) and (37d), which the hearer has to supply if the interpretation is to be consistent with the principle of relevance. Strong implicatures, such as (38a,b) – (39a,b), are strongly encouraged, but do not necessarily have to be supplied. The weaker the encouragement, the wider a range of possible interpretations is open to the hearer, and there will be a point at which there is no encouragement supplied by the speaker to construct a particular interpretation.

Thus an utterance with a small range of strongly implicated premises or conclusions strongly encourages the hearer to use all these assumptions, and to regard them as forming part of the speaker's beliefs. An utterance with a wide range of weakly implicated premises or conclusions encourages the hearer to use some subset of these assumptions, and regard some subset of them – but not necessarily the same subset – as part of the speaker's beliefs. The weaker the implicatures, the greater the possible discrepancy between the thoughts actually entertained by speaker and hearer.

Weak implicatures play a special role in the interpretation of all types of figurative speech (see Sperber and Wilson 1986a:217–43). In the course of the book I will discuss a number of examples. Here, I just want to give one example of metaphor to show how weak implicatures may play a role. Consider (45):

(45)   a. Michael is a mouse.

On Sperber and Wilson's analysis of metaphor, (45a) would express the proposition that Michael is a mouse, but would not explicate it: the speaker does not expect to be understood as guaranteeing that this proposition is true. The speaker does, however, implicate some of the contextual implications drawn from the cultural stereotype of a mouse. Thus (45a) would typically implicate premise (45b):

(45)   b. Mice are timid.

Combining (45a) and (45b), the hearer can draw the contextual implication (45c), which would be an implicated conclusion:

(45)   c. Michael is timid.

Examples (45b) and (45c) are strong implicatures. It is hard to see how the utterance could achieve optimal relevance unless some such implicatures were derived. Considerations of relevance ensure that the hearer will use only those encyclopaedic properties of mice which can also be attributed to humans – thus something like *Michael is a rodent* or *Michael lives in a mousehole* would be ruled out as inconsistent with common-sense assumptions. However, for reasons already given, the speaker would not have achieved optimal relevance if he had only wanted to convey (45c) by saying (45a), since he could have conveyed this more economically by saying *Michael is timid*. By using a metaphor, the speaker therefore encourages the hearer to draw further weak implicatures. In the case of (45a) these may include, for example, assumptions about Michael's drabness or insignificance of appearance. It is clear that these implicatures are much weaker than (45b) and (45c).

Sometimes all the implicatures of an utterance are weak. In the case of the commercial slogan (46), mentioned in the first chapter,

(46)   The Peugeot 405 takes your breath away.

there is no one strong implicature which the hearer is expected to recover. Rather, there will be an array of weak ones to the effect that the Peugeot 405 has a lot of astonishing qualities, and should therefore be an attractive car to buy.

In this section I have introduced a view of pragmatics which differs from the traditional view in a number of respects. On the one hand, it provides a clear criterion for the identification of propositional form and implicatures. On the other hand, it does not ignore the fact that there may be indeterminacy in utterance interpretation; indeed, it offers a theoretical framework in which such indeterminacy can be accepted and explained. In the next section, I will make some more detailed comparisons between relevance theory and alternative pragmatic approaches.

2.4   Relevance theory versus coherence theory

One fundamental difference between relevance-based and coherence-based approaches is that, while coherence is a relation between *linguistic units* (utterances, elements of a text), relevance is a relation which is defined not only for utterances but also for assumptions, i.e. units of information or thought. Relevant assumptions may be acquired from text, but also from isolated utterances, from non-verbal communication and indeed from situations in which no communication takes place at all. For example, I may discover that I have dropped my purse by being told it, by someone tugging at my arm and pointing it out or by simply opening my handbag and noticing that it is gone: the information will be equally relevant to me whatever its source.

A second major difference is that the criterion of consistency with the principle of relevance does not encounter difficulties in dealing with many examples that are problematic for coherence-based approaches.

Returning to Hobbs' example (12) in chapter 1, repeated here as (47), we can now see how the hearer might go about picking out the right referent for the pronoun *he*:

(47)   John can open Bill's safe. He knows the combination.

The information that John can open Bill's safe is likely to raise immediately in the hearer's mind the question of how John comes to be able to open Bill's safe: is it because he is a safecracker, or a dynamiter, or because Bill has given him permission, or what? On the assumption that *he* refers to John, the second clause of (47) achieves optimal relevance by providing an immediate answer to these questions. Hence, by the criterion of consistency with the principle of relevance, this is the interpretation that should be chosen.

Here it might be argued that the principle of relevance does no more for the analysis of (47) than Hobbs' own account in terms of coherence. However, it can easily be shown that the criterion of consistency with the principle of relevance gives the correct account for utterances such as (27) and (28) of chapter 1, repeated here as (48) and (49), in which the most appropriate answer may be one that does not preserve coherence relations:

(48)   The man who has made a bomb may use it.
(49)   A. What did Susan say?
         B. You've dropped your purse.

The generic interpretation of (48) ('Any man who has made a bomb may use it') will be selected in two different situations: (a) when it is more accessible than the specific interpretation and has an adequate range of contextual effects; or (b) when the specific interpretation, though more accessible, has few or no contextual implications, and is thus not relevant enough to be worth the hearer's attention. To illustrate how this second situation might arise, consider the following exchange:

(48')   A: Do you think that man may use his bomb?
         B: Yes, he may. The man who has made a bomb may use it.

In these circumstances, it is the specific interpretation of (48'B) that is most likely to come first to mind. However, the speaker has just given this information in the first part of her answer. Sperber and Wilson (1986a:219–22) show that a repetition may be relevant: for example, if there is some doubt about whether the hearer has heard, believed or adequately processed the original remark. If no such doubt is reasonable, then the repetition in (48'B) will be irrelevant, and the generic interpretation should be selected instead.

In the case of (49) the non-coherent interpretation will be made more accessible than the coherent interpretation if the speaker, say, turns round to look at the ground, or points at the hearer's open bag: clearly, the information that the speaker has dropped her purse will have an enormous number of contextual implications in an immediately accessible context, and is not the sort of information that can wait.

Similarly, isolated utterances and discourse-initial utterances, for which, as we have seen, accounts in terms of coherence fail, are satisfactorily dealt with by the criterion of consistency with the principle of relevance. These are, like other utterances, interpreted in a context. Thus *Trespassers will be prosecuted*, example (2) of chapter 1, may yield adequate contextual implications in a context of general assumptions about trespassing and its penalties, which the criterion of consistency with the principle of relevance picks out.

The first sentence in a book, as with example (26) in chapter 1, repeated here as (50) for convenience will, as always, be interpreted in an easily accessible context:

(50)   It is a truth universally acknowledged that a single man in possession of a good fortune must be in want of a wife. (Austen, *Pride and prejudice*)

Here the proposition expressed by the utterance is likely to contradict manifest assumptions about what is universally acknowledged, and is therefore unlikely to be accepted as an explicature. An ironical interpretation at that point becomes obvious, and will be confirmed by subsequent ironies in the text.

Let me return to one more example, mentioned in chapter 1, example (35), repeated as (51a), which had the two possible interpretations (51b) and (51c):

(51)   a. The baby dropped the toy and cried.
            The mother picked it up.
        b. The mother picked up the baby.
        c. The mother picked up the toy.

A speaker of (51a) who intends to convey (51b) must assume that this will be the first interpretation tested and found consistent with the principle of relevance; and similarly for (51c). If the hearer does not have appropriate contexts immediately accessible, the utterance is inconsistent with the principle of relevance. The speaker should have reformulated her utterance so that the first interpretation consistent with the principle of relevance is the one she intended to convey.

Relevance theory thus accounts for the interpretation of utterances which coherence theory cannot account for and shows why even when there is a co-text, interpretation almost invariably involves the use of background assumptions not derived from the co-text. In this sense, relevance theory is clearly a more adequate theory of how utterances are understood.

2.5   Relevance theory and textuality

2.5.1   Text and relevance

In this section I will argue that just as relevance, rather than cohesion or coherence, is the key to comprehension, so it is relevance relations, rather than cohesion and coherence relations, which underlie judgements of textual well-formedness. The fact that there is generally a degree of connectivity between utterances in conversation is simply a result of the fact that speakers aim at optimal relevance. But as I showed in chapter 1, utterances and texts may be perfectly appropriate without exhibiting obvious coherence relations at all.

I will look first at a number of examples which do not exhibit obvious coherence or 'topic continuity', and show how they would be handled in a relevance-based framework. Consider (52):

(52)   a. What are you doing after eight o'clock?
        b. Marceline: Let's talk business.

Example (52b) is neither obviously coherent nor topic-preserving; yet it is clearly appropriate. Why is this? Relevance theory suggests the following answer: (52b) is not a direct answer to Pierre's question; nor would it imply an answer in any normally accessible context. However, the fact that Marceline has refused to answer Pierre's question would, given a set of contextual assumptions which any socially adept speaker could supply, be highly relevant. Thus the intuitive connection between (52a) and (52b) is not explainable in structural terms, or by examining the semantic content of these utterances, but it is explainable in a relevance-based approach.

In fact, there are many well-formed conversations which do not exhibit the connectedness between utterances that a coherence-based approach to textual well-formedness would lead one to expect. Consider (53):

(53)   a. He: Tomatoes have been cheap this year, haven't they?
        b. She: Look who's coming.
        c. He: Tony! Well I never.

Clearly such exchanges happen all the time, and would not normally be regarded as either uncooperative or defective. Yet intuitively there is no connection between the remarks in (53a) and (53b), and such an exchange would be ruled out on a coherence-based approach.

Within relevance theory, exchanges of the above type are readily explained: there is no *requirement* of topic continuity. The speaker of (53b) knows that the fact that Tony is coming will be relevant enough to be worth the hearer's attention, more relevant in fact than any other information she can give him. The idea that in a well-formed text each utterance *has* to connect up with the immediately preceding one is not borne out. Indeed it is easy to think of circumstances in which maintaining connectivity with previous discourse would be highly inappropriate. Suppose a friend comes up to you in the street and asks if you have time for coffee. As she speaks, you see behind her someone who is apparently about to snatch her handbag. Clearly, the most relevant – and the most appropriate – remark you could make in the circumstances is to warn her about this; the coherence-maintaining response would be entirely inappropriate.

Sometimes, indeed, the most appropriate, and relevant, response to some remark will be silence. I may indicate my displeasure at your question not by changing the subject, as in (52) above, but simply by saying nothing at all. Because relevance is defined for phenomena in general rather than texts, such examples present no problem for relevance theory. Here, for example, the fact that I have remained silent would be relevant in its own right. Coherence and topic, by contrast, are regarded as primarily properties of utterances or texts, and examples where relevant information is conveyed by non-linguistic means are problematic for coherence-based approaches. More generally, the more rigidly text-based an approach, the less adequate it will be to account for non-verbal and paralinguistic aspects of communication, which, by contrast, are readily handled within relevance theory.

As far as topic is concerned, it may indeed be useful to think pretheoretically of speakers or discourses as sometimes having topics. However, topic is not a necessary theoretical notion; comprehension can succeed even where there is no notion of topic, as the above examples show.

How are intuitions about topics then to be explained? Sperber and Wilson (1986a:216–17) argue that the notion of topic is derivative in relevance theory: a 'topic' merely gives access to an encyclopaedic entry which plays a relatively central role in comprehension, being drawn on, say, in the interpretation of each utterance in a stretch of discourse. Intuitions about topic can be seen as intuitions about homogeneity of context. Thus titles, often claimed to identify the topic of a discourse, can be seen as providing access to encyclopaedic information necessary for processing the text they introduce, the topic being the conceptual address at which the required encyclopaedic information is stored. However, not all well-formed and appropriate discourses can be easily provided with topics or titles, as the above examples have shown. Relevance theory can not only handle utterances or discourses with a relatively homogeneous context, as is needed for topic theory, but it can also handle utterances which are relevant in a non-homogeneous context: contexts which are derived from a variety of encyclopaedic and environmental sources, and for which intuitions for a common topic are lacking. On this approach, intuitions about topic-relevance are like intuitions about coherence: where they exist, they can be illuminated by a relevance-based framework, but they are neither necessary nor sufficient for comprehension. The basis for discourse analysis is not topic or coherence but relevance.

One of the main claims of text analysis is that texts have a structure which it is the task of the analyst to discover and display. I have already shown with example (29) of chapter 1 how relevance theory provides a better framework. It is worth noting too that in many cases these structures are themselves determined by considerations of relevance. Consider, for example, the fact that narratives generally begin by setting the stage, introducing the characters and then taking them chronologically through a sequence of events leading up to a climax. For a narrator aiming at optimal relevance, this procedure is quite reasonable. It is the aim of the speaker to optimise relevance over a discourse; that is, to achieve adequate contextual effects for the minimum justifiable processing effort. This makes it reasonable to introduce all contextual assumptions needed to establish the main point of the discourse before the climax itself is reached; where there are several peaks of relevance, perhaps culminating in a single, overall peak, the result should be the sort of paragraph structure so often noted in narrative texts.

Paragraph structure, like overall textual structure, has generally been approached in terms of cohesion or coherence. There is an intuition that just as the utterances which make up a single text must display connectedness or unity of meaning, so the utterances which make up a single paragraph should be more closely connected to each other than to utterances belonging to neighbouring paragraphs. I have already argued that connectivity between utterances is neither necessary nor sufficient for textual well-formedness, at least in conversation. However, the phenomenon of connectivity in a discourse certainly exists, and I would like to suggest a way of approaching it in the framework of relevance theory.

The problem with cohesion- or coherence-based approaches to connectivity is that they look for connections primarily at the level of utterance content. However, as I have shown, context has a crucial effect on the way utterances are understood, and it may not be possible to see the connection between one remark and another without considering the context in which they are processed. Thus, what makes (53b) above intuitively unconnected to (53a) is the fact that in establishing its relevance the hearer needs to use no information derived from the interpretation of (53a). What makes (52b) above intuitively connected to (52a), despite their apparent disparity of content, is the fact that in establishing its relevance, the hearer needs to make crucial use of information derived from the interpretation of (52a).

Typically, within a paragraph of narrative, there is a continuity of context in the following sense: information made easily accessible by the interpretation of the first utterance is used in establishing the relevance of the second; information made easily accessible by the interpretation of the second utterance is used in establishing the relevance of the third, and so on indefinitely. Which information will that be? In the framework Sperber and Wilson have developed it will be, first, the contextual assumptions used in establishing the relevance of an utterance, second, the content of the utterance itself, and third, its contextual effects.

For instance, relevance theory has more to say in the analysis of (54) than that there is connectivity between semantically similar concepts and a connective *but*.

(54)   The world of the happy is not the world of the unhappy, as Gerard often says, quoting some philosopher. But what that philosopher did not realise was that the happy can sometimes kidnap the unhappy and carry them kicking and screaming into the world of happiness. (Iris Murdoch, *The book and the brotherhood*)

Connectivity is primarily established through the search for adequate contextual effects. Thus the use of *but* suggests to the hearer that the relevance of the second utterance lies partly in the fact that it is designed to contradict and eliminate an assumption conveyed by the first. Where each utterance in a sequence makes use of information made easily accessible by the interpretation of the immediately preceding utterance, some degree of connectedness should be perceived. This is the case with example (52b) above, but not with example (53b), where information made easily accessible by (53a) makes no contribution to the context in which (53b) is processed.

Relevant units of text do not need to occur as a block but can occur interwoven. They would still be units of relevance, though they would cease to be paragraphs. Consider the following more complex example:

(55)   a.   He: Did you know that Upper Volta has a new name?
       b.   She: Bother! The fridge has stopped working.
       c.   Quick, fetch a bowl!
       d.   It's a long name isn't it? Something with F, or ...?
       e.   He: The bowl.
       f.   Yes, Burkina Faso and the people are the Burkinabè.
       g.   She: What a mess, the meat is all thawed. I'll have to fry it immediately.
       h.   What is the meaning of Burkina Faso?

 i. He: 'The land of the people of integrity.'
 j.   Let's have steak for lunch, then.

Here there are intuitively two interwoven conversations being conducted simultaneously. This intuition can be explained along the lines just suggested. Remarks (55a), (55d), (55f), (55h) and (55i) are intuitively connected, and also exhibit the sort of cumulative development of context just described; the same goes for remarks (55b), (55c), (55e), (55g) and (55j). The lack of connectedness between, say, (55a) and (55b) is explained by the fact that the interpretation of (55a) makes no contribution to the context needed to establish the relevance of (55b).

However, as my example (23) in chapter 1 was designed to show, the mere existence of connectivity between successive remarks in a discourse does not necessarily make it well-formed. It is easy to think of fictitious discourses in which each utterance bears some connection to the immediately preceding one, but in which the discourse as a whole displays no 'unity of meaning'. However, it is also easy to think of ways in which more global notions of relevance and continuity of context might be defined. In the case of a planned narrative, for example, it seems reasonable to assume that the speaker tries to optimise relevance over the narrative as a whole. In this case one could talk of the narrative as a whole as consistent or inconsistent with the principle of relevance. To the extent that extraneous material is introduced into a narrative – that is, material which, by the end of the narrative, has made no satisfactory contribution to relevance, either in its own right or by contributing to the context in which some later part of the narrative will be relevant – the text will be inconsistent with the principle of relevance. In other words, every part of a narrative must be there for a reason, and within relevance theory there are only a few possible reasons to consider: either it must be relevant in its own right, or it must contribute to the relevance of later stretches of discourse. Any narrative which is consistent with the principle of relevance should, I maintain, be seen as displaying unity of meaning in this sense.

A further aim of discourse analysts has been to isolate different types of discourse: conversational, procedural, narrative, expositional, hortatory and so on. The claim is that each is stylistically different and exhibits structures characteristic of its type, which can be described and classified (Callow 1974; Longacre 1983).

If discourse analysis is seen as investigating the formal part of text only, then this is the natural conclusion to come to, because discourses which have different functions exhibit different structuring to some degree. On closer investigation, though, it becomes clear that these 'types' are not always so clear-cut. Thus narrative may contain conversation, procedural discourse may have hortatory elements, conversation may have elements of all of these. Moreover, just setting up these types does not say anything about the function of these discourses nor why they have the particular structures they do. This approach is like comparing different games such as football, cricket and polo just by their outward appearances and forgetting that players are actively involved in achieving particular goals, the goals being different in each case.

It has also been assumed that there is a greater difference between conversation and the rest of the 'types' than there is between the narrative text 'types'. The reason for this is that conversation is much more loosely structured, in that there may be frequent contextual changes, and it is said to be typically governed by rules of 'turn taking' and co-operation, or other social rules.

This is not the only possible approach to discourse analysis. Conversation is not only a turn-taking type of activity, subject to social rules; it is also a cognitive activity, and can be investigated from a cognitive point of view. I have illustrated above how the cognitive, relevance-based approach can shed light on dialogues which do not conform to rules of turn-taking, because information has arisen which it is urgent to impart. In relevance-theoretic terms, the goals of communication are the same for all formal types of discourse: to achieve adequate contextual effects with least justifiable processing effort. In the end many structural variations can be explained in these terms, but to go into detail is far beyond the scope of this book.

To sum up, the aims of coherence- and topic-based approaches are quite different from the aims of relevance theory: coherence- and topic-based approaches look at purely textual connectivity: relevance theory is based on the relation between information content and context. Moreover, discourse analysis within relevance theory is not a purely formal matter, but involves a consideration of how texts are understood, how they are processed and what effects are achieved. Context is viewed as actively constructed in the course of the comprehension process, rather than given in advance. A unit of text is a unit of relevance if relevance is optimised over it. Thus relevance theory suggests criteria for well-formedness judgements which other theories do not.

2.5.2   Aspects of text analysis in Sissala

2.5.2.1 Paragraphs
In the last section I discussed the theoretical basis of paragraphs. Let us now consider some Sissala examples. The following is taken from an oral description of Abidjan:

(56)   a. ʊ tɔ́ɔ   sɪɛrʊ   jıısɛ   náŋá,
           its town inside houses some
        b. 6a   pí   simiti   ní   a   sɔ́   wɔ́
           they take cement SDM and build them
        c. ká   6áséwɔ́   wuu   arí   céŋsé.
           and nail them all   with zinc
           'Some of the houses in town are built with cement and have zinc roofs.'
        d. ʊ jıısɛ   wɪ   jııyolli   kené.
           its houses NEG mud-roofs have
           'Its houses do not have mud roofs.'
        e. Abijan   jıısɛ   náŋá ká jııtukni   ní.
           Abidjan houses other are storey-houses SDM
           'Other houses of Abidjan are storey houses.'

The topicalised element in (56a) 'Some of the houses in town' makes the encyclopaedic entries for 'houses' and 'town' available to the hearer, providing the main context against which the subsequent stretch of discourse is to be processed. The interconnections among the units of discourse are revealed by examining the intended contextual effects. For example, consider the intended effects of (56d): to establish these, the background assumptions of the intended audience have to be taken into account. The point of uttering (56a–c) is that the people to whom this description of Abidjan was addressed have a stereotype of houses being built of mud with flat mud roofs. They rarely encounter houses built with cement and roofed with zinc. Thus, that *all* the houses of Abidjan should have zinc roofs is quite unusual. On hearing (56a–c) the hearer will modify his expectations about houses in Abidjan, but may still preserve enough of his stereotype to assume that none the less *some* houses in Abidjan will have mud roofs. The effect of (56d) is to contradict and eliminate this residual assumption. Thus (56d) is relevant in a context directly created by (56a–c). Example (56e), by contrast, is the beginning of a new paragraph. A new concept, 'storey-houses', is introduced, and (56e) has no contextual effect in the context directly created by (56a–d).

Of course the two units of relevance, (56a–d) on the one hand and (56e) on the other, are also related to each other. They both provide answers to the same question: *What is Abidjan like?* which is intuitively the topic of the whole discourse.

I have deliberately started with a paragraph which does not have a typical initial 'paragraph marker' to show that the unit of paragraph can be defined in terms of contextual effects alone. However, sometimes there seem to be overt markers used only in written text, but in most cases, 'paragraph markers' also occur in conversation. In relevance theory such markers are naturally analysable as guiding the interpretation process. As was shown above, breaks between paragraphs tend to coincide with breaks in the continuity of context. A marker at the beginning of a paragraph has the function of preparing the hearer for such breaks. They thus fall into the class of linguistic expressions which Blakemore (1987) calls 'semantic constraints on relevance' (see chapter 4).

Consider (57) in Sissala:

(57) a. Pılɛkɛ   má kúsɛ ʋ ɓıɛ,   amá taŋa ʋ mıɛ́ wı káŋ
          chameleon also cut his things but really his millet NEG a-lot
          'The chameleon harvested his things but his millet was not much.'
       b. Ɛ né pıléké   dé   ko   kɛsɛ nancʋʋsɛ...
          then chameleon INT come catch flies
          'Then the chameleon caught flies...'

Ɛ né (literally: 'that being it') in (57b) is a fixed expression, which can also occur in other positions (not only paragraph-initially). Its presence may give rise to a temporal interpretation. It indicates that the hearer has to be prepared for a quite different context – in this case, from 'millet harvesting' in (57a) to 'catching flies' in (57b). Although there is a new paragraph starting with *ɛ né* the expression does not *mean* 'here is a new paragraph'. It merely alerts the hearer to a particular type of break in the continuity of context.

Relevance theory also sheds light on other traditional notions in discourse analysis, as is shown by the following example:

(58) a. Zaŋ ɓıɛ   ná né   ŋ má colli.
          Jean things the SDM I also like
       b. Ʋ há   maŋ́sɛ́ háálɔ́ há   mɔhɛ́ ʋ-ʋ   tuŋ ɛ́
          he how teach woman what must COMP-she work that
          nibiine sísıɛrʋwa,
          society in

c. háálɔ́ há mɔhɛ̄ rú-ú   a   ɛ́ ná ʊ rí rú
woman how must COMP-she make that there she and her
bala   wɔ́llí nɑ́ŋɑ́ mɛ́.
husband can others at
'Jean's speech I also liked. How he taught which role the woman
has in society, what the woman must do so that she and her
husband have a good relationship with each other.'

The main intended effect of (58b) and (58c) is to strengthen the
proposition expressed by (58a). According to one traditional view, (58a)
would be 'mainline' information in discourse and (58b) and (58c) would
be 'peripheral'. In the terms of Hopper (1979), (58a) is 'in the foreground' and (58b) and (58c) are 'in the background'. However, little
explanation has been given of our intuition that some propositions
describe mainline events and others do not, or that some are in the
foreground and others are not. Relevance theory sheds some light on
these distinctions. The so-called background propositions have the
characteristic contextual effect of strengthening so-called foregrounded
propositions (although they may also have contextual implications in
their own right). Since the relationship of propositions in discourse to
each other and the context are much more rigorously analysable in terms
of contextual effects, I regard terms like 'mainline' and 'periphery',
'foreground' and 'background' as theoretically superfluous.

2.5.2.2 *'Discourse-unit marker'?*
Having seen the importance of considerations of relevance in discourse
processing and discourse analysis, it is no surprise to find devices in
language which guide the hearer's attention to crucial passages of the
discourse: that is, passages on which the main point of the discourse
depends. Longacre (1976:468–75) saw the occurrence of such devices as
an indication that discourse is a genuine grammatical unit, similar to a
sentence. I would like to suggest an alternative to this approach.

Consider the use of the particle *dé* (introduced in chapter 1, example
(29)), in a folk story:

(59)   The chameleon and the spider went and made farms next to each other.
           The spider harvested a lot,
        the chameleon harvested little.
        The chameleon *dé* caught flies,
        and made a pretty garment.
        He asked the spider whether he
        wanted the garment in exchange for

millet. The spider said 'Yes'.
The spider made his wife bring
millet to the chameleon and filled
all his granaries.
    One day the spider went to his
mother-in-law's funeral. He greeted
all the people. All of a sudden, the
flies *dé* of the garment flew away,
and *dé* left, and left him *dé*
sitting naked. The chameleon walked away.

Dé is used to mark important sections of the text. The first proposition marked with *dé* is one the hearer should keep easily accessible, as it will be crucial in what follows: as we notice at the climax of the story, the fact that the garment is made of flies is important. Then at the climax there are three utterances marked with *dé* which constitute the main point of the story: i.e. they carry the main contextual effects.

My hypothesis is that *dé* is used in order to minimise processing effort by guiding the hearer to the most important information, i.e. information which is crucial to the main intended contextual effects. Such expressions should naturally arise in a framework where the speaker is constantly anxious to spare the hearer processing effort, and thus increase his willingness to go on listening.

Many more Sissala examples could be provided to show how the speaker tries to facilitate processing over stretches of discourse in order to optimise relevance over the text as a whole. To treat the subject fully would make a book on its own. The examples I have discussed are intended to do no more than give an idea of how relevance theory sheds interesting light on more global aspects of a text.

2.5.3   Text, context and culture

I have already pointed out that communication depends to a large extent on the fact that humans can recover implicit contextual assumptions and derive implicit conclusions. What we say explicitly is only a fraction of what we actually communicate. The number of implicit assumptions which a hearer is expected to supply will depend to a large extent on how much information speaker and hearer share. Some implicit assumptions can be expected to be recovered by all humans; others are much less widely shared. Thus when someone refers to 'the moon' or 'the sun' all humans should be able to identify the referent, even when these terms are used for the first time in the discourse. On the other hand, (60) most probably does not communicate anything to the majority of English-speaking people:

(60)   Bounding theory poses locality conditions on certain processes and related items. The central notion of government theory is the relation between the head of the construction and categories dependent on it. (Chomsky 1982:5)

To make sense of these remarks one would have to attend a number of lectures in linguistics and acquire a fair amount of specialised knowledge.

Variation in potential assumptions is especially great between different cultures. Example (61) is probably quite comprehensible to any Westerner:

(61)   He went to McDonald's. The quarter pounder sounded good and he ordered it.

A Westerner immediately knows that implicit assumptions about restaurants must be used in processing this utterance, that the definite noun phrase refers to a type of hamburger, which in turn is supposed to be sold in this type of restaurant. All this information is immediately accessible to a Westerner in the encyclopaedic entry for 'McDonald's'. It would therefore detract from relevance to mention it explicitly. It would be unbearable for a Westerner to have to spend the time needed to process the following account, in which these assumptions are made explicit:

(62)   He went to a place where food is cooked and sold. It is called 'McDonald's'. There he saw ground meat which was formed into patties, fried and put into something baked with flour . . .

Yet to someone unfamiliar with the fast-food industry – for example, a Sissala person – this might be the only relevant way of giving this information, since he may have no encyclopaedic entries for 'McDonald's', 'hamburgers', 'bread buns', etc. In Western culture (62) would be far less relevant than (61), because much of it is already known, and thus yields few contextual implications in return for the effort spent in processing it. For a non-Westerner, by contrast, the rewards of processing (62) would be much greater, and he might find (61) entirely incomprehensible.

Similarly there may be information from other cultures which could pose a problem to us if it was not made explicit. Thus while any Sissala would be immediately able to recover the background assumptions needed to understand (63), these would have to be made explicit to a Westerner:

(63)   The river had been dry for a long time.
        Everybody attended the funeral.

This utterance is relevant in a context containing the following assumptions:

(64)   a. If a river has been dry for a long time then a river spirit has died.
        b. If somebody has died there is a funeral.

Everything hinges on the hearer's ability to supply the appropriate contextual assumptions. What seemed to be unconnected utterances in isolation become a coherent text when the appropriate background is supplied.

This helps to explain why anthropologists like Malinowski thought that other cultures have languages which are more 'context-dependent' than European languages. The fact that he would share background assumptions to a much higher degree with Europeans than with Trobriand Islanders may have helped to lead him to this conclusion, and allowed him to overlook the fact that Europeans 'imply' a lot as well.

On the other hand it is quite conceivable and explainable in relevance-theoretic terms that people of some cultures – of close-knit communities – share so many assumptions about the world that they indeed leave more implicit than people from less homogeneous cultures would, and that their discourses typically include less text than the same discourses would in less homogeneous cultures.

The following sections will be devoted to the subject of 'implicitness' in Sissala. How does the Sissala speaker exploit the existence of shared information in his search for optimal relevance? Here I want to justify my claim in chapter 1 that while cultural background may vary widely, the process of utterance comprehension is universally the same.

2.5.4   Sissala text and implicit import

2.5.4.1 *Text and implicature*
In section 2.3.2 I discussed the notions of contextual assumption, contextual implication and implicature. The purpose of this section is to show that this approach to the recovery of implicit import works as well for natural Sissala texts as it does for the artificial English examples I have so far discussed.

Consider (65):

(65)   Yıbiŋ   dʋʋnɛ zuɪ   mɛ́, duoŋ dé púl ko   wérí rí.
       rainy-season begin entering at   rain INT start come well IM
       Ba dé du   ɓıɛ   wuu.
       they INT plant things all
       'At the beginning of the rainy season the rains started to come well.
       (So) They planted all their things.'

Although there is no explicit marker indicating an inferential connection between the two propositions, it is clear that such a connection exists: the planting had only been done because the rains had come.

However, those who did the planting did not decide to plant solely because the rains had come. That decision would be based on additional background assumptions, such as the following:

(65′)   a. Plants only grow when the ground is wet.
        b. Rains make the ground wet.

With these extra premises in the context, the hearer can understand the inferential connection in (65) by constructing an argument based on (65′a), (65′b) and (65′c) to the conclusion that the planting could begin.

(65′)   c. The rains came.

(65′)   d. Conclusion: The planting could begin.

It is clear that without the extra implicit assumptions (65′a) and (65′b) there would have been no grounds for the conclusion in (65′d).

The next example is a case in which the speaker explicitly presents some premises and leaves the conclusion implicit:

(66)   a. ɪ zaa iso   ká tá   ŋ dʋŋɔ rí ya-a?
        you today get-up and leave me alone IM or-Q
        'Are you leaving me alone today?'
     b. Anɛ Luc ha sɛ́   ŋ́ é dí kıŋkaŋ.
        as   Luc   said I F eat a-lot
     c. ʋ keŋ taŋa   rɛ́.
        he has wisdom IM
        'As Luc said, I eat a lot. He is right.'

The above utterances were produced in a situation in which the speaker was the only one still eating. Example (66a) is a rhetorical question, drawing attention to this fact. The speaker then supplies premises which might explain why she is still eating. From the premises 'I eat a lot' and further assumptions to the effect that people who eat a lot need a lot of time for it, the hearers can draw the implicit conclusion (66′):

(66′)   X is still eating.

This conclusion was already accessible to them: what the additional premises do is offer a possible explanation of the fact.

However, X did not really want to communicate that she eats a lot; rather she was being ironical in mentioning what Luc had said about her. She knew that it was manifest to everyone that she had prepared the meal and was the last person to sit down and eat. She just had not had as much time to eat her meal as others had. Therefore, though X suggests a possible explanation of the fact that she is still eating, she expects them not to believe it, because of other assumptions she is confident her hearers have available. (For further treatment of irony see chapter 3.)

The next example is a typical case of an indirect answer, where the hearer is expected to draw contextual implications in order to derive the direct answer:

(67)   A: ʊ wa-á   hónsí-i?
        he not-IPF bark-Q
        'Does he not bark?'
       B: Tɔɔ́ dé biri ʊ dé pɛ́ ɛ́nɛ́,   tʊna!
        town INT black he INT sleeps like-this touna
        'At night he sleeps like this, touna!' (Description of a certain way of sleeping.)

B does not directly answer A's question, rather he supplies more information about what the dog does. A takes for granted that this information is intended to be relevant to him, and to yield an answer to his question.

To derive a direct answer from (67), A would have to have something like the following contextual assumption accessible:

(67′)   a. A dog who sleeps at night does not bark at night.

From assumption (67′a), together with (67B), A can derive the conclusion in (67′b):

(67′)   b. B's dog does not bark at night.

This is the conclusion B expects A to be able to draw, and it directly answers A's question. As we see, though B demands more processing effort than would have been needed to process a direct answer, he suggests that extra information, in the form of weak implicatures, is derivable from the indirect answer: for example, the information that the dog does not bark because he is asleep.

The next example involves a more complicated indirect answer. L's question is relevant in the following context: most people in West Africa travel either in lorries or in bush taxis (station wagons). The lorries are not very comfortable, unless one is invited to take the seat next to the driver. L knows that J normally refuses to travel in the back of a lorry, though she would travel in the back of a bush taxi. In Sissala the words for both car and lorry are the same *lɔɔlɛ* (from English *lorry*). When J says that she would take the 'market *lɔɔlɛ*', L thinks that she means 'a big lorry'. He becomes curious and wants to know whether J would compromise her principles:

(68)   L: a. Yɔwɔ lɔɔlɛ síɛ   kéŋ dıkéní rí-í.
            market lorry front has seat   IM-Q
            'Does the market lorry have a seat in the front (near the driver)?'

        J: b. Péézó   ní,
             Peugeot SDM
             'It is a Peugeot,'

           c. u sıɛ há wéro.
              it so P good
              'so it is good.'

J's answer is indirect. By uttering (68b) she makes a number of assumptions accessible to L, one of which she subsequently makes explicit herself:

(68')   a. Peugeot cars are bush taxis.
        b. Bush taxis are far more comfortable than big lorries.
        c. J would not mind being in the back of a bush taxi.

A direct answer to L's question becomes superfluous, given the assumptions which L now has accessible. Since J is going in a Peugeot car, it is not important to her whether there is a seat available in the front.

    L might continue the argument in (68') by adding the following assumptions:

(68')   d. If J takes a Peugeot car, she will take any seat available.

From this, together with what J has said, the contextual implication (68'e) can be drawn:

(68')   e. J would take any seat.

Having this information, L can draw implications to the effect that it is irrelevant whether the market car has a seat in the front or not.

It is interesting that J independently confirms with her utterance (68c) an assumption she expects L to have been able to infer from her utterance 'so it is good'. It seems that a lot of what we say is said for the purpose of strengthening – providing additional evidence for – our hearer's assumptions, and this is the reason for this kind of conversational contribution.

The four examples in (65)–(68) were meant to show that Sperber and Wilson's analysis of implicatures can be applied to very different languages. We can also observe that economy of processing effort and the search for adequate contextual effect are just as rigorously exploited in Sissala as they are in European languages. These examples provide no support for the view that different cultures use different kinds of logic.

2.5.4.2   *Explicature and ellipsis*

As was mentioned in section 2.3.1, few utterances explicitly encode a unique propositional form. It seems that disambiguation, reference assignment and various types of pragmatic enrichment of the explicitly encoded logical form are almost invariably required. However, utterances vary in their degree of explicitness: that is, in how much pragmatic enrichment is required. In some cases the speaker gets by with just one word, such as *yes* or *Shakespeare*, which is enough to enable the hearer to recover the full propositional form; in others, much more of that form is explicitly encoded.

As we will see with Sissala examples, the way content is encoded can vary considerably from language to language. There are more differences here than there are in the interpretation process used for implicatures. The reason is, of course, that the encoding of propositional content is a strictly linguistic matter, whereas the recovery of implicatures is not.

The following three examples from Sissala will illustrate some of the cross-linguistic differences I have in mind:

(69)   Tɔ́ɔ bírí u yɔwɛ muiwa a   pɔ [e] ʋ háálɔ ná. ʋ cɔ́
        day dark he buy   rice   and give [e] his wife DEF she cook
        [e]. ʋ sɛ́: 'La [e] mʋ́ pɔ́ [e] ŋ házoŋ.'
        [e] he said Take [e] go give [e] my lover.
        'In the evening, he bought rice and gave it to his wife. She cooked it.
        He said: "Take it and give it to my lover."'

In (69), there is a missing direct object of the verbs 'cook' and 'give' (indicated by [e]). The omission is optional in Sissala. In English, of course, the pronoun *it* would have to be used with these verbs, though with other verbs (e.g. *eat*) the omission would have been permissible in English too. Thus the Sissala hearer has no pronoun as a help or clue to facilitate reference assignment. He has to perform this task by pragmatic means alone.

Consider another example where the temporal indication in English would be made explicit but is left implicit in Sissala:

(70) a. Ba pa   a   tuki tɔɔ   mɛ́
         they collect and pound mortar in
      b. núúla ná   wuu bɪrmɛ mɪŋ
         fat   DEF all turns flour
         'They collect (nuts) and pound (them) in a mortar (*until*) all the fat becomes flour.'

The speaker expects the hearer to understand the event described in (70a) as lasting until (70b) becomes true. In English, of course, this would be made more explicit by use of the temporal marker *until*.

Consider one more example, in which the English speaker would either have to employ a preposition, or form a whole sentence with subject and verb:

(71) Ɔŋ   ká ballɛwié   rí   nyúú gilégilé, síɛ kórwóró,
      monkey is animal-small TDM head round   eyes crossed
      múdúŋ ɓɪgóó.
      tail   long
      'The monkey is a small animal, (with) a round head, (with) crossed eyes, (with) a long tail.'

In (71) the hearer has to realise that these noun phrases are to be interpreted as describing the monkey. The English speaker would make this relation explicit by using *with*.

The above examples show how language-specific syntactic constraints may affect the explicit encoding of propositional forms. They also show how pragmatics can account for the recovery of implicit import in Sissala. I argued that the way implicatures are recovered is very similar to the way they are recovered in English. I also showed that the explicitness of propositional form may vary considerably from language to language.

2.6   Conclusion

In this chapter and the last, I have concentrated on general issues, in an attempt to decide on a suitable framework for the analysis of discourse. I have argued that Sperber and Wilson's relevance theory currently offers the best account of the utterance-interpretation process, solving many problems which receive no satisfactory treatment in alternative accounts.[3] Here I would like to stress two fundamental assumptions of relevance theory that will play an important role in the remainder of this book.

First, the linguistic form of an utterance grossly under-determines its interpretation. What an utterance communicates vastly exceeds what it linguistically encodes, and this is true both at the level of what is said and at the level of what is implied. Second, the gap between what is linguistically encoded and what is communicated is not filled by a further layer of pragmatic coding. It is filled by an inference process constrained by a single, powerful pragmatic criterion, which yields at most a single interpretation for any utterance: the criterion of consistency with the principle of relevance.

In the remainder of this book, I shall be dealing with more specific issues concerning the relation between linguistic form and pragmatic interpretation. I shall be looking particularly at some possible analyses of 'non-content words' – i.e. determiners, conjunctions, complementisers, etc. (for which I shall sometimes use the cover term 'particles' or 'markers'). I shall approach the data with two central questions in mind. First, what do these particles encode? In particular, do they encode truth-conditional content or some more abstract form of processing instruction? Here, I shall argue that some particles are truth-conditional and others are not, and I shall suggest how one might decide between a truth-conditional and a non-truth-conditional approach.

The second question I shall bear in mind is: what are the implications of my analysis for the description of other languages? In the next chapter, for example, I shall look at a so-called 'hearsay' particle in Sissala and argue that what it encodes is rather different from what one would expect on traditional accounts of 'hearsay' particles in other languages. My analysis strongly suggests a reconsideration of such traditional accounts. In a later chapter, I shall argue that my analysis of the Sissala particle *má* 'also' has interesting implications for the analysis of the German particle *auch* 'also', and for the typology of particles in general. Thus, I hope that the move from general issues to specific ones will lead to no loss in relevance.

3 *The interpretive-use marker* ré

3.1 Introduction

A number of linguists have used the notion of a 'hearsay' particle in analysing particular languages, e.g. Ballard (1974), Barnes (1984), Chafe and Nichols (1986), Derbyshire (1979), Donaldson (1980), Givón (1982), Haviland (1987), Hewitt (1979), Höhlig (1978), Laughren (1981), Levinsohn (1975), Lowe (1972), Palmer (1986), Slobin and Aksu (1982), Thomas (1978), Willet (1988). While the exact uses of 'hearsay' devices vary from language to language, it is said that their main function is to mark information which the speaker got from somebody else. The data on hearsay particles have generally been rather fragmentary, and the notion of a hearsay particle is typically left unanalysed. My aims in this chapter are twofold: first, to provide a fuller range of data on one particular hearsay particle – ré, from Sissala: and second, to use ré to choose between two competing accounts of the nature and function of hearsay particles in general.[1]

What is the minimal hypothesis one might make about hearsay particles, given only the informal observation, noted above, that hearsay particles are used to mark information that the speaker got from somebody else? The minimal hypothesis would be, I think, that they should be used only for reporting actual speech. Reported thought would be excluded, and the status of paraphrase, or speech that is attributed by inference without actually being heard, would be unclear. Typically, work on hearsay particles reports a number of uses which do not fit the minimal hypothesis. My data provide clear counter-examples to it.

Apart from the minimal hypothesis, I know of two main accounts of the nature and function of hearsay particles. The first is offered by Palmer (1986:7,9). He sees the main function of hearsay particles in terms of the intention of the speaker to express his degree of commitment to the information being conveyed: this degree being most certainly

93

less high with hearsay particles than something experienced at first hand. For Palmer, therefore, a 'hearsay' particle is a kind of 'modal' or 'evidential', falling into the same semantic class as 'may' and 'might'.

There is some justice in this intuition. Compare (1b) and (1c) as responses to (1a):

(1)   a. Is Tokyo worth visiting?
       b. It is.
       c. They say it is.

The speaker of (1b) takes responsibility for the truth of the proposition expressed; the speaker of (1c) is responsible not for the truth of the proposition 'Tokyo is worth visiting', but only for the faithfulness of her report. This account will be considered in more detail in section 3.2.

The alternative account, which I hope to develop here, is based on the framework of Sperber and Wilson (1986a), who draw a fundamental distinction between *descriptive* and *interpretive* uses of utterances. In this framework, hearsay particles function as grammatical indicators of interpretive use, and fall together with other linguistic devices adapted for this function. This account will be considered in more detail in section 3.4. I will argue that the data from *ɾέ* in Sissala are compatible with neither the minimal hypothesis nor Palmer's evidential account, whereas they fit, in often surprising ways, with the assumptions of the Sperber–Wilson framework. In other words, I will argue that the grammatically definable particle *ɾέ* in Sissala is specialised to act as an indicator of the pragmatic phenomenon of interpretive use. This is what I shall mean when I talk of 'grammaticalisation of interpretive use'.

The form of this chapter will be as follows. In section 3.3, I shall outline Palmer's view of hearsay markers as evidential. Next, I shall present the Sissala data, assuming that *ɾέ* is a minimal hearsay marker or evidential. In section 3.4 I shall introduce the notion of interpretive use and its function within relevance theory. In sections 3.5–3.7 I shall argue that *ɾέ* is a marker of interpretive use which is found not only in true 'hearsay' constructions, but also in constructions involving propositional-attitude verbs, in irony, and in questions and echoic answers to questions, all of which are analysed by Sperber and Wilson as involving interpretive use. In section 3.8 I will discuss some further examples which also fit an analysis in terms of interpretive use.

I shall draw two main conclusions: first, that 'hearsay' constructions are best analysed, not as a type of modal or evidential, weakening the speaker's commitment to the truth of the proposition expressed, but as a variety of interpretive-use marker, with all the functions attributed to interpretive use by Sperber and Wilson; second, that other so-called 'hearsay' particles might be usefully re-examined to see whether they, like *ré*, occur in other than true 'hearsay' constructions, and should thus be reanalysed as markers of interpretive use.[2]

3.2   Cross-linguistic 'modal' systems

According to Palmer (1986:53), there are two different systems of epistemic modality found in the languages of the world: judgements and evidentials. Judgements involve speculation and deduction: evidentials include perceptives and quotative (hearsay) devices (e.g. particles and morphological marking). This fits well with the widespread view that there are three types of propositions expressible in language. For example, Givón (1982:24) proposes the following classification:

1   Propositions which are taken for granted, via the force of diverse conventions, as unchallengeable by the hearer and thus requiring no evidentiary justifications by the speaker.
2   Propositions that are asserted with relative confidence, are open to challenge by the hearer and thus require – or admit – evidentiary justification.
3   Propositions that are asserted with doubt as hypotheses and are thus beneath both challenge and evidentiary substantiation.

Type 1 propositions are usually described as declaratives; type 2 as evidentials; and type 3 as judgements.

Palmer suggests that there are two grammatical systems of epistemic modality. Some languages, like English, have a system only of judgements: apparently Tuyuca (Barnes 1984) has only evidentials. Other languages have a mixture of judgements and evidentials: Palmer refers to Inga (Levinsohn (1975:14–15)) and German. Consider (2), an example from Inga:

Inga (Levinsohn 1975:14–15)
(2)   a. nis   pununcuna-mi
            there they-slept-AFF
            'There they slept.'
        b. chipica diablo-char ca
            there   devil-DED it-was
            'A devil was presumably there.'
        c. chacapi-si   yallinacú
            on-bridge-REP they-were-crossing
            'They were crossing on the bridge.'

In (2a) the speaker is presenting a fact, which is marked with what Levinsohn calls 'affirmative' (AFF). Example (2b) is a conclusion which was drawn: it is not said on the basis of which evidence. The speaker marks this with what Levinsohn calls 'deductive' (DED); Palmer would list it under 'judgement'. Example (2c) has a marker 'reported' (REP), which indicates that the speaker got this information from somebody else. Markers of this kind have also been referred to as 'hearsay' markers.

In German there are similar phenomena, only in this case it is the verbal system itself which indicates the difference in speaker commitment. The verbs *wollen* and *sollen* may be used in such a way that they have a 'hearsay' effect, i.e. the speaker indicates that she is reporting what somebody else said. Compare (3), a straightforward declarative, with the 'reportative' (4):

(3)   Er ist in die Schweiz gegangen.
         'He has gone to Switzerland.'
(4)   Er soll in die Schweiz gegangen sein.
         'Apparently, he has gone to Switzerland.'

A pure system of evidentials has been described by Barnes for Tuyuca (1984). She introduces a system of five evidentials, which she calls 'visual', 'non-visual', 'apparent', 'second-hand' and 'assumed'. In some languages, e.g. Hixkaryana (Derbyshire 1979) and Nambiquara (Lowe 1972), the use of a 'hearsay' marker is obligatory when the speaker passes on anything that he heard from somebody else. Looking at the data of languages with obligatory 'hearsay' systems, it is surprising how much of what we communicate is not 'first-hand' information.

According to the standard accounts, *ré* in Sissala should be a 'hearsay' particle, or perhaps an 'evidential' with further uses than just 'hearsay'. However, does it fit the 'evidential' or 'modal' pattern as outlined in Palmer (1986)? In the following section I shall introduce the Sissala data, assuming first that it is a minimal 'hearsay' particle or 'evidential'. In subsequent sections, I shall revise this initial assumption.

3.3   Uses of *ré*

3.3.1   Origin of *ré* and phonological realisation

The 'hearsay' marker *ré* and its free variant *έ* in Sissala have most likely developed from the locative/demonstrative *ré* 'here, this', which is invariant in its phonological form (i.e. it is not influenced by the vowel qualities of its environment). Consider (5):

(5)   ʊ sɛ́: 'ko rɛ́'
        he said come here
        'He said: "Come here!"'

In (5) *ré* is used as a locative. It may also occur as a deictic demonstrative, to indicate in which direction to go. Its phonological form is not affected by the vowel quality of the preceding word.

By contrast, the hearsay marker *ré* (or *ɛ́*) is phonologically affected by both its syntactic and its phonological environment. Primarily, it is influenced by a form of vowel harmony which is sensitive to the value plus or minus of the feature 'advanced tongue-root' (ATR). Thus the vowel is *ɛ* or *ı* (depending on the position in the sentence) whenever *ré* (or *ɛ́*) is affected by the [−ATR] value; and the vowel is *i* whenever it is affected by the [+ATR] value. Secondly, it is influenced by its position in the sentence, with *ré* (*ɛ́*) occurring in NP-, VP- or S-final position and *rí* (*í*) elsewhere. The following display illustrates the vowel system of Sissala, the two harmonic vowel sets and the various forms of *ré*:

i	u	ı	ʊ
e	o	ɛ	ɔ
		a	

[+ATR]	[−ATR]
rí (í)	*ré (ɛ́)* in NP-, VP- or S-final position
rí (í)	*rí (í)* elsewhere

In S-medial and -final position the vowel of *ré* harmonises with the vowel quality of the *preceding* word; in S-initial (COMP) position it harmonises with the *following* word, specifically to the quality of the immediately following vowel: thus *ré* (*ɛ́*) before the pronoun *ʋ* will become *rʋ́-ʋ́* (*ʋ́-ʋ́*); *ré* before *a* will become *rá-á* (*á-á*). However, whenever there is an intervening consonant, the vowel of *ré* (*ɛ́*) is only affected by vowel harmony and position in the sentence: thus *ré* plus *wɔ* in S-initial position becomes *rí-wɔ*.

3.3.2   Uses related to 'hearsay', and their grammatical function

Ré can fulfil two main grammatical functions: as a complementiser (COMP) in sentence-initial position, and as a particle, occurring in other positions. Both uses have a 'hearsay' function; I shall argue that both are properly analysed as indicators of interpretive use. Their uses are illustrated below.

The most obvious occurrence of the hearsay marker *rɛ́* is as a complementiser introducing direct and indirect speech. Most commonly, *rɛ́* is positioned at the front of the embedded sentence, as in (6) and (7):

(6)   Ba sɛ rí   Ɓa yálá há kúé   makɛ doŋ pɪnɛ weri
       they said COMP their aunt who has-come show sleep lying well
       pa wɔ.
       give them
       'They say that their aunt who has come will show them how to sleep properly.'

(7)   Ʊ háálɔ́ ná líɔ́ bʊl rí   Ŋ-ŋ́ mú ŋ bozóŋ dihī ní.
       his wife DEF left said COMP I-IPF go my lover   place SDM
       'While leaving his wife said: "I am going to my lover".'

Ré may also occur utterance-finally, with or without a complementiser, as in (8):

(8)   Ʊ ké kénó   ʋ-ʋ́   sɛ́ rʋ́-ʋ́   tʊwɛ
       she sit sitting-thing IPF-she say COMP-she-IPF go-down
       mɪnɔ ne ná rɛ́.
       thing this see P
       'She sat on the sitting-thing, and said that she would go down into this well and see.'

I shall call this utterance-final *rɛ́* a particle rather than a complementiser, mainly because it can occur in simple sentences in that position. This particle I will call an 'interpretive-use marker' (IM), for reasons to be given in section 3.4.

Ré may also occur with a number of other speech verbs. However, it is often used without any speech verb at all. When the speaker is sure that there is no ambiguity as to who is speaking, and to whom, she may just leave out any speech verbs and indicate with *rɛ́* that free indirect speech is introduced. This use is illustrated in (9) (taken from a conversation) and (10) (taken from narrative):

(9)   Ʊ ko   ɛ́nɛ́ Ɓa pi   muiwa arí sikili hé a
       he come then they took rice   and sugar put and
       pii pɔ́-ʋ́ í   Ɓa má-á bɔ́llɛ́ rɛ́
       take give-him COMP they also-IPF greet IM
       'When he came, they gave him rice and sugar. (That) they wanted to thank him.'

In narrative, reported speech may be introduced in this way when it is clear who is speaking to whom. While in a normal sequence of events, temporal or aspectual indication is given only once at the beginning of the narrative, in free indirect speech, as in English, the verb is 'non-present': in Sissala it is marked with perfective aspect. Consider (10):

(10) Ɛ né ɓa bɪr   fá ko   rí   ɓa mú-ɔ́ ja
      then they return flee come COMP they go-PF search
      nyii gul í   niŋ kú-ó   pi nyii ná
      water fail COMP fire come-PF take water DEF
      wuu ní   di.
      all SDM eat
      'Then they ran away back (and said) that they didn't find any water,
      that all the water had been consumed by the fire.'

In examples (9) and (10) the complementiser is the main indicator of reported speech. As the next example shows, the particle ré may also be used as the only indicator of reported speech. The background of this example is a report by a griot about the slave trade. Amongst other things, he talks about people being tied to the tails of horses and dragged along. Somebody asks whether the tail did not tear. The griot does not really answer the question, but goes on to say in (11) that people did indeed die that way. Perhaps because he senses some disbelief in the audience, he marks his utterance with ré, thus giving it the evidence of hearsay:

(11) Náŋá sʊsɛ. Ba kaa konni yo   ta   ré
      some died they took cut   throw leave IM
      'Some died and were untied and left there. (It is said.)'

So far the data have fitted in very well with the 'hearsay' data of other languages; there was always reported speech of some sort involved. However, ré also occurs embedded under such propositional-attitude verbs as 'believe', 'think', 'hope', 'want' and so on. Their uses are considered in the next section.

3.3.3   Other uses

There is ample evidence that ré occurs in a range of constructions which are, strictly speaking, not hearsay, since they involve not verbs of saying but verbs of propositional attitude.

Consider (12) and (13):

(12) Ɛ-né-tɛ   Sísaala múmúré sɪɛrʊ ɓa bʊnɛ rí   balla
      this-is-why Sissala stories in   they think COMP animals
      wuu sɪɛrʊ rí   cuomo ka líntɪŋ ré.
      all in   COMP rabbit is sly   TDM
      'This is why the rabbit in the Sissala stories is seen as sly.'

(13)   ɩ   zɪŋ   rí   wífıɛŋ   ré   jaa
      you know COMP matter-IMP TDM house
      né   tínáwa   co   rí   ɓa   túmɔ́.
      this owners want COMP they manifest
      'You know that this is an important matter which the owners of this
      house want to make manifest.'

The verb *bunɛ* in (12) means 'think' or 'assume'. In (13) there are two
verbs of propositional attitude, 'know' and 'want'. As we see, they
function very much like the speech verbs previously discussed. This
suggests that the minimal hypothesis – that hearsay markers are only
used for reporting speech – is wrong.[3]

A further difference from the minimal 'hearsay' particle is the fact that
ré is frequently used in questions, and sometimes in their answers.
Consider (14) and (15):

(14)   J: ɩ   lísɛ́   namíɛ́ ná   ré-ɛ́?
        you taken-out meat   DEF IM-Q
        'Have you taken out the meat?'
      C: Oó, á   lísɔ́   ré   hāā   ká   tá
        yes we taken-out IM AH and left
        'Yes we have taken out (some) and left (some).'

(15)   S: Ɓa   fa-á   pɛ   ɛré   ré?
        they PAST-IPF sleep how IM
        'How did they sleep?'
      A: Ɓa   fa-á   pɛ́   dáhá   ré
        they PAST-IPF slept standing IM
        'They used to sleep standing.'

The last segment in a yes–no question is always lengthened; this,
together with special intonation, is how yes–no questions are marked. *Ré*
itself is therefore not a question particle. Nor would an analysis of *ré* as a
question particle shed any light on its occurrence in the answers (14C)
and (15A).

The occurrence of *ré* in questions is unexpected on Palmer's evidential
account. In asking a question, the speaker does not commit himself to the
truth of the proposition expressed, so how could the addition of *ré*
weaken the speaker's commitment? Thus, even the limited data presented in this section cast doubt on the validity of both the minimal
hypothesis and Palmer's evidential account.

In the next section I shall propose my own analysis of *ré*, which, I shall
argue, provides a better explanation of the full range of data than the
claim that it is mainly a 'hearsay' particle or a 'modal'.

3.4   *Ré* as interpretive-use marker

3.4.1   Interpretive use and relevance

All the uses of *ré* so far discussed represent phenomena which Sperber and Wilson (1986a:224–31; see also Wilson and Sperber 1988b) would analyse as examples of interpretive use.

Sperber and Wilson introduce a distinction between descriptive and interpretive uses of language and thought. An utterance or assumption can be descriptively used to represent a state of affairs – that state of affairs which would make it true. Or it can be interpretively used to represent another utterance or thought which resembles it. The notion of descriptive representation is familiar from truth-conditional semantics. The notion of interpretive representation, or representation by resemblance, is less familiar, and needs some introduction here.

Communication often involves an exploitation of resemblances. For example, when I am thirsty and I do not speak the language of a country I am visiting, I may mimic the act of drinking, in order to indicate that I would like something to drink. In other situations I may draw a sketch of my house, to enable you to recognise it; I may imitate the way someone speaks, in order to make fun of him. What Sperber and Wilson call 'interpretive representation' is a special case of representation by resemblance: a thought or utterance is used to represent another thought or utterance, which it resembles in content. The most obvious example is free indirect speech, but Sperber and Wilson give many more.

Representation by resemblance is not, of course, the only type of representation. Utterances are used to represent not only other thoughts or utterances which they resemble in content, but also actual or conceivable states of affairs. This truth-conditional type of representation involves no exploitation of resemblances: utterances do not *resemble* states of affairs. Utterances used in this way are, in Sperber and Wilson's terminology, *descriptively* used.

According to Sperber and Wilson, every utterance is, in the first instance, interpretively used to represent a thought of the speaker's: the proposition expressed by the utterance is put forward as resembling a thought that the speaker wants to communicate. The interesting question is whether that thought is itself entertained as a description of a state of affairs – in which case I shall regard the utterance itself as descriptively used – or as a representation of some further thought or utterance, which it resembles. In this latter case, the original utterance is doubly interpretive: the proposition expressed is put forward as resembling a thought of the speaker, which is in turn entertained as a representation of some further utterance or thought, which it resembles. When I talk of an utterance as interpretively used, I shall mean that it is doubly interpretive, in the sense just described. In understanding an utterance, then, the hearer has to decide whether it is being descriptively or interpretively used.

The most commonly noticed interpretive use of utterances is in reporting speech. Consider the exchange in (16):

(16)   A to B: The water board has turned off the water.
        (later)
        C to B: Why is the water not coming?
        B: The water has been turned off, I hear.

Here B produces, in response to C's question, an utterance similar to the one A produced. B does not tell C that she got the information from A, but she does indicate that she is using her utterance interpretively, to represent an opinion which she attributes to someone else. According to Sperber and Wilson, reported speech is a typical example of the interpretive use of language.

Let us say that when somebody uses an utterance interpretively, to attribute an utterance or thought to someone else, then he *echoes* the other person's utterance or thought. Echoic utterances involve a resemblance relation between the original thought or utterance and the propositional content of an utterance currently being processed. Minimal hearsay markers would be markers of echoic interpretive use. For other important aspects of echoic use, see Sperber and Wilson (1986a:237–43); I shall discuss this notion further below.

Notice that the degree of resemblance presumed to exist in echoic utterances may vary. A direct quotation is put forward as resembling the original in all linguistic properties, including semantic properties. Example (5) above includes an illustration of direct quotation. In indirect quotation, the degree of resemblance presumed to exist may be much less.

To illustrate, let us assume that A, before talking to B, had a long explanation from one of the water-board men, pointing out that a pipe had been broken and that as a result they had had to take a number of measures, which he described in bureaucratic detail. In reporting this conversation, A might produce the following utterance to B:

(17)   The man said that the water board has turned off the water.

A is in this case merely giving a summary of what the man said. The proposition expressed by his utterance is different from the original, but it resembles the proposition expressed by the original; that is, the two have semantic or logical properties in common. According to Sperber and Wilson, in order for an utterance, or the proposition it expresses, to be used interpretively, it must share some logical properties with the original it represents, i.e. it must have partially identical logical and contextual implications.

Another example of the interpretive use of utterances is for the attribution to another person not of utterances, but of thoughts. Consider (18) and (19):

(18)   A: He doesn't want a surprise shower, he thinks; this is why he wants to turn the water off.

(19)   After ten years of separation James saw her again for the first time. How beautiful she was.

In (18) the thought 'He doesn't want a surprise shower' is explicitly attributed to the water-board man; in one reading of (19) the thought 'How beautiful she was' is implicitly attributed to James. According to Sperber and Wilson, both (18) and (19) would be examples of interpretive use.

Sperber and Wilson also show that utterances which are interpretively used may achieve relevance in various ways. As in the examples considered so far, they may be used merely to report that someone said, or believed, a certain thing. However, the speaker may, in reporting someone else's views, indicate his own attitude to, or opinion of, those views. As Sperber and Wilson (1986a:239) show, there is no limit to the attitudes that a speaker can express to an opinion echoed. Consider example (20):

(20)   a. He: It's a lovely day for a picnic.
            (They go for a picnic and the sun shines.)
          b. She (happily): It's a lovely day for a picnic, indeed.

In (20b) the utterance is used echoically and the speaker of (20b) endorses the opinion echoed. Of course, as Sperber and Wilson show, a speaker could also reject the opinion echoed. I will discuss the theoretical implications of such examples further on.

Notice, though, that example (20b) already undermines the view that the main function of echoic utterances is to weaken the speaker's commitment to the proposition expressed. It is quite possible to echo someone's opinion in order to endorse it; or to use the authority of the original speaker to support one's own opinion, as when citing one's teacher's views. If hearsay markers are found in such echoic utterances, it is hard to see how Palmer's analysis of them can be correct.

The phenomena described in this section present a problem for the hearer. How does he decide, for any given utterance, whether it is to be understood descriptively or interpretively; whose thought or utterance is being represented; what attitude the speaker is experiencing; and how faithful a representation has been attempted? That is, which logical and contextual implications of the representation are shared by the original being represented? As always, the criterion of consistency with the principle of relevance plays a decisive role: the first interpretation tested and found consistent with the principle of relevance is the *only* interpretation consistent with the principle of relevance, and is the one the hearer should choose. The speaker should therefore try to formulate her utterance so that the first interpretation tested and found consistent with the principle of relevance is the one she intends to convey. In this connection, Sperber and Wilson note that it might be useful for a language to possess explicit indicators of interpretive use, to guide the hearer towards the intended interpretation. My proposal is that *rɛ́* (in both COMP and IM position), and other 'hearsay' particles in other languages, have the function of indicating to the hearer that the utterance which contains them is interpretively used. In other words, *rɛ́* is an explicit linguistic indicator of interpretive use.

Let us now return to *rɛ́* in Sissala, and look at it in the light of this hypothesis. The most obvious example of echoic use is where the speaker echoes the immediately preceding utterance. I shall therefore look at some instances of this from my Sissala data, before returning to the examples presented in the last section.

3.4.2   Evidence for grammaticalisation of interpretive use

Many echoic utterances are straightforward repetitions of preceding utterances. Repetitions can be made for various reasons. As indicated above, they are often made in order to express somebody's attitude towards the opinion echoed. Consider (21) and (22):

(21)   M: Ba   dʊla   á   wérí.
                they   this-year   done   well
                'They have done well this year.'

```
        A:  Ba  há  keŋ  séminέré ná      mʊ Buro.
            they who took seminar   DEF go Boura
            'They, who conducted the seminar at Boura.'
        N:  Ba  ɓɪέná á      weri é rí.
            they really done well F IM
            'They have really done well.'
(22)    D:  l    ɓínɔ  ná    sɪέ keŋ  susi fέ.
            your thing DEF so catch pity much
            'Your thing (taperecorder) arouses pity.'
        N:  Susi rí.  U  má  nɪɪsɔ  nέ.
            pity IM  its also make SDM
            'Pity. It is just its make.' (Things of that make are always small.)
```

While M's utterance in (21) and D's in (22) are examples of descriptive use, N's utterance in (21) and N's in (22) are examples of echoic interpretive use. They are not *reports* of speech, used to inform the hearer of what has just been said; rather, they indicate the speaker's own attitude to what has just been said. If *ré* is an echoic interpretive marker, its use in these examples is explained.

While in (21) N endorses what has just been said, in (22) the speaker repeats the preceding utterance in order to dissociate herself from it. Intonation, facial expression and contextual factors will help to identify which attitude the speaker is actually taking – 'agreeing' or 'disagreeing'. In neither case does repetition function in the way that the analysis of 'hearsay' particles as evidentials would lead one to suspect. The speaker is not expressing a weakened commitment to the proposition expressed. In one case she is endorsing it, and in the other she may be rejecting it entirely.

Consider now another clear case of echoic use:

```
(23)    Ba  sɛ  ʊ  ká lúrí      é  rí  amá . . .
        they say it is medicine F IM but
        'It is said that it (the chameleon) is medicine, but . . .⁴
```

Example (23) is a case where a thought is not attributed to any particular person, but the utterance echoes the opinion of a great majority of people in the Sissala culture. As we have seen, (23) may be merely a paraphrase of what people actually say. Is this use compatible with the minimal hypothesis about hearsay particles? Should we expect such particles to be restricted to literal reproductions of the content of some actual utterance? Standard accounts of hearsay particles are so vague that such a question can scarcely arise. It is clear, though, that the use of *rέ* in (23) is compatible with the hypothesis that *rέ* is a marker of echoic interpretive use.

Echoing the thought of people in general is what happens with proverbs and wise sayings such as (24):

(24)   ʟ-ı   máŋsέ wíwie,   wıı   wuu   pɛ-ı   tıı
        if-you learn   thing-small matter every give-you self
        cie   ı   é di ʋ   yʋɔrɛ   rέ
        tomorrow you F eat your fruit   IM
        'Whatever small thing you learn, tomorrow you will eat its fruit.'
        (You will gain from it.)

This utterance is an interpretation of traditional wisdom, and the interpretive marker *rέ* is used. Traditional wisdom is not the particular thought of anybody, but of people in general.

As we suspected, the use of *rέ* in echoing traditional wisdom does not always square with the analysis of.'hearsay' particles as evidentials. One may just as well invoke traditional wisdom, or some other authority, e.g. the Bible, to *strengthen* one's commitment to the proposition expressed – or at least to give it greater strength than would have been derived from one's own unsupported word.

Sometimes, the speaker uses *rέ* in passing on information which she attributes to the general opinion of a certain group of people. Consider (25):

(25)   Moto   ori   má kó   ŋ   jaa   rıı nyέ?
        motorbike which also come my house to this
        'What kind of a motorbike is coming to my house like this?'
        ʋ dé   nɛ   Amadu rí.
        it exactly like Amadu IM
        'One would say it is Amadu.'

In (25) my informant, translating the example into French, explicitly indicated, by using the conditional form of *say*, that the utterance was interpretively used. In Sperber and Wilson's framework, the reportative conditional in French would be analysed as a further example of a grammaticalisation of interpretive use, and would thus fall together with the Sissala particle *rέ*.

A speaker may also echo not a proposition explicitly expressed but an implicature of a previous utterance. Implicatures may again be echoed with various attitudes. Consider example (26):

(26) D: Ba né pɔ́wɔ́   ná   kaa lɛ   ɓa-á
          they SDM gather-them there take leave they-IPF
          kaa lí   tá   ká baa zʊ́   ja   bɪfɛlɛ
          take leave leave and again enter house new
          a   baa cɛsɛ, cɛsɛ a   baa cíínɛ lɛ
          and again break break and again carry leave
          'They (ants) gather them (grains) and take them out and leave
          them there. They enter the house again, break (grains) again and
          take them out.'
      A: E! cuŋcumó tʊŋ   ré!
          eh ants   work IM
          'Eh! Ants work!'

A's comment does not echo anything that D said explicitly – and as such
it presents problems for the minimal hypothesis. Rather, A echoes a
contextual implication – that is, an implication not derived from the
content of the proposition expressed alone, but from the proposition
expressed together with the context – of what D said. A is confident that
D is aware of this contextual implication. He reasons as follows:

(26') If ants break grains and carry them out of the house all the time then
       they work hard.

However, the purpose of D's utterances was not only to convey that ants
work hard, but that they have worked hard in his house and are very
effective in destroying his grain. A's utterance, which is relevant against
the same context, also conveys this contextual implication and therefore
confirms the implicature conveyed by D. This example is again incompatible with the evidential analysis.

3.5   Figurative speech

Ballard (1974) reports on some uses of *hearsay* particles in the Philippines which he could not explain. The 'hearsay' particles *kono* or *daw* are
found in a number of Philippine languages, and are obligatory whenever
the speaker reports information which he got from somebody else.
Although Ballard does not provide any further data, he mentions that
these particles have to be used in Bible translation in cases of sarcasm and
irony in the following way:

(27) He saved others *kono*, but he cannot save himself. He is *kono* the king
      of Israel, so let him come down from the cross. (Matthew 27:42)

The question is whether the above use of the 'hearsay' marker really is an 'odd sidelight', as Ballard calls it, i.e. whether this use is unrelated to hearsay. Following Palmer (1986) and Givón (1982), who treat evidentials as a type of modal, we would have to say 'yes'. Recall what Givón (1982:24) says about propositions that require 'evidentiary justification': 'ii. Propositions that are asserted with relative confidence, are open to challenge by the hearer and thus require – or admit – evidentiary justification.' After all, a translation which would communicate for Matthew 27:42 that the chief priests and the scribes believed with relative confidence that Jesus was the son of God, would definitely be a bad representation of what was originally meant. The truth is that the chief priests and scribes did not believe *at all* that Jesus was the son of God. Surely *kono* does not mark the proposition expressed with the speaker's relative confidence in its truth.

On the other hand, if we assume that these utterances are interpretive, and more specifically echoic, then *kono* in the above translation makes very good sense and falls in with all the other uses of interpretive marking we have discussed so far. Surely what *kono* does in the above case is attribute the thoughts expressed to somebody, but this somebody is *not* the speaker – nor does the speaker endorse the proposition expressed.

Sperber and Wilson (1986a:239) show that there is no limit to the attitudes that a speaker can express to an opinion echoed. Let us return to example (20) and compare it with a second example (28) (these are Sperber and Wilson's examples (111) and (112)):

(20)   a. He: It's a lovely day for a picnic.
            (They go for a picnic and the sun shines.)
        b. She (happily): It's a lovely day for a picnic, indeed.
(28)   a. He: It's a lovely day for a picnic.
            (They go for a picnic and it rains.)
        b. She (sarcastically): It's a lovely day for a picnic, indeed.

In both (20b) and (28b), the utterance is used echoically. However, while the speaker of (20b) endorses the opinion echoed, the speaker of (28b) rejects it with scorn. Example (28b) is, of course, a typical case of irony. According to Sperber and Wilson, irony is an example of interpretive, and more specifically, echoic use. The speaker echoes an opinion which he rejects with mockery and scorn.[5]

Using a 'hearsay' marker, or in our terms an interpretive-use marker, in ironical utterances, seems to make good sense, once the nature of irony is understood; on the other hand, treating it as a type of modal would make no sense at all. Thus, the analysis of 'hearsay' particles as echoic interpretive markers seems to make more sense than the modal or evidential analysis.

In languages where interpretive use is grammaticalised, and where its use is obligatory, irony will have to be expressed with an overt marker. This is obviously the case in languages of the Philippines; it has also been mentioned by Slobin and Aksu (1982), who report that the morpheme *-mis* in Turkish is used in hearsay as well as in cases of irony. Consider (29):

(29)   Bu sarkı- nın söz- ler- i-   ni   ne   de   iyi   bil-
        this song gen. word pl. poss. acc. how emph. good know
        iyor-mus-um.
        pres.   1sg.
        'How well I know the words to this song!'
            (1982:195)

Slobin and Aksu suggest that what is conveyed by this utterance is something like (29'):

(29')   I'm supposed to know the words of this song.

and that there is an ironic assertion that it is general knowledge 'that I should know these words'. However, though Slobin and Aksu's observations are right, they fail to notice that irony in general *is* 'hearsay', i.e. it involves echoic attribution of a thought; they therefore see this example as a particular case of hearsay which, interpreted against a particular context, may just happen to be ironical. Their findings provide further confirmation of Sperber and Wilson's claim that irony is a case of echoic interpretive use.

As we would expect, ironical utterances in Sissala are also marked with *ré*. Consider example (30) (see also example (66) in chapter 2):

(J is upset that C uses his torch.)
(30)   J: ι   né   yɔwɛ ŋ   mınɔ pa ŋ-ŋ?
           you SDM buy   my thing give me-Q
           'Did you buy that torch for me?'
      C: Ɗ yɔ́wɛ́ ŋ   tιι ré.
           I bought my self IM
           'I bought (it) myself.'
           Ɗ sιɛ́ guɔrɛ yɔwɛ tɔrswaa?
           I so walk buy   torches
           'So I should go and buy torches?'

J's question is meant to be a reminder of what he takes to be a generally accepted generalisation, a piece of background knowledge, namely (30'):

(30′)   One only has the right to use what one has bought oneself.

However, C does not agree with J's assumption, and she echoes J's question in such a way as to make it clear that she is annoyed and does not agree with J at all. In the final utterance she explicitly formulates her disagreement as a question. The echoic utterance is marked with *rέ*. *Rέ* in this case makes it clear that C's utterance is not descriptively, but interpretively used.

Echoing somebody's thoughts can be done in such a way that one takes the original beliefs as a basis and draws all sorts of conclusions from them, which one would expect a person holding these beliefs to draw. The echoic utterance, marked with *rέ*, would again be used to attribute these beliefs to the person in question. The background to example (31) is that it is used in a conversation about sacrificial meat from Mecca, which had been given to the Sissala people during the time of famine. All the participants in the conversation had eaten this meat and started to mock what they held to be the Muslim belief that these animals have divine, life-saving power. The following utterances are based on inferences from that belief:

(31)   a. S: A   e   bírmɛ   súwέ   luri   ri.
              we F   turned   death   medicine   IM
              'We have become immortal.'
        b. J: ʊ túwɛ   baŋjírá.
              it fell   toilet
              'It fell into the WC.'
        c. T: ʊ ha   káánɔ́ rέ, lɔ ú   cέ.
              it still left   IM let him stop
              'It is still left inside us, you stop!'
              ʊ mínɔ́   rέ.
              it is-there IM
              'It is still inside us.'

Again we find that the 'mocking' utterances (31a) and (31c) are marked with *rέ*, to indicate that the opinions expressed are attributed to other people, opinions which the speakers do not endorse.

Where there is an explicit indicator of interpretive use, and therefore also of irony, it is easy to see that the proposition expressed is attributed to somebody. However, *whose* thought exactly is expressed is not explicitly indicated, and is left to the hearer to infer. A speaker aiming at optimal relevance must assume that the hearer will have a context available, which makes it clear to him *whose* opinion is being echoed.

The hearer makes the most accessible, i.e. the most natural, assumption about whose opinion is being echoed, and rejects it only if the result is inconsistent with the principle of relevance. Thus the use of *ré*, though it adds an element of explicitness to free indirect speech, still does not fully determine what proposition the speaker should be taken to have expressed.

Metaphor is not normally marked with *ré* in Sissala. However, when the metaphorically used utterance echoes another utterance or thought, then it is also interpretively marked in Sissala, as we would expect. Consider (32), which is taken from an oral free paraphrase of 'the prodigal son':

(32) ŋ bio ná fa há yúksέ ʋ nέ
      my child the PAST who lost he SDM
      báá bírέ ko έ
      again return come like-that
      'My son who was lost, he has come back again.'
      ʋ fa súwɔ́ ré, ʋ sɪέ báá híésú ri.
      he PAST dead IM he so again live IM
      'He was dead, he now lives again.'

'Being dead' and 'being alive' are used metaphorically, and also echoically: they echo the preceding utterances 'He was lost' and 'He has come back'. The utterances in which the metaphorical expressions occur are therefore marked with *ré*. This draws the hearer's attention to the relation between being lost and being dead, coming back and being alive. The use of echoic *ré* thus gives the hearer access to implications which he might otherwise have missed.

As Sperber and Wilson show, interpretively used propositions come with a guarantee not of truthfulness but of *faithfulness*: the guarantee is that the utterance is a faithful enough representation of thoughts to which the speaker wants to draw the hearer's attention. Considering metaphor and irony in this way, 'figurative speech' does not need to be treated as violating any maxim of truthfulness, as Grice (1975) and others seem to think. Nor should metaphor and irony be seen as very closely related phenomena. As Sperber and Wilson show, there is a fundamental difference between irony and metaphor. While irony is always echoically used, i.e. a thought is attributed to someone, metaphor can, but does not have to, be used attributively. In Sissala, it would not normally be marked with *ré*.

This section offers considerable evidence against a modal or evidential analysis of 'hearsay' phenomena. Use of *ré* does not invariably indicate a weakened degree of commitment to the truth of the proposition expressed. It is thus not just a matter of different terminology when we call *ré* an interpretive-use marker rather than a modal particle. In the next section I will consider another use of *ré* which fits in well with the view that it is an echoic interpretive marker, and less with the view that it is a hearsay or modal particle.

3.6   Beliefs and desires

So far, we have been concerned with the use of *ré* for reporting or attributing belief. In fact, the range of propositional attitudes which can be embedded under *ré* is much wider than this. Consider (33)–(37):

(33)   Ŋ é sé ʋ: 'Sí   á ré.'
        I F told her IMP-NEG do IM
        'I told her: "Don't do it!"'

(34)   . . . rí   ŋ ka káántıɛ́ ná   ko   yee.
        . . . COMP I take bush-knife DEF come please
        '(He said) that I should please take a bush-knife.'

(35)   Ŋ sé ı   wıısɛ sı   tɛ   tɛŋgıɛ́l.
        I say COMP God FUT give peace
        'I say that God may give peace.'

(36)   Ʋ sé ʋ-ʋ́   ko ŋ dıhı̄ rı́í yá.
        he said COMP-he come my place to P
        'He promised to come to me.'

(37)   Ŋ má sé bio ná   má á bátɛm ré.
        I also said child DEF also do baptism IM
        'I also believed that the person had also been baptised.'

Here, although verbs of saying are involved, different speech acts are reported. In traditional speech-act terms it could be said that (33) reports an order, (34) a request, (35) a wish, (36) a commitment and (37) a belief.

   Although the above examples are all embedded under verbs of saying, the embedded clauses represent not only beliefs but other propositional attitudes too. In this section, I will show that *ré* in Sissala – in both its complementiser and its particle use – can introduce a variety of propositional attitudes, not all of which fit well with the traditional 'hearsay' or 'modal' analysis.

3.6.1   *Ré* and belief

There are various terms in Sissala which represent thought, belief and knowledge, under which clauses containing *ré* may be embedded. Consider (38):

(38)   Nɪɛ́   kánɔ́ kɪŋkáŋ, ɓa   bué   rí
       people many very   they believe COMP
       lunne ni   ja   háálá   pá   wɔ́.
       shrines SDM marry women give them
       'Many people believe that it is the shrines which give them their wives.'

The verb *bu* 'believe, respect', in (38) is to be understood as 'hold true'. The speaker explicitly indicates whose beliefs are being echoed; it is implicit that the speaker himself does not endorse those beliefs.

The verb in the following utterance represents belief with some emotional content. It has the interpretation of 'to trust, have confidence in.'

(39)   . . . ká   a   yardá rú-ʋ́   já   íwa toló.
             and have trust   COMP-he marry your daughter
       '. . . and you trusted that he would marry your daughter.'

The subordinate clause echoes a belief that certain states of affairs would come about. However, the 'trust' is placed in a particular person, who is in a position to make things true. The above expression is also used for 'believe in God'.

The next example involves the verb 'think' together with 'take', whose use is rather similar to English 'gather':

(40)   ʋ pio bɪɪnɛ   ʋ wí   gbee ri.
       he took thought he NEG play IM
       'He gathered that he (Kofi) was not joking.'

The speaker indicates that the person referred to by the third-person pronoun has come to the conclusion that Kofi is not joking. The use of *pio* in this case shows that the belief reported is not at the lowest level of strength or confirmation. In this case the *ré* is not a COMP but an interpretive-use marker.

Many abstract concepts in African languages are expressed metaphorically: 'belief' in Sissala is also expressed as 'to take something (what you believe) and eat it'. Consider (41):

(41)   ʊ pi   ʊ háálɔ́ wɪɛ́   di rʊ́-ʊ́   bél   u   bio.
       he took his wife's words ate COMP-she watch her child
       'He believed his wife's statement that she watched the child.'

Just like single verbs *bunɛ* 'think' and *bu* 'believe', the above complex
idiom can take a sentential complement, introduced with *ré*. There is
also an expression for 'know', as in (42):

(42)   ι   zιŋ   rí-í   ká ánáwa ré.
       you know COMP-you are parents IM
       'You know that you are parents.'

This utterance, which again contains the particle *ré*, was used at a
wedding to remind the parents of the couple to be wedded that being a
parent has all sorts of obligations attached.

The occurrence of *ré* with 'know' is particularly surprising, given the
traditional analysis of 'hearsay' phenomena, since 'know' is a factive
verb, which entails the truth of its complement clause. To use the verb
'know' is, if anything, to make a stronger commitment to the truth of the
proposition expressed than would be achieved by the speaker's mere
unsupported assertion. By contrast, on the interpretive-use analysis,
such examples are to be expected.

3.6.2   *Ré* and desire

In this section, I will look at the use of *ré* with propositional attitude
related to desire. As in English, desires in Sissala may be embedded
under such verbs as 'want' and 'like, love'. Consider (43) and (44):

(43)   ι   yálá kúrsɔɔlé há   keŋ   hĩɛ̃   ŋ má
       your aunt baskets   since have beauty I also
       có   rí   ŋ yɔwɛ náŋá.
       like COMP I buy   some
       'Since your aunt's baskets are pretty, I would also like to buy some.'
(44)   Ŋ zaa   bɔ́lɔ́ pááá. Ŋdé   có   ŋ mʊ́ɔ́ pí   ré.
       I today tired very   I INT like I go   sleep IM
       'I am very tired today, I would like to go and sleep.'

In (43) *ré* appears in the form of a COMP and in (44) as a particle. We
therefore find the same grammatical pattern of *ré* marking amongst the
different propositional-attitude examples as with the speech-verb
examples.

Sperber and Wilson argue that the notion of *desirability* plays a crucial role in linguistics. In imperatives, for example, the speaker presents a certain state of affairs as desirable from someone's point of view, not necessarily her own. As always, this semantic indeterminacy will be pragmatically resolved by reference to the criterion of consistency with the principle of relevance.

A further term from Sissala which will illustrate the notion of desirability is *lo* 'let'. Consider (45) and (46):

(45)   Lo rá-á   jʊɔsɛ.
       let COMP-we rejoice
       'Let us rejoice.'

       (Taken from an instruction on how to grow yams.)
(46)   . . . sí   ló rí   nyɔɔ́ ná   wuu mi
       IMP-NEG let COMP weed DEF all   there
       a makɛ rʊ́-ʊ́   sí   hílʊ́.
       in order COMP NEG dry
       'Don't leave the weeds there so that it (yam plant) does not get dry.'

In (45) the speaker indicates that it is desirable, from his own point of view and that of his hearer, to rejoice. In (46), which is a word of advice, the speaker indicates that it is desirable from his hearer's point of view not to leave the yam plants to get dry. In both examples, the complementiser *ré* is used.

The term *lo*, introduced above, often expresses permission. However, there is also an idiomatic expression which more commonly expresses permission, and with this expression the complementiser *ré* is used:

(47)   ɪ   wóllí pɔ́-ʊ́   ŋménɔ́ rʊ́-ʊ́   tʊŋ   ɛ́   tʊtʊmí.
       you can give-him road   COMP-he works that work
       'You can permit him that he does that work.'

In the case of (47) the state of affairs described is represented as desirable to the person to whom permission is being given.

These are only a few examples to show how *ré* is used with propositional attitudes of desire, but they suffice to show that these constructions fall in well with all the other cases of interpretive use. Again, they fall in much less well with the traditional modal or hearsay analysis.

In the next section I will consider a further range of constructions which appear to present problems for the traditional account.

3.7   Questions and answers

As already mentioned, questions may also be marked with *ɾɛ́*. This is not surprising if *ɾɛ́* is a marker of interpretive use. According to Sperber and Wilson, interrogatives, unlike declaratives and imperatives, are specialised for interpretive use.

Speech-act theorists usually analyse interrogative utterances as a special subtype of directive speech act: specifically, as requests for information (see Bach and Harnish 1979:48; Searle 1969:69). However, as Sperber and Wilson (1986a:251) show, there are a variety of interrogatives (e.g. rhetorical questions, expository questions, self-addressed questions and indirect questions) which are not easily analysed in this way.

Sperber and Wilson distinguish between yes–no questions, which not only have a logical form but also a fully propositional form, and wh-questions, which have only incomplete logical forms. They claim that both types of question are interpretively used to represent their answers. More precisely, they claim that utterances can be interpretively used to represent not only attributed thoughts, but desirable thoughts, i.e. thoughts that the speaker regards as relevant, to himself or to someone else. The function of an interrogative utterance is not to describe a state of a crisis, but to represent a thought that the speaker regards as relevant, if true.

To take an example: suppose Mary asks Peter *Do you live in London?* Her question expresses the proposition that Peter lives in London, and indicates that a proposition which resembles it would be relevant, if true. The hearer, in interpreting her utterance, must decide which proposition she has in mind, and who she thinks would find it relevant. In this, as always, he is guided by considerations of relevance, and accepts the first assumption tested and found consistent with the principle of relevance. In this case, as with most yes–no questions, he is likely to assume that the proposition expressed by the utterance is the very proposition which would be relevant if true; and in this case, as with many questions, he is likely to assume that it is the speaker herself who would find this proposition relevant.

Wh-questions do not have a complete propositional form, but only an incomplete logical form. Sperber and Wilson claim that wh-questions, like yes–no questions, are interpretively used to represent relevant answers: they communicate that some fully propositional completion of their incomplete logical form would be relevant, if true.

The occurrence of *ré* in interrogatives in Sissala raises an interesting question. All the examples of *ré* so far discussed have been echoic. Questions in Sissala – as in any language – may be echoic, but they are not always: they may represent their answers without necessarily suggesting that anyone *has* the answer. The question is: does *ré* occur only in echoic questions in Sissala – in which case it would be a marker of echoic use – or does it mark both echoic and non-echoic questions – in which case it would clearly be a marker of interpretive, but not necessarily echoic, use?

Example (14) (repeated here for convenience) is a case where the question could be interpreted either way – as echoic or non-echoic.

(14) J: ʅ lísέ   namíέ ná   ré-έ?
          you taken-out meat DEF IM-Q
          'Have you taken out the meat?'
      C: Oó, á lísɔ   ré hǎǎ ká tá.
          yes we taken-out IM AH and left
          'Yes we have taken out (some) and left (some)'.

If non-echoic, it would just be a normal question; if echoic, it would mean something like 'Am I right to think that you've taken out the meat?' or 'Am I right to attribute to you the belief that you've taken out the meat?' In the answer of (14) the speaker echoes the proposition expressed by the question, indicating that she endorses it. However, she adds a further non-echoic conjunct, which is not marked with *ré*.

Questions are not obligatorily marked with *ré*. It is possible that the presence or absence of marking is due to dialectal variation, because in one dialect it is not found in questions at all. However, whenever the question is echoed in the answer, the answer is obligatorily marked with *ré*. Consider (48), where the question has no *ré* but the echoed answer does:

(48) A: ʅ hé pilwa-a?
          you put batteries-Q
          'Did you put batteries in?'
      B: Ŋ he pilwa   ré.
          I put batteries IM
          'I did put batteries in.'

An argument that *ré* is not solely an echoic marker might be built around the fact that *ré* may be used with wh-words: e.g. *nεε ré* 'where', *ɛrɛ ré* 'how', *bee rí* 'what', *aŋ ré* 'who', and also with *bεŋmε ré* 'how much/many'.[6] Example (49) uses 'how much/many':

(49)   N: Nɪɛ   bɛŋmɛ   rɛ́?
              people how-many IM
              'How many people (are there)?'
        E: Botoro ni   ɛ́ ná.
              three   SDM like that
              'There are three like that.'

Here the speaker of (49) represents a thought that would be relevant to
him, if true. He expects the hearer to complete the logical form of (49)
into a fully propositional form. In the answer, we find no *rɛ́*. Although E
knew the answer, he did not *echo* it: that is, he put it forward without
attributing it to anyone else.

Example (15) (repeated below for convenience) is a wh-question with
rɛ́:

(15)   S: Ɓa   fa-á   pɛ́   ɛrɛ́   rɛ́?
              they PAST-IPF   sleep how   IM
              'How did they sleep?'
        A: Ɓa   fa-á   pɛ́   dáhá   rɛ́
              they PAST-IPF   sleep standing IM
              'They used to sleep standing.'

The answer is a completion of the incomplete logical form 'they slept in
——— way'. It has a *rɛ́* marker because it echoes a legend – received
knowledge. The answer echoes a thought attributed to someone else.

Rhetorical questions are very widely used in Sissala. According to
Sperber and Wilson (1986a:251–2), rhetorical questions often function
not as requests for information, but as reminders of information that the
speaker regards as relevant to the hearer. Consider (50):

(S speaks angrily to another woman, who had taken dawa dawa
pods from her tree before S had had the chance to take any
herself.)
(50)   S: Súúsɛ́   tínáwa kuó ɓɔ́rɛ́ rɛ́-ɛ́?
              dawa-dawa owners come pluck IM-Q
              'You think the owners of the dawa dawa tree have harvested?'
              Ɛ nɛ ríwa ko   luɔrɛ   zɛ́   a-á   ɓɔ́rɛ́.
              then you come secretly climb and-IPF pluck
              'And you (can) come secretly, and climb in order to harvest.'

In (50) both the speaker and the hearer know the answer to the question.
The question is used sarcastically to attribute to the hearer a belief from
which the speaker is dissociating herself, but which a hearer obeying
society's rules would have had to hold to do what she has done. The

utterance in (50) makes explicit the offensive act as if to say: 'you knew the rules and yet you disregarded them, you behave as if you didn't know.' The answer, although known, is therefore relevant to the hearer.

Ré is also used in echoic questions. These can serve various purposes: to have part of an utterance repeated because one did not understand it the first time; or to express surprise about a previous claim. They may also serve to invite further elaboration on a subject just talked about, and can be used to gain time for formulating an answer to a question. Answers to echoic questions are generally presented as relevant to the speaker, except where a previous utterance is being echoed: in that case the answer is presented as relevant to the hearer.

Consider (51)–(53):

(51)   L: Ba há sɛ́ rá-á   bɪ bɪsɛ   í
               they P said COMP-we talk conversation COMP
               Níkólá sɪɛ́ a   ɓɪdíílí pá raa.
               Nicolas so   makes food give us
               'It was said that we should make conversation, and that Nicolas therefore makes food for us.'
      J: ʊ-ʊ́   a   beé pɛ́-íwa-a?
               COMP-he makes what give-you-Q
               'It was said that he makes what for you?'

(52)   M: Ŋ jaa   Márkɛ́-ɛ́?
               my house Mark-Q
               'Our Mark? (Is he well?)'
      N: ʊ dúókó.
               he strong
               'He is well.'
      M: ʊ dúókó rí-í?
               he strong IM-Q
               'Is he well?'
      N: Oó
               yes
               'Yes'

(53)   (A: There were many dead bodies.)
      S: Ba baa wo nyaŋ a-á   wii?
               they still can these and-IPF cry
               'Is it (still) possible to mourn all these?'
      A: Bɪwiilé   rí baa fa   ká nyaŋ?
               things-crying IM still PAST are these
               'Were these mourned (in spite of the big number)?'

In example (51), the woman of the house, J, is surprised (and annoyed) that her husband was supposed to provide a meal for many people, of which she had not known anything. She airs her surprise by echoically questioning part of the proposition expressed by the preceding utterance. *Ré* is in this case in initial position, echoing the complementiser of the preceding sentence (*ι* to *v* assimilation because of the pronoun *v*).

In (52) the proposition that Mark is well is echoed to invite confirmation, perhaps in the form of further evidence.

In (53) a question is itself echoed. However, the echoed question is rephrased. The content of most of the utterance is rephrased as an NP, which is marked with *ré*, and the question marker is separate. It is typical for repeated utterances to be rephrased so that the repeated part is in initial position. This is done either by preposing or by restructuring the utterance so that the main information of the preceding utterance is the content of the subject NP. Here the function of the echoic question is to request confirmation that this was, in fact, the question asked. One ulterior motive might be to gain time for thinking about an answer.

The occurrence of *ré* in Sissala interrogatives makes very good sense on the assumption that *ré* is a marker of interpretive use, whereas it is much less easily understood in terms of the minimal hypothesis or the analysis of hearsay particles as evidentials. Although many yes–no questions containing *ré* could be analysed as echoic, there is some evidence from the occurrence of *ré* in wh-questions that *ré* is here merely a marker of interpretive, but not necessarily echoic, use. If this evidence could be undermined, nothing would stand in the way of analysing *ré* as a marker of echoic interpretive use. And this is how I suggest that the 'hearsay' phenomena of other languages might best be approached.

3.8   Other evidence

In this section I want to mention a few cases which suggest that the use of *ré* extends to perceptual phenomena – which again makes problems for a traditional 'hearsay' analysis. *Ré* is found in subordinate clauses embedded under a term of perception such as *na* 'see' or *nɛ* 'hear'. It may also be used with verbs such as *v nɛhē* 'it seems', *la* or *pi* 'gather' and *ja* 'is about to'. Can these be analysed as verbs of propositional attitude, involving interpretive use?

As mentioned under section 3.2, there are languages which mark perceptually derived information with a special perceptual marker (see Barnes 1984), which is the strongest evidential marker in the language, indicating the highest possible degree of commitment to the truth of the proposition expressed. In Sissala, as in English, such information does not need to be embedded under an explicit perceptual verb. Where such a verb is used, however, the embedded clause is treated within the Sperber and Wilson framework as interpretively used. In Sissala, this analysis is confirmed by the fact that such clauses are introduced with *ré*.

Consider (54) and (55):

(54)   Záá né kál wuu ŋ ná nɪɛ́   rí   wɔ pú   ráŋ.
       now this day every I see people COMP they assemble there
       'Now every day I see the people gathering there.'

(55)   Ŋ níɔ́ rí   6a sí   kɛ́rɛ́ barás̪e-zeno Burɔ́ mi.
       I heard COMP they FUT build dam-big   Boura at
       'I heard that they will build a big dam at Boura.'

The verb in (55) is ambiguous between 'perceive (a sound)' and 'hear (and understand) what was said'; in this case the 'hearsay' sense is clearly involved, since the tense is future. There are languages in Africa, such as Engenni (Thomas 1978:44), which have a special complementiser for perceptual material: the speaker will use the complementiser *ga* for embedded propositions under 'hear' if they are second-hand (hearsay) and he will use the complementiser *na* if they are first-hand, i.e. perceptual.

Na 'see' in Sissala, as in European languages, may also have the interpretation 'come to understand'. In that case, a proposition embedded under *na* represents an inference made by the speaker on the basis of some evidence. Consider (56):

(56)   Ʋ nó rʋ́-ʋ́   baa wɪ ɛ́ wíɛ́   duusi
       he saw COMP-he again NEG those matters way
       mi wo a   í-a.
       at can and IPF-do
       'He saw that he could no more do this kind of deed.'

'Saw' in (56) has to be interpreted as 'came to understand' or even 'knew'. The embedded clause represents a thought attributed to the referent of 'he'.

The following example provides a case where the opinion of a certain village is represented. The opinion is a result of observation of the people of that village. The proposition is embedded under 'take', which could be interpreted as 'they gather':

(57)   Tɔ́ɔ́ nɪɛ wuu sɪɛ́ de la rí   Buune,
       town people all so INT took COMP people-of-Boura,

> rí-í   né   kír   nɛrɔ   gúl,   í-í   pi   kéyé
> if-you SDM chase person fail, COMP-you take rubber
> í   Buune   maafa né   ká kéyé.
> COMP people-of-Boura gun   SDM is rubber
> 'The people in the surrounding villages think (understand) that if one
> fails to catch a person, the gun of Boura is "rubber" (sling shots).'

Another speaker then takes up the same subject. This time he does not
embed the thought of the other villagers under *la*, but similarly introduces it with *ré*. It is left open whether the speaker in this case wants to
indicate 'they say' more literally, or whether he wants to express the
same as the speaker of (57) which is 'they gather':

(58)   ι   buune   maáfa né   ká téyé.
       COMP people-of-Boura gun   SDM is rubber
       'They say/gather that Boura's gun is a sling shot.'

My texts provide many more examples of this type, with *ré* being used as
both a complementiser and a particle under the verbs *υ nɛhɛ̃* 'it seems',
and *ja* 'wants to, is about to'. On an evidential analysis of *ré*, these
examples are rather surprising, since the type of evidence being offered is
quite distinct from hearsay. By contrast on the analysis of *ré* as an
interpretive-use marker, these examples fall naturally into place.

3.9   Conclusion

The main aim of this chapter has been to show how Sissala grammatica-
lises a certain mode of representation – interpretive use. I have argued
that an analysis in these terms fits the data better than the standard
analysis of 'hearsay' phenomena as belonging to a modal/evidential
system.

As we have seen, to assign to *ré* a modal function, indicating the
degree of the speaker's commitment to the truth of the proposition
expressed, distorts the real function of the particle, and cannot accom-
modate the full range of data. I suggest that so-called 'hearsay' particles
in other languages might not be modal indicators either, but might be
more fruitfully analysed as markers of echoic interpretive use.

The main evidence for the interpretive analysis and against the modal
analysis was the following: the use of *ré* with irony; the use of *ré* under
verbs of propositional attitude, such as belief and desire; and the use of *ré*
in questions and answers to questions. All these uses are predicted by the

interpretive analysis, and conflict with the predictions of the standard modal analysis.

In the light of the Sissala data, it would be interesting to look at English and see whether there is something like an interpretive-use marker. The COMP *that* is one obvious candidate.

It would also be interesting to know whether so-called 'hearsay' phenomena in other languages – particles, verbs, etc. – are more commonly restricted to echoic use – after all, 'hearsay' implies 'echoic' – or whether they have wider application to other cases of interpretive use, as I have argued they do in Sissala.

As regards the overall argument of this book, this chapter is intended to make two substantive points. It shows how a particular theoretical distinction – the distinction between descriptive and interpretive use – can suggest new lines of empirical investigation. If these prove successful, they in turn lend indirect support to the theory. In this case, the theoretical distinction between descriptive and interpretive use is unique to relevance theory, which is thus uniquely confirmed. In the next chapter, I will show how the relevance-theoretic notion of contextual effect suggests new lines of empirical analysis, and receives similar confirmation from a further range of Sissala data.

Second, this chapter is intended to illustrate one sort of contribution that a particle may make to the relevance of utterances in which it occurs. In this case, the contribution is an explicit, truth-conditional one. Sissala has a means of explicitly indicating whether a certain utterance is intended as an ordinary assertion or a free indirect report of speech. What in other languages would be a genuine ambiguity, resolvable only by the criterion of consistency with the principle of relevance, can be eliminated in Sissala by the use of *ré*. *Ré* may thus be regarded as an indeterminacy-reducing device, which operates to reduce an indeterminacy at the level of explicit truth-conditional content, or the proposition expressed. This, in turn, suggests further possibilities of analysis. In utterance interpretation, indeterminacies arise not only at the level of explicit truth-conditional content, but also at the levels of context and contextual effects. One might thus expect to find explicit linguistic devices whose function is to resolve indeterminacies at these levels. In the next chapter, I shall show that such devices do indeed exist.

4 *Constraints on relevance and particle typology*

4.1 Introduction

The area of non-truth-conditional particle phenomena as discussed by Grice (1975), Karttunen and Peters (1975) and Blakemore (1987) is a relatively new field of research. Little is known about how such phenomena arise, their range of possible functions and their distribution across the languages of the world.

If it is true, as was suggested in chapter 1, that all humans have the same logical abilities, and that communication creates a presumption of adequate contextual effects for the minimum justifiable effort, should we not expect to find in every language similar linguistic phenomena which save the hearer processing effort by guiding him towards the intended range of contextual effects? In other words, could the very fact that humans are constrained by considerations of relevance be the basis for a typology of non-truth-conditional particle phenomena? This chapter is an attempt to show that this could well be the case.

After reviewing some theoretical accounts of non-truth-conditional particles in English, I will look in detail at the behaviour of a variety of such particles. I will discuss at some length the analysis of *also* in English, *auch* in German and its equivalent *má* in Sissala. I will argue that *auch* and *má* have a range of functions not shared by *also* in English, and I will offer an explanation of this fact in relevance-theoretic terms.

Other particles I will look at more briefly are *so, after all, you see* and *even* in English, and their equivalents in Sissala. I will try to show that relevance theory sheds light on the analysis of such particles.

My conclusion will be that the function of non-truth-conditional particles, in order to facilitate processing by guiding the hearer towards the intended range of contextual effects, may create surprising similarities in the function of particles in quite unrelated languages. However, there are various possible ways of grammaticalising these functions: that

124

is, giving some explicit linguistic indication of the way the utterance is to be processed, the direction in which relevance is to be sought. This is why there may be diversity as well as similarity in the use of particles in different languages. Thus relevance theory suggests a new and interesting approach to the typology of some linguistic phenomena.

4.2   Non-truth-conditional particles

4.2.1   Conventional implicatures

In section 1.4 I outlined Grice's theory of conversation and I mentioned his notion of conversational implicature. However, Grice introduced another type of implicature, which he called 'conventional implicature'. The main difference between the two being that 'conversational implicatures' are said to be calculated on the basis of the conversational maxims, while so-called 'conventional implicatures' are said to be determined not by inference and pragmatic principles, but by the content of particular lexical items.

Grice discusses two lexical items which, according to him, must be analysed as carrying conventional implicatures: *therefore* and *but*. His analysis of *but* involves a truth-functional *and* and an additional conventional content which is non-truth-conditional. In the case of *therefore* he argues that, though the speaker of (1), for instance,

(1)   He is an Englishman; he is, therefore, brave,

indicates that his being brave is a consequence of his being an Englishman, he could not have been accused of speaking falsely should the consequence in question fail to hold. He assumed, in other words, that *therefore* conventionally implicated a certain type of consequence relation, rather than actually entailing it.[1]

Karttunen (1974) and Karttunen and Peters (1975) have taken up the notion of conventional implicature and applied it to what have been referred to by Stalnaker (1974, 1975) and others as 'pragmatic presuppositions', carried by words such as *manage, fail, again, even* and *too*. Karttunen and Peters argue that such words are 'rhetorical devices', whose presence or absence does not have any bearing on what proposition the utterance containing them expresses, but rather relates the sentence 'to a particular kind of conversational context' (1974:12).[2]

The idea that these words are primarily designed to impose constraints on the context in which utterances containing them are interpreted has been taken up by Blakemore (1987), who analyses them as imposing 'semantic constraints on relevance', and whose account I have chosen as a basis for the analysis of the Sissala and German data. In the next section I will review Blakemore's proposals in more detail.

4.2.2   Constraints on relevance

Blakemore diverges from Karttunen and Peters' views in two main respects. One is that she does not share their view that the semantics/ pragmatics distinction coincides with the distinction between truth-conditional and non-truth-conditional meaning. According to Blakemore (1987:72–104), the content of constraints on relevance is both semantic and non-truth-conditional. Blakemore (1987:72–7) also differs from Karttunen and Peters as to the nature of context and context choice. According to the latter, contexts are drawn from the 'common ground' of assumptions mutually known by speaker and hearer, but they offer no clear account of how exactly this happens. Blakemore (1987:75) follows Sperber and Wilson in arguing that the context is not restricted to common ground, and that context choice is governed by considerations of relevance. (See chapter 2.)

Blakemore's hypothesis about non-truth-conditional particle phenomena is that they contribute to optimal relevance by guiding the interpretation process, and in particular by specifying certain properties of the intended context and contextual effects. They are not truth-conditional: they do not make any contribution to the content of the proposition expressed; but they facilitate the interpretation process by, on the one hand, economising on processing effort, and, on the other hand, decreasing the risk of misunderstanding.

Why should such expressions be necessary, given that all utterance interpretation is constrained by a single general principle – the principle of relevance? Blakemore (1987:76) argues that it is just this principle that provides an explanation for the existence of non-truth-conditional part-icles. The presumption of relevance encourages the hearer to process an utterance in the smallest and most accessible context which yields adequate contextual effects. Thus, if a speaker wants to be sure that the hearer will arrive at the intended interpretation of an utterance, it is in her interest to make the intended context immediately accessible. The particles, on Blakemore's account, enable her to direct the hearer to a particular set of assumptions in an economical way. These expressions therefore make good sense in a relevance-based framework, where the aim is to minimise processing costs. Their function is to constrain or guide the hearer's search for optimal relevance. Hence the name 'semantic constraints on relevance'.

I will now review some of the constraints on relevance discussed by Blakemore (1987), before turning to similar constraints in Sissala.

4.3   Inferential constraints

4.3.1   Inferential constraints in English

Imagine we had to interpret two utterances of a discourse. Without any further information, we would be faced with the problem of discovering not only how each one is relevant, but also whether or how each of them is related to the other. Consider (2) and (3):

(2)   Romeo likes to please Juliet.
(3)   He is Juliet's favourite.

These two utterances could be construed as being in a variety of relations to each other: for instance, they could just be a list of two facts or beliefs; or one could be construed as providing evidence for the truth of the other. In that case, one of the two propositions would be a conclusion, and the other evidence to support the conclusion. The problem is that either proposition could be a conclusion, and either could be supporting evidence, depending on the circumstances and the speaker's intention. It is, of course, possible that in some circumstances only one interpretation is possible, given the presumption of relevance. However, this is by no means always so. In cases where misinterpretation is a possibility, Blakemore argues that constraints on relevance can play a vital role.

She claims, for instance, that *after all* and *so* may have this function. Thus, if we preface (3) with *after all*, or with *so*, we know immediately which utterance is to be taken as conclusion and which as evidence:

(4)   a. Romeo likes to please Juliet.
         b. After all, he is Juliet's favourite.
(5)   a. Romeo likes to please Juliet.
         b. So he is Juliet's favourite.

Although the two original utterances remain in the same order in (4) and (5) they are related in different ways. In (4) it is (4a) which is the conclusion, for which (4b) provides evidence: while in (5) it is (5b) which is the conclusion, for which (5a) provides evidence. In both cases the speaker expects the hearer to have further contextual assumptions available, and these are not the same for (4) as they are for (5). Thus in (4) the speaker expects the hearer to access assumption (4'):

(4')   If x is someone's favourite then x likes to please this person.

In (5), on the other hand, the implicit assumption is different:

(5')   If x likes to please a person then x may become this person's favourite.

Thus *after all* and *so* constrain the processing of the two utterances in different ways.

Of course *after all* and *so* could give evidence for the same conclusion if the order of the propositions was reversed in one case. Consider (6) and (7):

(6)   Romeo is polite to Juliet.
       After all, Juliet loves him.
(7)   Juliet loves Romeo,
       so Romeo is polite to Juliet.

In both cases it is 'Romeo is polite to Juliet' which is the conclusion and 'Juliet loves Romeo' which is the evidence. However, as Blakemore points out, there may be special reasons for delaying the evidence until after the conclusion has been given, as is usually the case when *after all* is used.

Before I discuss this further, let us consider another of Blakemore's observations. Not only *after all*, but also *you see* may be used to preface evidence for a conclusion, as in (8) and (9):

(8)   Juliet was distressed.
       You see, Romeo had not seen her.
(9)   Juliet was distressed.
       After all, Romeo had not seen her.

However, these utterances are not understood in the same way. As Blakemore (1987: 81–2) points out, *after all* is used as a reminder: it is used to introduce propositions assumed to be already known to the hearer. By contrast, *you see* is used to introduce propositions assumed not to be already known to the hearer. Thus in (8), *Romeo had not seen her* is introduced as new to the hearer; while in (9) it is treated as an assumption which the hearer already has available.

On this account, *after all* seems to have two processing instructions, or one complex instruction, attached: it encourages the hearer to treat the proposition expressed as an item of evidence for some prior conclusion – an item which was already part of his set of assumptions in memory. However, this does not seem to me the way the reminding function of *after all* should be analysed. Historically, *after all* appears to have arisen as part of a clause which is still used sometimes: *after all is said and done.* I suggest, therefore, that what *after all* contributes, as an additional explicature, is that the proposition introduced with *after all* is known. Although this does not affect any of Blakemore's other observations about *after all*, it does suggest that a device with non-truth-conditional functions may make an independent contribution to truth-conditions. In fact, if non-truth-conditional devices develop from truth-conditional devices, as I will argue in the next chapter, then we might expect there to be in-between cases, which make truth-conditional as well as non-truth-conditional contributions.

The particles *after all* and *so* have an interesting relation to the notion of contextual effect, in terms of which relevance is defined. In chapter 2 I showed that, according to Sperber and Wilson, there are three types of contextual effects: contextual implication, strengthening and contradiction. In a relevance-based framework assumptions about the world come with varying degrees of strength, and logical computations assign strength to conclusions on the basis of the strength of the premises from which they are derived. These premises include, of course, not only those explicitly given, but also those provided by the context, such as (4′) and (5′). As Blakemore (1987:84–5) points out, where a newly presented proposition, together with supplementary premises, entails the proposition expressed by a preceding utterance, it is naturally interpreted as providing confirmation of the preceding utterance. Where a newly presented proposition, together with supplementary premises, entails the proposition expressed by some subsequent utterance, then it is naturally taken as providing evidence for the proposition expressed by that utterance. There is thus an important connection between the notion of evidence and inferential connection needed for the analysis of the particles discussed in this section, and the notion of strengthening and contextual effect which are central to relevance theory. In the next section, I will argue that a similar connection exists in Sissala.

4.3.2   Inferential constraints in Sissala

Having introduced the notion of semantic constraint on relevance, and discussed its role in a relevance-theoretic framework, I will now examine the role of some constraints on relevance in Sissala.

The particle *sɪɛ́* in Sissala is similar in function to English *so* and *therefore*. Consider (10):

(10)   a. Ba há sɛ́ ra-á bɪ   bɪsɛ   pá rá,
           they since say that-we make conversation give us
           'Since they have said we should make conversation,
     b. í   Níkólá sɪɛ́ a   ɓidíílí,
           that Nicolas so make food
           and so Nicolas provides food,
     c. a   kénó tíkʋ né   sɪɛ́   ɛ́.
           we sit   wait SDM therefore that
           we are therefore waiting for that.'

The example contains two occurrences of *sɪɛ́*, and I will explain the use of the second one, in (10c), first. The function of *sɪɛ́* in (10c) is to indicate that (10c) is a conclusion; the natural assumption is that (10a) and (10b) are the evidence for it. The function of *sɪɛ́* in (10b) is to indicate that (10b) is a conclusion; the natural assumption is that (10a) is evidence for it. However, in this case further premises are needed. Example (10b) is a contextual implication of (10a) in a context containing the further assumption (10'):

(10')   Whoever is asked to make conversation can expect to be provided with a meal.

As we see, the function of *sɪɛ́* is very much like that of *so* in English.

As Blakemore (1987:86) points out, *so* in English can be used without an explicit antecedent: that is, without the evidence for the conclusion it introduces being explicitly expressed. Consider (11):

         (Jane takes a big envelope to the letter box.)
(11)   Janice: So you've finished your chapter.

Here, the hearer is expected to access the required evidence via visual perception, rather than recovering it from a preceding utterance. Similar examples occur in Sissala. Consider (12):

(12)   (Preceding conversation:
         J: Have you taken out the fish?
         C: Yes, we have taken some and left some.)

J: l   sɪɛ́ wɪ   ŋ weri ɛ́.
      you so NEG me well done
      'So you haven't treated me very well.'
      Náŋwulí gɔ́kɔ́.
      fish   neck
      'The neck of the fish.'

Sɪɛ́ indicates that the proposition in which it occurs is a conclusion. The evidence for the conclusion is left implicit: J knows that everybody can see that there was not much edible fish left; hence it was not necessary to state this fact explicitly.

In fact, the speaker later goes on to state explicitly that the only thing left is the neck of the fish. But of course, this premise is not enough on its own to explain J's complaint that they treated her badly. The hearer must also have access to assumptions like (12′a) and (12′b):

(12′)   a. The neck of the fish has very little flesh.
        b. The person who gets the neck will have very little flesh.

With these background assumptions added to (12′c), the hearer can draw the conclusion (12′d):

(12′)   c. J was left the neck of the fish, which has very little flesh.
        d. J was left very little flesh.

The contextual implication 'She was left very little flesh' still does not justify the conclusion 'They have not treated her well.' For that, further assumptions have to be supplied, such as:

(12′)   e. If somebody leaves an unfair share of food to somebody else then they do not treat her well.
        f. The neck of the fish is an unfair share of food.

These combine with (12′d) to yield the conclusion (12′g)

(12′)   g. They did not treat her well.

And this is exactly the conclusion required. We can see how *sɪɛ́* facilitates the interpretation process by specifying the type of inference process the hearer is expected to go through.

In fact, *sɪɛ́* in Sissala, like *alors* in French and *also* in German, has a wider range of functions than *so* in English. It can have a similar interpretation to *well* in English. Consider (13):

(13)   (Background:
        J: If those from down there also came (to join in making conversation), would you like them as well?)

L: a. Ɲ é sɪɛ́   wʊ-ʊ́   có.
I F well NEG-it like
'As for me, well, I don't like it.'

J: b. Ɲ é sɪɛ́   có-ú.
I F well like-it
'As for me, well, I like it.'

L: c. Ɲ é sɪɛ́   wʊ-ʊ́   có.
I F well NEG-it like
'As for me, well, I don't like it.'

The French translation of *sɪɛ́* (provided by my French-speaking informant) was in each case *alors*. Should we consider *sɪɛ́* as having a different
sense in this case, or can some common core of meaning be found? The
fact that *so* and *well* have the same form in Sissala, French and German
suggests that there might be some similarity between the uses of *sɪɛ́* in
(11) and (12), on the one hand, and in (13), on the other.

What is striking about the use of English *well*, Sissala *sɪɛ́*, French *alors*
and German *also* is that they often occur in replies, as in the above
example. It seems that these particles suggest the following line of
interpretation to the hearer:

(13′)   You want my opinion, so my opinion is . . .

In answering a question, the speaker can rely on the hearer's interest,
since he would not otherwise have asked the question. Notice that in
German, in cases where he is not sure of the hearer's interest, the
speaker may actually make the premise explicit and use *also*:

(14)   Also, wenn Du mich fragst, ich würde es tun.
       If you asked me, I would do it.
       Well, I would do it.

Either *well* or the explicit statement *if you asked me* . . . yield an adequate
translation into English.

My suggestion is, then, that the conclusion introduced by *sɪɛ́* in (13) is
a proposition only partially encoded by the utterance: a proposition of
the form 'My opinion is the following: I like/don't like it.' Relevance
theory, which allows for such partial encodings of the proposition
expressed by an utterance, thus makes it possible to treat this use of *sɪɛ́* as
having the same sense as the other inferential uses discussed earlier in the
section.

Are there devices in Sissala which have similar functions to *you see* and *after all* in English, discussed above? Consider (15), where *ná* 'see' (*voilà*) constrains the hearer's search for relevance:

(15) a. Vaa cʋʋlé né   ɓɪɛná.
        dog stupid SDM really
        'It is really a stupid dog.'
     b. Ná, tɔɔ́biri ŋ lɪsɛ, ʋ lɛ   ziŋbal.
        see night I loosen he leave courtyard
        'You see (*voilà*), at night, I let him loose outside the courtyard.'
        (English translation of continuation: He comes and pulls and pulls
        at the door, in order to enter. He tries in vain, and then sleeps in
        the middle of the doorway. And I sleep in the courtyard and hear
        the howling of all the dogs, but I never hear his howling, never,
        never. I don't see him.)

Ná in this case introduces a number of premises which provide evidence for the conclusion that the dog is stupid. As with *you see* in English, the speaker does not expect the hearer to have these premises already available.

There is no expression in Sissala which translates as *after all* and always indicates that the evidence is known to the hearer. The particle *má* may be used to introduce known premises, but the fact that the premises are known has to be inferred, and is not stipulated as part of the meaning of *má*. Consider (16):

(16) a. N: Ií gbé, ʋ-ʋ́   kó   rʋ́-ʋ́ súl rá né.
          perhaps he-IPF come that-he ask us SDM
          'Perhaps he is coming to ask us.'
     b. E: Ʋ jaa   ná wɪɛ́.
          his house DEF matters
          'Concerning his house.'
     c. N: Oó, má ʋ die   má kúó rírá   fa   pa
          yes also he yesterday also came that-we should collect
          cɛrɛ ná.
          wood DEF
          'Yes, after all, he also came yesterday to ask us to collect wood
          for him.'

The initial *má* in (16c) indicates that the proposition expressed by this utterance is evidence for the proposition expressed by (16a). As we would expect, the hearer has to supply additional premises which support the conclusion in (16a):

(16') a. If somebody came yesterday with a certain intention, then it is likely
          that he will come a second time with the same intention.

b. If he came yesterday in order to ask us for help, then he will come today in order to ask us for help.

The hearer knew in this case that the person had a reason for coming in connection with repairs to his house. He most likely knew that the person had come the day before. Thus (16c) functions as a reminder.

In (16c), there is another *má*, which translates as *also*. So *má* has different interpretations. Should it be considered as ambiguous? Both potential senses involve constraints on relevance. I will not discuss the answer at this point; in the next section I will provide a detailed analysis of *má* in all its uses, and compare it with related expressions in English and German.

In this section my aim was to review the inferential constraints introduced by Blakemore (1987), and apply them to phenomena in Sissala. As I have shown, the phenomena in Sissala and English are very similar, and where they differ, there are similarities to phenomena in other languages, as in the case of Sissala *sιέ*, which covers the functions of French *alors* and German *also*, and of both *so* and some uses of *well* in English.

We have also seen how such non-truth-conditional particles help to achieve the speaker's aim of achieving adequate contextual effects for the minimum justifiable processing effort. Particles such as *therefore, so* and *after all* indicate the inferential role of the proposition they intro-duce: that of strengthening other propositions or implied assumptions. Thus we have some evidence for the hypothesis that relevance theory may shed interesting light on non-truth-conditional particle typology.

In the next section I want to consider two particles which may shed further light on this hypothesis – the particles *má* in Sissala and *auch* in German.

4.4   *Má, auch* and contextual effects

4.4.1   The traditional problem of '*auch*'

Auch in German is traditionally analysed as having both 'modal' and 'conjunctive' or 'adverbial' uses (see, for example, Franck 1980; König 1977; Weydt 1977, 1979, 1983). The adverbial uses, illustrated in (17) below, are essentially those of *also* in English; the so-called 'modal' uses, illustrated in (18), are not shared by *also* in English, and are traditionally seen as performing functions of the same general type as modal verbs:

(17)   Klaus hat fünf Autos und auch eine Jacht.
       'Klaus has five cars and also a yacht.'
(18)   A: Deine Schuhe sind genau richtig für dieses Wetter.
          'Your shoes are just right for this weather.'
       B: Sind sie auch.
          Lit.: 'Are they also.'
          'Indeed, they are.'

Some linguists treat the two uses as homonyms with disparate semantic and pragmatic functions. Others leave the possibility open that there is some relationship between them, but no satisfactory theoretical account of the relation has been given. Further uses of *auch*, such as that in (19), have usually been ignored completely.

(19)   Wer auch immer nach Amerika geht wird erstaunt sein über die vielen Wolkenkratzer.
       'Whoever goes to America will be amazed at the many skyscrapers.'

Recently, two factors have come to light, which cast doubt on the assumption that the so-called adverbial and modal uses are a conventionalised peculiarity of some Germanic languages. First, it has been found that there are quite unrelated languages, such as Sissala, which exhibit the same phenomena. Consider (20), (21) and (22), which are very similar to (17), (18) and (19), respectively:

(20)   A múré múmúré ré   a   púŋsé má.
       we told   stories IM and written also.
       'We have told stories and also written.'
(21)   A: Zimpaalé Kiele   bio   ni.
          Zimpaale Dagaati child SDM
          'Zimpaale is a Dagaati.'
       B: Má ŋ ῡ-ʋ   rí yá, ŋ naŋnɔ́ŋɔ́ nέ.
          also I know-him IM P   my friend   SDM
          'Indeed, he is; I know him, he is my friend.'
(22)   Tíná   má cókó, ʋ-ʋ́   pii hé   ʋ nuɔ   mέ nέ,   yá?
       owner also cuts   he-IMP take put his mouth into SDM or
       'Whoever suffers does it for his own good, does he not?'

Surely it would be an extraordinary coincidence if the above uses in Sissala and German were only accidentally related.

The second factor which casts doubt on the assumption that the so-called adverbial and modal uses are genuinely homonymous is that relevance theory suggests a possible relationship between the two major uses. The notion of a confirmatory role in the processing of information, and, more generally, of the various methods by which relevance is established, are at the heart of the solution, which I shall now proceed to outline.

4.4.2   The parallel use

4.4.2.1   Parallelism and focus

Examples (17)–(22) show that English *also* has a more restricted range of functions than its counterparts in Sissala and German. I will concentrate first on the uses of *má* and *auch* which can be translated into English with *also*. Consider the following:

(23)   a. Cilla knitted a **cardigan**.
       b. She also knitted a **jumper**.
(24)   **Bernd** fährt einen Audi, Jens fährt **auch** einen.
       'Bernd drives an Audi, Jens also drives one.'
(25)   ʊ sɪɛ́ kénó ká de   isi   kal nɔ́ŋɔ́ bʊlɛ́, ʋ́-ʋ́   sí
       he so sat and INT get-up day other saying COMP-he FUT
       ko   ná Lʊʊ ká daarɛ   ko   ná Buro barááse má.
       come see Léo and continue come see Boura dam   also
       'One day he decided to come and visit Léo and to continue to Boura
       in order to see the dam also.'

The above use of *also* is traditionally referred to as the adverbial or conjunctive use. Blakemore (1987:97–104) draws attention to the fact that *also* in English interacts with focusing devices, and she bases her analysis of this interaction on Wilson and Sperber's (1979) account of ordered entailments.

Wilson and Sperber suggest that the proposition expressed by an utterance has grammatically specified entailments, entailments which can be obtained by substituting a logical variable or proform for a syntactic constituent. The grammatically specified entailments of (23a) are represented in (26):

(23)   a. Cilla knitted a cardigan.
(26)   a. Someone knitted a cardigan.
       b. Cilla knitted something.
       c. Cilla did something in connection with a cardigan.
       d. Cilla did something.
       e. Something happened.

Wilson and Sperber argue that though the speaker commits herself to the truth of all the entailments of her utterance, she does not expect them all to be relevant in the same way.

They draw a distinction between background and foreground entailments, background entailments helping to determine context, and foreground entailments contributing to the main point of utterance. Thus if (26a) is taken as background, the hearer is expected to process the utterance in a context in which it is relevant to know the identity of the person who knitted a cardigan; with (26) as background, the point would be to know *what* Cilla knitted, etc. The foreground entailments of the utterance specify the information that has to be added to the background to obtain the proposition as a whole.

Wilson and Sperber (1979) claim further that the speaker may use special linguistic devices to indicate the foreground entailments. Clefting is one such device, and stress assignment is another. Consider (27) and (28):

(27)   It was Cilla who knitted the cardigan.
(28)   **Cilla** knitted the cardigan.

In both cases (26a) is the main background entailment, and the point of utterance is to give the information that the person in question was Cilla.

Now compare (29) and (23b):

(29)   Cilla knitted a **jumper**.
(23)   b. She also knitted a **jumper**.

The main background entailment of both utterances is (26b). What *also* does is provide the further information in (23'):

(23')   b. Cilla knitted something other than a jumper.

Suppose the hearer asks himself what this something else might be. In (23), there is an immediately accessible hypothesis, namely (23a):

(23)   a. Cilla knitted a cardigan.

This utterance shares with (23b) the background entailment (26b). In other words, *also* in English seems to be used in the second of two syntactically parallel utterances with identical backgrounds. According to Blakemore, the two utterances stand in a relation of *addition*.

Similar remarks apply to (24). *Auch* is used in the second of two syntactically parallel utterances with identical background entailment 'someone drives an Audi'. The point of (24), in Blakemore's view, would be to indicate that it is relevant for the hearer to know that Jens drives an Audi, in addition to knowing that Bernd drives one.

The focus in the English and German examples is often indicated by stress. In the Sissala example (25), where the focus is 'the dam at Boura', there is some indication that the syntactic position of *má* helps to determine the focus. However, just as stress placement in English and German need not determine a unique focus, so the syntactic position of *má* is only a rough indication to the hearer as to what the focus is supposed to be. Thus *má* in final position may have either NP, PP or VP in its scope; *má* as part of the subject NP has that NP in its scope; and *má* in presentential position has S in its scope. Examples (20) and (25) have *má* positioned finally. In (20) the whole VP is in the scope of *má*, and in (25) the object NP only.

On this account, the function of *also* is to pick out two syntactically parallel clauses and indicate that they stand in the relation that Blakemore calls 'additional'. As she points out, this relation is not obviously inferential, the central feature of the use of *also* seems to be a relation of parallelism, and it is to this relation that I now turn.

4.4.2.2   *Parallelism and contextual effects*

As we saw in section 4.3 with the discussion of *after all* and *therefore*, particles may encourage the hearer to look for certain types of inference relation, giving rise to certain types of contextual effect. As we have seen, the primary uses of *also, má* and *auch* as discussed in the last section seem to occur in utterances involving a certain type of parallelism. That in itself does not say anything about the particular contextual effects that such utterances may achieve. However, let us have a closer look at utterances with *also*, and see what contextual effects they may have.

Consider the use of *auch* and *also* in example (17).

(17)   Klaus hat fünf Autos und auch eine Jacht.
          'Klaus has five cars and also a yacht.'

If processed in a context containing assumption (17a), the first clause of (17) would yield the contextual implication in (17b):

(17)   a. People who own five cars are rich.
(17)   b. Klaus is rich.

If processed in a context containing assumption (17c) the second clause of (17) would yield this same contextual implication (17b):

(17)   c. People who own yachts are rich.

In other words, the second clause of (17) achieves relevance by strengthening, or providing additional evidence for, a contextual implication already derivable from the first clause.

Could we generalise this observation, and claim that in these adverbial uses involving parallelism, the propositions introduced by *also, auch* and *má* are invariably expected to achieve relevance by strengthening, or providing evidence for, a contextual implication already derivable from the first of the two parallel clauses? Unfortunately, things are not quite this simple. Although *also* does sometimes have this function, which I shall call parallel confirmation, there are other cases involving parallelism where the intended effect seems to be one of disconfirmation.

Parallelism in processing is achieved when two utterances or assumptions are processed in the same or similar contexts, yielding the same or similar conclusion. For an utterance to achieve relevance by parallel confirmation, two conjuncts must be processed in parallel contexts, by parallel inference processes, to yield the same or similar contextual implication. This does not happen in examples (30)–(31), which might be called a case of parallel disconfirmation or contradiction:

(30)   A: a. Klaus ist reich,   b. er spielt Tennis
            'Klaus is rich,   he plays tennis.'
(31)   B: a. Ich bin nicht reich b. und spiele auch Tennis.
            'I'm not rich   and I also play tennis.'

In (30b), A wants to strengthen his claim that Klaus is rich. A's utterance (30b) is intended to be relevant in a context containing assumption (30′):

(30′)   People who play tennis are rich.

In (31), B explicitly contradicts this assumption, and disconfirms A's claim that Klaus is rich, which depends on it. The parallelism here consists in the fact that the conclusion 'Klaus is rich' which (30b) is intended to strengthen, is contradicted or disconfirmed by the parallel utterance (31b). Here *auch* has nothing to do with the contradiction as such, it merely encourages the hearer to look for a certain type of parallelism in processing the utterance (31).

However, the claim that *also* in English and its equivalents in German and Sissala merely encourage the hearer to look for *some* form of parallelism in processing is rather vague. Let us try to make it more precise.

Recall that relevance can be achieved in three different ways or by three different types of contextual effects: contextual implication, confirmation and contradiction. We have already seen that an utterance may achieve relevance by contradicting, and hence eliminating, a proposition expressed or implied by a preceding utterance. In (31) the effect of the contradiction was to undermine the support for a previously established conclusion, thus disconfirming or contradicting this conclusion too. This is the type of case I have called parallel disconfirmation or contradiction.

Now consider (32):

(32)   A: John lives in Edinburgh.
        B: **Karen** lives in Edinburgh.

The speaker of (32B) could intend it to stand in one of two quite different relations to (32A): she could intend it to be treated in parallel to (32A), as an additional fact that the hearer should bear in mind; or she could intend it to contradict and eliminate (32A), with the implication that it is Karen rather than John who lives in Edinburgh. Let us call this second relation 'backwards contradiction'. Clearly, it would be useful for a speaker to have some linguistic device for indicating which way she intends her utterance to be understood – which type of relevance she has in mind.

My claim is that the function of *also*, and of *auch* and *má* in their parallel use indicates to the hearer that relevance is not to be achieved by backwards contradiction. Thus, the addition of these particles to (32) automatically rules out one of its two possible interpretations.

Clearly, this device will only be used where there is a risk of misinterpretation. Typically, such a risk will only arise when – as in (32) – the second of two utterances or clauses is similar enough to a preceding one to be misconstruable as a case of backwards contradiction.

Now consider (33):

(33)   A: Klaus is very rich.
        B: He has five cars.

Again, the speaker of (33B) could intend it to stand in one of two quite different relations to (33A): she could intend it to be treated in parallel to (33A), as an additional fact that the hearer should bear in mind; or she could intend it to confirm, or strengthen (33A), by providing evidence for its truth. Let us call this second relation 'backwards confirmation'. Clearly, it would be useful for a speaker to have some linguistic device for indicating which way she intends her utterance to be understood – which type of relevance she has in mind.

My claim is that *also* in English, unlike *auch* in German and *má* in

Sissala, is to indicate to the hearer that relevance is not to be achieved by either backwards contradiction or backwards confirmation. It follows that the two conjoined utterances must be treated in parallel: that the second should not be treated as modifying (i.e. confirming or contradicting) the first. Thus, the parallelism required by the *also* can be analysed as a result of prohibition on its use with backwards contradiction and backwards confirmation.

It is interesting to note that Sissala, which does not use contrastive stress as English and German do, has a particle *é*, which can be used as an explicit indicator of backwards contradiction. Consider (34):

(34) A: Háálɔ́ tuku muɪwa nɛ́.
   woman pounding rice SDM
   'The woman is pounding rice.'
  B: Kapalɛ é ʋ tuku ri.
   fufu F she pounding IM
   '**Fufu** she is pounding.'
   (i.e. she is pounding fufu, not rice)

Sissala, then, has a marker *é* for cases involving, amongst other things, parallelism of form and backwards contradiction, and a marker *má* for cases involving parallelism of form and some method of processing other than backwards contradiction.

So far, I have only discussed the contextual effects achieved by adverbial uses of *also, má* and *auch*, cases which, as we have seen, involve some form of parallelism in processing; we still have to consider the 'modal' use of *auch* and *má*. Before I take up this issue, I would like to look at some further examples of adverbial use.

4.4.2.3 *Parallel answers to the same question*

The examples given so far have involved only two parallel clauses. There are cases, however, where a cluster of clauses are involved. In Sissala, especially, *má* is often used to induce global parallelisms, or parallelisms among clusters of propositions. Consider (35):

(35) a. Kénco ká túú ri.
   nim is tree TDM
   'The nim is a tree.'
  b. Ʋ gbésó . . .
   it tall
   'It is tall . . . '

   c. ʋ zénó má.
     it big   also
     ' . . . and also big.'
   d. Ʋ paarʋ má ká yɛ́sɛ́ yɛ́sɛ́.
     its leaves also are small small
     'Its leaves are also very small.'
   e. Kénco daborsi rírʋ́   paarʋ   má haakí wɪ   déké.
     nim   bark   and-its leaves also bitter NEG compare
     'The nim's bark and its leaves are also bitter without comparison.'
   f. Diwiisi má di wó nɔna.
     birds   also eat their fruits
     'Birds also eat its fruits'.
   g. Niɛ   náŋá má coki dɪhí a   cɔ́ŋsɛ́ kénco.
     people some also clear place and plant nim-tree.
     'Some people also clear their place and plant the nim tree.'

Syntactically, *má* is positioned finally and is in the scope of the VP in (35c). In all other cases it is positioned preverbally and is in the scope of S.

In this example, every utterance containing a *má* induces a parallelism with the preceding utterances. The proposition expressed by each utterance provides a partial answer to the same question: 'What is the nim tree like?' The function of *má* is to encourage the hearer to look for parallelisms of context and contextual effects throughout the text. Each new occurrence of *má* indicates that the subsequent stretch of text is to be processed and understood in a parallel way to the preceding cluster of propositions, all of which provide answers to the same question.

It is not surprising that *also* can be perceived as a paragraph marker in this type of use, since it prefaces a cluster of propositions which are processed in the same or similar contexts. This example suggests that what have been called paragraph markers may not have the function of marking a paragraph as such; their paragraphing functions may be a by-product of their more general functions as constraints on relevance, which are the same for both global and non-global uses.

In European languages, it is stylistically unacceptable to use 'also' as often as in the example from Sissala just discussed. However, *auch* in German and *also* in English have a global function as well. The following example is taken from an article in *Der Spiegel* (No. 19, 5 May 1986), in which the dissatisfaction of the farmers with the agricultural policies of the EEC is expressed. The theme of the article is:

    Bauern: 'Die Unruhe ist einfach da.'
    'Farmers: "The disquiet is just there."'

Every paragraph in the text describes a particular point of dissatisfaction of the farmers. Only one paragraph is prefaced with *auch* and it expresses a further reason for the worry of the farmers:

(36)   *Auch* die Verwendung von Getreide, Kartoffeln und Zuckerrüben für die Produktion von Bio-Sprit bringt den bayrischen Kleinbauern eher in Zorn. Er hat nichts anzubieten, was sich für den großindustriellen Einsatz eignen würde.
'*Also* the use of grains, potatoes and sugar-beets for the production of bio-spirits rather annoys the small Bavarian farmer. He does not have anything which could be suitable for large-scale industrial use.'

As in the Sissala example, *auch* indicates that the following propositions form a unit, which is to be understood in a way parallel to the question 'Why are the farmers worried?'

The following English example is rather more complicated, in that a conjunct is implicated:

(Interview in *Time Magazine* (6 May 1985) with Chancellor Kohl, concerning the Bitburg affair.)
(37)   a. T.R.: Do you recall any other occasions on which German–American relations have been so tested?
        b. K.: No. The debate over deployment of course *also* had its strong emotional elements.

Although (37a) elicits the answer in (37b), it does not directly express a background assumption 'Something else had its strong emotional elements', which is required by the use of *also*. Rather, the speaker assumes that the hearer will have assumptions available to the effect that it is in the nature of tested relations to have strong emotional elements. His utterance suggests that there have indeed been other occasions on which relations have been tested, although not to the same degree as the Bitburg affair. Therefore the implicit assumption which the hearer is encouraged to recover is (37'):

(37')   The Bitburg affair had its strong emotional elements.

In principle, any number of incidents could be added, which would all provide partial answers to the same question, 'Which occasions of tested German–American relations have there been?'

The examples discussed in this section all involve parallelisms in processing, although they do not necessarily amount to cases of parallel confirmation or contradiction. Their parallelism consists in the fact that they are to be understood as providing partial answers to a single question. They are clearly compatible with the claim that *also* is to be given a purely negative characterisation – as excluding an interpretation involving backwards contradiction. In the next section, I will look at some more typical cases of parallel confirmation.

4.4.2.4   Parallel premises

The examples discussed in the last section involved parallelisms of context and contextual effects among a variety of independently processed propositions. These parallelisms fell well short of the identity of contextual effects. However, as Blakemore shows, there is one use of *also* in English which is a synonym of *moreover*, and which encourages the hearer to look not merely for similar, but for identical, contextual effects. Consider first an English example:

(38)   a. Bill didn't come for lunch today.
       b. He has a cold.
       c. Also, he doesn't like fish.

In (38c), the proposition expressed must be understood as providing additional support for the conclusion which has been derived from (38b). The conclusion is, of course, the proposition expressed in (38a). Example (38) is thus a standard case of parallel confirmation, as discussed in section 4.4.2.2 above.

The following Sissala example illustrates a similar use of *má*. It is part of a discussion concerning the use of sacrificial animals for food, which happened when frozen sheep had been sent from Mecca to areas of famine. The utterance states the two reasons why the Sissala people cannot be blamed for having eaten sacrificial animals (wrong as it may be under normal circumstances):

(39)   a. Ba há   kene ko   ı   ha wʊ-ʊ   mʊl   ɛ̄.
          they when took come you still NEG-its meaning knew
          'When they brought it, you didn't know what its meaning was.'
       b. Má zilé ni   vele a   ko   yáá.
          also gift SDM go   and come P
          'Also, it was a gift, which came along.'

As in (38), the hearer must draw the same conclusion from the premise in (39b) as from the premise in (39a), namely (39′):

(39′)   The Sissalas cannot be blamed for having eaten sacrificial meat.

Or consider the following German example from *Der Spiegel* (No. 28, 1985), which exhibits the same function of the particle as in the preceding example:

(40)　a. Der Bürger in Deutschland, der kauft eins [ein Auto] mit Katy
　　　　　[Katalysator],
　　　b. nicht nur wegen der steuerlichen Förderungen,
　　　c. sondern weil das einfach **auch** im Trend der Zeit liegt.

　　　a. 'A citizen in Germany buys a car with a catalytic converter,
　　　b. not only because of the tax advantages
　　　c. but **also** because it is simply the trend of the time.'

Again, both the premises and the conclusion are explicitly stated in the
text. The function of *auch* is to encourage a search for parallelisms, with
propositions (40b) and (40c) providing independent support for proposition (40a).

In this section I have compared a variety of adverbial uses of *also,
má* and *auch*. In the next section I want to look at the so-called modal
uses of *má* and *auch*, which cannot be translated into English by *also*.

4.4.3　*Ma, auch* and confirmation

4.4.3.1　*The role of backwards confirmation*
Examples (18)–(19) and (21)–(22) in section 4.4.1 contained uses of *má*
and *auch* which could not be translated into English using *also*. In this
section I will concentrate on examples of this type. Consider (41):

(41)　A:　You didn't sow early, therefore you will be well off. As far as we
　　　　　are concerned, ours will all be bad.
　　　B:　Nyamέ siláárɛ ɓɪɛ　　náá e wuu sɪέ　hɪlɔ.
　　　　　perhaps first　　things the F all　　then dry
　　　　　'Maybe the first are dry.'
　　　C:　Má náŋá　e dé　caasɛ hɪl.
　　　　　also others F INT really dry
　　　　　'Yes, some are really dry.'

A translation of (41C), using *also* would be inappropriate:

(41′)　　?Also some are really dry.
　　　　　(In a boutique)
(42)　A:　Ich werde den Pulli und nicht die weiße Bluse zum Kostüm nehmen.
　　　　　'I'm going to take the jumper and not the white blouse for the suit.'
　　　B:　Vielleicht haben Sie noch eine weiße Bluse.
　　　　　'Maybe you still have a white blouse.'
　　　A:　Habe ich auch.
　　　　　Lit.: Have I also.
　　　　　'I have indeed.'
but: * Have I also.

Although confirmation or strengthening plays a role in these examples, it is not the type of parallel confirmation so far discussed. In (41) and (42), and in all the so-called 'modal' uses, there are not two utterances processed in parallel contexts, by parallel inferences, to yield parallel conclusions. In (41) C confirms B's suspicion that the first crop will be dry; in (42) A confirms B's guess that the customer might have a white blouse. Thus the utterances containing *má* and *auch* achieve relevance by strengthening or confirming a proposition previously expressed. Though there may be parallelism in form, the formally similar utterances are not processed in parallel ways. I have called this type of relation 'backwards confirmation'.

What, if anything, is common to the adverbial and 'modal' uses of *má* and *auch*? It would be puzzling if the two uses were unrelated, since they are found in such widely different languages. My suggestion is that *má* and *auch* have the same function in both their 'modal' and their adverbial uses. Their function is simply to exclude the possibility that backwards contradiction is involved. If this is so, then we have indeed a common relationship between the 'adverbial' and 'modal' uses and a possible explanation for the striking similarity in form and function of these expressions in Sissala and German. Let us now consider the full range of 'modal' uses.[3]

4.4.3.2   Confirmation of explicatures

Although the 'modal' functions of *má* in Sissala and *auch* in German are very similar, in Sissala a yes–no question may be answered with *má*, which is not permissible in German. Consider (43):

(43)   A: ι   má die   dáárέ ráŋ   ríí   kέ?
               you also yesterday pass   there near F
               'Did you also go down there yesterday?'
        B: Má á die   de   mυ   ráŋ ˙né   nyáŋ.
               also we yesterday INT went there SDM back
               'Indeed, we were back down there yesterday.'

A's question expresses a proposition which he hopes B will confirm. B indicates by the use of *má* that what A thought possible, is indeed the case.

Now consider another example where the proposition expressed by a question is confirmed with *má*:

(44)   a. N: ι   ha-á   bınυ bır   mυí   rí   yá-á? Abidjan ná.
               you still-IPF think again going IM P-Q Abidjan DEF
               'Are you still thinking of going? To Abidjan.'

b. E: Abidjan ná é, dʋla   é ŋ wa-á   wolli.
       Abidjan the F this-year F I NEG-IPF can
       'Abidjan, this year, I cannot.'

c.   Má amá taŋŋa ŋ ha-á   bííné   é rí.
       also but really I still-IPF believe F IM
       'Although, I'm actually still thinking about it.'

This example is somewhat more complicated than the previous one, in that the proposition (44a) being confirmed is not the one expressed by the utterance immediately preceding (44c). The immediate reaction to N's question is a negative answer in (44b) by E, who then goes on to confirm that though he is not going to Abidjan this year, he is still thinking about going. In this case the intended relevance of *má* in (44c) is to confirm (44a). Thus we have the interesting phenomenon of one proposition being constrained in two different ways, by two different constraints on relevance, *amá* 'but' and *má*.

In Sissala no wh-question can be answered with *má*. In both German and Sissala, the use of *má* in backwards confirmation appears to be restricted to propositions which already have a certain degree of strength; this degree seems to be higher in German than in Sissala, since Sissala permits propositions expressed by yes–no questions to be confirmed with *má*.

Example (21) in section 4.4.1 is a case where the proposition to be confirmed is not identical to the one prefaced by *má*. However, B's answer, together with the contextual assumption (21'a), yields (21'b) as a contextual implication.

(21')   a. If one knows somebody well, one knows where he comes from.
        b. B knows where Zimpaale comes from.

And this yields the required effect by backwards strengthening: B's utterance confirms what A has said.

Now let us return to example (16), repeated here for convenience, where *má* is understood as meaning *after all*:

(16)   a. N: Íí gbé, ʋ-ʋ́   kó   rʋ́-ʋ́   sʋ́l rá né.
             perhaps he-IPF come that-he ask us SDM
             'Perhaps he is coming to ask us.'

       b. E: Ʋ jaa   ná   wɪé.
             his house DEF matters
             'Concerning his house.'

    c. N: Oó, má ʋ die   má kúó rírá   fa   pa
          yes also he yesterday also came that-we should collect
          cɛrɛ ná.
          wood DEF
          'Yes, after all, he also came yesterday to ask us to collect wood
          for him.'

The second *má* in (16c) is the familiar parallel use discussed in previous
sections. The first *má* in (16c) is a case of backwards confirmation: the
proposition expressed by (16b) is intended to confirm (16a). The extra
assumptions which the hearer is supposed to supply are something like
(16'):

(16')   a. If somebody came yesterday with a certain intention, then it is likely
          that he will come a second time with the same intention.
    b. If he came yesterday in order to ask us for help, then he will come
          today in order to ask us for help.

Thus *má* in its interpretation *after all* fits in as a case of backwards
confirmation. As already mentioned, it is not part of the meaning of *má*
that the proposition used as evidence is already known. In Sissala the
hearer has to infer by considerations of relevance whether the proposition prefaced by *má* is known or not.

    Similar remarks apply to the German use of *auch* in backwards
confirmation. However, in German the speaker may indicate with a
second particle *ja* whether the proposition expressed is known or not.
Consider (45):

(45)   A: Klaus hat den Vortrag gut gehalten.
        'Klaus has given a good presentation.'
    B: Er ist *ja auch* Lehrer.
        'After all, he is a teacher.'

B's answer is relevant in a context (45'):

(45')   All teachers know how to give a good presentation.
        If Klaus is a teacher, then he knows how to give a good presentation.

The contextual implication is (45'a):

(45')   a. Klaus knows how to give a good presentation.

With this contextual implication B's utterance provides backwards confirmation of A's assertion. Thus, every example in this section has shown
how 'modal' uses of *má* and *auch* suggest that relevance is to be sought
via backwards confirmation. In the cases so far discussed the proposition
to be confirmed has always been explicitly expressed. However, I will

show in the next section that *má* and *auch* may be used to confirm implicit assumptions.

4.4.3.3 Confirmation of implicatures

If it is the case that our existing assumptions constantly undergo strengthening or weakening as a result of the processing of new information, it is to be expected that devices such as *má* and *auch* will not be restricted to confirming assumptions that have been explicitly expressed. I will now consider a few cases in which *má* and *auch* are used to confirm implicit or implicated assumptions. Consider (46):

(46)   ʟ   fá   súl   ŋménɔ́   ko   rí-í   má   tʊŋ?
       you PAST beg road   come COMP-you also work
       'Did you ask for permission to work, then?'
       'Hast Du auch um Arbeitserlaubnis gefragt?'

This example can be directly translated into German with *auch*, which is indeed used in this way quite frequently. My suggestion is that in (46) the speaker is indicating that an answer containing *má* or *auch* would be relevant to her. How could such an answer be relevant? It would be relevant as a case of backward confirmation only if the speaker already thought that the hearer might already have permission to work. Thus (46) would be appropriate where the hearer was behaving as if he had in fact permission to work, but it is doubtful that he actually has.

The implicatures carried by such utterances with *má* and *auch* may even be informative. Thus if, for instance, the hearer of (46) had not realised that it was important to have permission to work, he could discover this information by processing (46). This illustrates how constraints on relevance can be used to generate 'conventional' implicatures.

A very similar German example is (47):

       (Mother to child going to the dinner table:)
(47)   Hast Du Dir auch die Hände gewaschen?
       'Have you washed your hands, then?'

Example (47) is relevant in a context in which the child knows that it is expected to wash its hands before coming to the dinner table. Going to the dinner table is normally an indication that one has washed one's hands. Hence (47) officially requests a positive answer, but by the very act of requesting confirmation, suggests that the speaker has some doubt about whether this answer will actually be forthcoming.

The knowledge that *auch* and *má* can be used to confirm implicated assumptions is necessary for an understanding of examples like the following in German:

(48)   A: Torsten nimmt Geigenunterricht seit Weihnachten.
        'Torsten has been taking violin lessons since Christmas.'
        B: Deshalb spielt er auch so gut.
        'So that is why he is playing so well.'

Here (48B) is a conclusion drawn from (48A). What, then, is the function of *auch*? My claim is that this is another case of backwards confirmation: B suggests that either he or A already has evidence that Torsten was playing well, and that they now have confirmation of, and an explanation for, this fact.

In order to understand better what is going on, let us assume that somebody had actually said (49):

(49)   A: Torsten spielt die Geige sehr gut.
        'Torsten plays the violin very well.'

Then a very natural reaction of B might be (49'):

(49')   B: Er hat auch Geigenunterricht seit Weihnachten.
        '(You see,) he has been having violin lessons since Christmas.'

In (49') the particle is positioned in the evidence, but it is really strengthening the same proposition as in (48). In both cases, what is being explained, and hence confirmed, is the fact that Torsten is playing so well.

Consider a similar example in Sissala:

(50)   a. l   né   tásıé sé   zíɓelo há-á   dé wii ʋ-ʋ́
           you SDM   before said cock   which-IPF INT crow he-IPF
           wí   ní.
           crow SDM
           'Before you have said that the cock will definitely crow.' (That you
           will talk until the cock crows.)
        b. Ɛ né   a   má sıé ja   zíɓelo ná wíílé   ní   zaa.
           therefore we also now want cock   DEF crowing SDM today
           'Therefore we (also) want the cock to crow.'

The proposition expressed in (50a) attributes a thought to the hearer, and functions as a reminder. The speaker then takes this reminder as a premise in an argument and draws (50b) as a conclusion. *Sıé* indicates that (50b) is to be considered the conclusion. To derive this conclusion, assumptions such as (50'a) must be used:

(50')   a. If somebody promises something then one can have expectations
           that the promise will be kept.

> If x promised to speak until the cock crows then they can expect that
> he will do so.

In this utterance, the function of *má* is to indicate that the speaker had a
prior expectation that the hearer would talk until the cock crows, an
expectation which she now wants satisfied.

In this section I have shown how utterances with the modal use of *má*
and *auch* can function in backwards confirmation. I have argued that the
modal and adverbial uses of *auch* can be unified in the framework of
relevance theory. In the next section I want to consider some examples
which have often been left out of discussions on 'modal' particles.

4.4.3.4 The 'different' cases

There are some uses of *má* and *auch* which seem different from both
'modal' and 'adverbial' uses, and require different translations into
English. Are we dealing with yet another function of *má* and *auch*,
distinctly different from the two major functions discussed so far? Let us
consider a number of examples.

As mentioned in the introduction to this chapter, sentences which in
English would be introduced by the words *wherever, whenever, however,*
etc., and which I shall refer to as 'pseudo-relatives', are expressed with
má in Sissala and *auch* in German.

(51)   Rı kóní   púló   mɔ   ɛ́rɛ́ má ɓa   wı   zɔ́krɛ́
         if antelopes multiplication equals how also they NEG damage
         wuu kené.
         all have
         'However much antelopes may multiply, they do not cause any
         damage.'

The proposition expressed by (51) is (51'):

(51')   If there is any number of antelopes they do not cause any damage.

The function of *má* appears to be an emphatic one, converting this
proposition into the stronger (51'a):

(51')   a. If there is any number of antelopes, however high . . .

How is this function to be analysed?

Or consider the following German example, with a similar pseudo-
relative function:

(52)   Wohin Du *auch* schaust in Holland im Frühling, da sind Tulpen über
         Tulpen.

'Wherever (also) you look in Holland in springtime there are tulips and tulips.'

This utterance expresses the following proposition:

(52')   If you look anywhere in Holland in springtime there are many tulips.

Auch appears to add an emphatic element, converting (52') to (52'a), which in turn implies (52'b):

(52')   a. If you look anywhere at all in Holland in springtime then there are many tulips.

(52')   b. There are tulips everywhere in Holland in springtime.

How are these examples to be analysed?

The pseudo-relative functions performed by *má* and *auch* are performed in English by *ever* and *at all*. German, in addition to *auch*, optionally uses *immer* 'ever, always'. How are these pseudo-relative expressions to be analysed?

The fact that it is hard to detect a truth-conditional difference between propositions such as 'if you look anywhere' and 'if you look anywhere at all' suggests that, in these pseudo-relative cases constraints on relevance are involved. The 'emphatic' function of pseudo-relatives is clearly related to the function of backwards confirmation, with its implication that something hitherto only suspected is indeed the case. Although this suggestion is rather vague, it at least opens up a line of further investigation.

There is another use of *auch* which could be looked upon as different from the others, since an element of scalarity is involved. Consider (53):

(53)   A: Ʊ-ʊ dé   ná moŋgo a   dé dí dí ʊ wa-á   já
            if-he INT see mango and INT eat eat he NEG-IPF want
            rʊ́-ʊ́   ta.
            that-he stop
            'If he sees mangoes, he eats and eats, he doesn't want to stop.'

        B: Mʊɔ́ nyɛ   má.
            little like-that also
            '(Not) even for a little while.'

B's utterance is meant to strengthen A's claim that X does not want to stop eating mangoes – and all the contextual effects of this claim – by emphasising that X does not want to stop eating even for a little time, i.e. by spelling out and confirming the import of this claim. The contextual implication of (53A) is (53'a):

(53')   a. X's liking for mangoes is extreme.

B confirms this contextual implication by indicating the scale of X's liking of mangoes: not being able to stop eating for a little while. When processed in a context containing (53'b),

(53')   b. Somebody who cannot stop eating mangoes for a little while has a very extreme liking for mangoes.

example (53B) achieves relevance by strengthening A's opinion that X's liking for mangoes is extreme.

This example could be translated into German with *auch*, but a translation into English using *also* would not work. Consider (54) and (55):

(54)   A: Wenn er Mangos sieht dann ißt und ißt er und will nicht aufhören.
           B: Auch nicht für eine kurze Zeit.
(55)   A: When he sees mangoes then he eats and eats and doesn't want to stop.
     *B: Also not for a short time.

While the grammaticality of *auch* in this case is expected, the ungrammaticality in English is predicted by the fact that *also* is not used in English for backwards confirmation.

The following example, taken from a natural text, illustrates the scalar use of *auch*. The example is taken from *Der Spiegel* (19 May 1986):

(Interview: Görlach to reporter concerning coalition of the SPD with the Greens:)
(56)   G: Ich will, daß der Johannes [Rau] Kanzler wird, und ich will das auch dann, wenn wir das optimale Ziel, allein regieren zu können, nicht erreichen.
          'I want Johannes Rau to become chancellor, and I even want it if we shouldn't reach the optimal goal of ruling alone.'

Görlach was accused in this interview of having the eccentric desire to form a coalition with the Greens. In (56) he justifies this desire. The conjunct including *auch* makes clear the strength of this desire by spelling out its consequences and explicitly confirming them:

(56')   Coalition with the Greens is not an optimal goal. However, Görlach would accept non-optimal goals in order to have Rau become chancellor.

As we see, there is again a function of backwards confirmation involved. The difference from other uses is that, because of the context in which the utterances are interpreted, a scalar interpretation of extremeness or unusualness is the result. English and French have special particles (*even* and *même*) which have as part of their semantic content the notion of extremeness. German uses particles with scalar content (*selbst, sogar*) in cases where the scalarity is not obvious from the context and Sissala adds other particles such as *wuu* 'all, completely' or *tu* 'self', which I will discuss in section 4.5.

We have now considered a whole range of uses of *má* and *auch* in which backwards confirmation is involved, and backwards contradiction ruled out. This confirms my claim that *má* in Sissala and *auch* in German can never be used in backwards contradiction.[4]

4.4.4   The relationship between the 'modal' and 'adverbial' uses

In section 4.4.2.2 I claimed that the adverbial use of *also, má* and *auch* excludes a certain type of interpretation: one involving either backwards contradiction or backwards confirmation. Similarly, in 4.4.3, I showed with many examples that the modal uses of *má* and *auch* yield interpretations involving backwards confirmation, never backwards contradiction. So the fact that *má* and *auch* cannot be used in backwards contradiction, must be what unites the modal and adverbial functions of these expressions in Sissala and German. What distinguishes English *also* from *má* and *auch* is simply how much they exclude: *also* excludes both backwards contradiction and backwards confirmation, whereas *má* and *auch* permit backwards confirmation and exclude only backwards contradiction. Sperber and Wilson's notion of contextual effect is crucial to this account. Relevance theory thus provides a means of uniting phenomena which are clearly related, but whose relations have never been satisfactorily explained.

It is perhaps worth emphasising that all the major uses of *má* and *auch* follow automatically from the fact that they are used to rule out interpretations involving backwards contradiction. Where their presence is optional, it follows from considerations of relevance (and in particular, of economy) that these devices will only be used when there is a risk of misinterpretation. Typically, such a risk will only arise when – as in (34) above – the second of two utterances or clauses is similar enough to a preceding one to be misconstruable as a case of backwards contradiction. And typically, utterances involving such similarity can only be relevant in two further ways: by backwards confirmation, or by one of the methods involving parallelism, e.g. parallel confirmation. From this it follows that the intended relevance must be via either backwards confirmation or parallelism. As we have seen, *má* in Sissala and *auch* in German are used in both these types of case, whereas *also* in English is restricted to cases involving parallelism, and different expressions are used to indicate backwards confirmation.

We can see now why a language such as English should turn out not to have one common particle for both 'modal' and 'adverbial' uses. There is indeed a difference between 'adverbial' and 'modal' function: adverbial uses never achieve relevance via backwards confirmation; modal uses always do. Hence relevance theory sheds light on both the similarities and the differences between *auch*, *má* and *also*.

Notice, incidentally, that languages may differ in the functions they assign to the particle *yes*. In English *yes* can be used for both backwards confirmation and backwards contradiction. Consider (57) and (58):

(57) A: The play is boring, isn't it?
      B: Yes, it is.
(58) A: The play isn't boring.
      B: Yes, it is.

In (57) B confirms what A said; and in (58) B contradicts what A said. Thus *yes* is not restricted to the function of confirmation. Consider the same examples in German:

(59) A: Das Stück ist langweilig, nicht wahr?
      B: Ja.
(60) A: Das Stück ist nicht langweilig.
      B: Doch.

Ja, like *auch* in German, can only be used to confirm. When denial or contradiction is achieved by a positive utterance, then another word – *doch* – has to be used. Similar phenomena are found in Romance languages.

I said above that English does not use *also* for backwards confirmation. However, *too* has this function, as Deirdre Wilson has pointed out to me.

(61) A: Susan is a nice person.
      B: She is too.

And it is interesting that *too*, unlike *má* and *auch*, can also be used in some dialects in backwards contradiction:

(62)   A: Susan is not a nice person.
        B: She is too.

Thus, *too* cannot perhaps be analysed like *also*, as excluding backwards contradiction. However, if a language has only one particle for backwards confirmation, which replaces particles like *indeed, after all, even*, as in Sissala, then it makes sense that it would rule out backwards contradiction, as does Sissala.

4.5   'Even' in English and Sissala

In section 4.4 I showed with examples (53) in Sissala and (56) in German, that *má* and *auch* can be understood as equivalents to *even* in certain types of scalar cases. In this section, I want to look at the use of English *even* and the Sissala compound particles *má wuú* and *má tu*, which perform many of the functions of *even* in English.

Even has been analysed as a non-truth-conditional particle by Altmann (1976), Karttunen and Karttunen (1977) and Karttunen and Peters (1979), Kempson (1975). Karttunen and Peters (1979) concentrate on the parallel use of *even* which interacts with focus, in a way similar to that discussed for *also* (see section 4.4.2.1); they point out that *even* has a scalar implicature, to the effect that the item or proposition in the scope of *even* is low on the scale of likelihood. It is easy to see that *even* has strong similarities to *also*, *too* and *either*, as Karttunen and Peters (1979:32) point out. All these items seem to induce an interpretation involving what Blakemore (1987) and others call an additional relation. Thus, consider (63):

(63)   John, Bill and even Michael came to the party.

The use of *even* encourages the hearer to use the assumption 'Somebody other than Michael came to the party' and suggests that it is unusual for Michael to go to parties.

I would like to question the claim that when scalar *even* is used, some form of parallelism or additional relation is necessarily involved. Consider (64):

(64)   a. Bill likes me a lot.
        b. He even cleans my shoes.

To understand (64b), the hearer does not need to access the assumption 'Bill does something else apart from cleaning my shoes.' Rather, (64b) is intended as a backwards confirmation of (64a); like *má* in Sissala and *auch* in German, *even* in English can be used in both parallel use and backwards confirmation.

In the above case the use of *even* has a very similar effect to *you see* and *after all*. Consider (65):

(65)   a. Bill likes me a lot.
          b. You see, he cleans my shoes.
(66)   a. Bill likes me a lot.
          b. After all, he cleans my shoes.

In examples (64), (65) and (66), the hearer has to have access to assumptions such as (67):

(67)   If somebody cleans shoes for somebody else, then he must like this person very much.

Even carries the additional implicature in (68):

(68)   Cleaning shoes is an unusual favour for another person.

The fact that both (67) and (68) could contain *even* confirms my claim that *even* need not have a parallel interpretation. As we have seen, these particles are typically used in backwards confirmation. *Even* would simply indicate the degree to which Bill likes X.

Or consider another example:

(69)   a. Jane is very tired.
          b. Not even coffee keeps her awake.

Again *even* does not have a parallel interpretation, if it is in the scope of the whole sentence. Example (69b) is designed to strengthen the proposition expressed by (69a), indicating how tired Jane is. The speaker expects the hearer to have assumptions available to the effect that coffee normally keeps tired people awake, and if that is not the case, then that person must be very tired.

To support my claim, let us consider another example, where the function of *even* is similar to that of *indeed*, with an additional scalar implicature:

(70)   A: Do you have a word processor?
          B: I even have a good one.

Here *even* has a backwards confirmatory function as well as the function of indicating unlikelihood. Obviously, A assumed that B would probably not have a word processor, let alone that he would have a good one. Thus B, taking A's point of view, confirms what A thought unlikely by using *even*. Thus, English too has a particle which is used in both parallel and backwards confirmation. However, I have not considered enough of the uses of *even* to be able to claim definitely that, like *má* and *auch*, it cannot be used in backwards contradiction.

Now let us consider some Sissala examples. I will start with the parallel confirmatory use:

(71)   a. Tié   wuu hɪl.
            earth all dry
            'All the ground was dry.'
    b. Mɪɛ   paarʊ wuu hil a   vɔwɛ náŋá   mɛ . . .
            millet leaves all dry and stick together at
            'The millet leaves are all dry and stick together . . . '
    c. lɛɛmɪɛ bónní ɓallɛ pɛ́ tíe . . .
            corn   broken fallen lie ground
            'the corn is broken, has fallen and is lying on the ground . . .
    d. síwié   paarʊ wuu gunni . . .
            groundnut leaves all   folded
            'the groundnut leaves are all folded . . . '
    e. ká píɛ́ é dé wɪ   nyʊ́ɛ́   má wuú.
            and yams F INT NEG germinated even
            'and as for the **yams**, they did not even germinate.'

All the propositions expressed by utterances (71a–e) indicate the bad effects of the famine, but (71e) is the worst on the scale, as indicated by *má wuú*.

Example (71) clearly expresses some form of parallelism. However *má wuú* or *má tɪ* may also occur where there is no parallel utterance or clause immediately preceding. Consider (72):

        (Background: X's funeral is discussed, and it is mentioned
        that they would dance at his funeral. However, X does not
        like the idea. So A says (72))
(72)   Ɓa de-é   gʊɛ́   ʋ má tɪ wa-á   saŋ.
      they INT-NEG dance he even   NEG-IPF agree
      'If they didn't dance, even he would not be in agreement.'

The use of *má tɪ* suggests that somebody else than X is not in agreement. Again, therefore, *má tɪ* 'even' involves the sort of parallel adding relation familiar with *also*.

Now consider example (73), in which there is a parallel relation expressed in (73a) and backwards confirmation in (73b):

(73)   a. A   fa   sı   bʊl   fafalı   má   tıı.
            we   PAST FUT   speak past-style even
            'We should even speak the old style.'
        b. Má tıı ré   nɔ́ŋɔ́   sɛ   í   Buuni   ra.
            even IM   some say   COMP   Boura-dialect NEG
            'It is even the case that some say that this is not the Boura dialect.'

In (73a) a parallel relation is involved and also a scalar implicature. The scalar implicature conveys the information that extreme care should have been taken in selecting the subjects for providing the text, even to the extent that only the old style (spoken by the elders) should have been recorded.

In (73b) *má tıı* is in sentence-initial position and therefore has the whole sentence in its scope. The utterance is meant to justify – and therefore backwards confirm – the claim in (73a). In addition to backwards confirmation it indicates scalarity: the claim that the dialect is not even from Boura is contrary to normal expectation.

In this section I have shown how *even* in English, like *má tıı* and *má wuú* in Sissala, can be used to constrain to parallel use, very much like 'also' in many languages, and how it can also be used in backwards confirmation. As far as I know, the latter has never been recognised by anyone for any language before. Most analysts seem to assume that 'even' has always parallel use. In addition to these two constraining functions, 'even' has a scalar implicature.

4.6   Conclusion

The purpose of this chapter has been to examine the function of a particular group of non-truth-conditional particles in Sissala.

I first discussed some theoretical accounts of these phenomena and then reviewed Blakemore's analysis of inferential constraints in English. I compared these with various inferential devices in Sissala, such as *sıɛ́*, *ná* and *má*, which indicate that some type of confirmation is involved, and which are further distinguished by the nature and type of the confirmation process. My conclusion was that there are many cross-linguistic similarities among these inferential devices.

I then drew attention to some differences between the use of 'also' in German (*auch*) and Sissala (*má*), on the one hand, and in English, on the other. 'Also' in the former languages has both adverbial and modal uses, whereas *also* in English has only the adverbial use. I argued that adverbial use involves some form of parallelism, whereas modal uses involve backwards confirmation.

Backwards confirmation, of course, exists in English, and can be explicitly indicated by the use of words like *indeed* and *after all* – thus strengthening the impression that modal and adverbial uses are unrelated. As I have tried to show, this impression is mistaken. There are both similarities and differences between the two types of use, and hence reasons for amalgamating them and for holding them apart. Different languages react to these possibilities in different ways.

I briefly discussed some aspects of the use of the scalar particle *even* in English and its equivalents *má wuu* and *má tu* in Sissala. I showed how *even*, unlike *also* in English, can be used in backwards confirmation, thus performing similar functions to *má* in Sissala and *auch* in German.

The result of this still limited research suggests a new approach to the typology of particle uses, based on the various methods by which relevance can be achieved. As we have seen, variation is to be expected in the choices made by different languages about how to correlate processing roles with form. However, it is to be expected that similar patterns of particle use will be found universally, due to the fact that humans have the same basic cognitive abilities and are constrained by the same general communicative principle, the principle of relevance.

5 'Baa': truth-conditional or non-truth-conditional particle?

5.1 Introduction

In the last two chapters I have shown that while some linguistic expressions can be analysed in purely truth-conditional terms, others – the semantic constraints on relevance – cannot. This raises an interesting theoretical question: how does one decide whether a given linguistic expression is truth-conditional or not? In this chapter, I will propose tests for distinguishing between truth-conditional and non-truth-conditional uses and look at a particle – *baa* – which appears to have both types of use. The existence of such particles raises a second interesting theoretical question: must they be analysed as genuinely ambiguous between truth-conditional senses, or can they be treated as merely vague?

My answer to these questions will be as follows. First, *baa* is not multiply ambiguous: it has two core meanings, one truth-conditional and the other non-truth-conditional, from which the full range of uses can be predicted. Second, it is genuinely ambiguous between truth-conditional and non-truth-conditional uses. However, the two core meanings are clearly related, and this type of ambiguity or polysemy between truth-conditional and non-truth-conditional senses is quite common. I shall end with some speculations on why such ambiguities are found.

5.2 Uses of *baa*

5.2.1 Temporal uses

Baa has a variety of temporal uses. In all of these, it is positioned consistently before the VP. Its semantic interpretations are discussed below.

5.2.1.1 The iterative and restitutive use
Both *baa* in Sissala and *again* in English may have an iterative or restitutive interpretation. What exactly I mean by this will be explained by

161

reference to the examples. The following examples have an iterative interpretation.

(1)   ι   wuse a   rí-í   ka teŋfiél wérí rá-á   wuu baa
      that God does COMP-you have peace much COMP-we all   again
      mıŋ naŋa   mé.
      there together at
      'May God give you peace and bring us together again.'

(2)   Midi ko   peri,   ɓa baa   ŋmɔwɛ téŋgɛré   Léo mé.
      noon come reach, they again beat telephone Léo at
      'At noon they again phoned Léo.'

The interpretation of *baa* in (1) and (2) is iterative in the sense that there is a time, t1, at which the proposition expressed by the utterance is true, a later time, t2, at which the proposition expressed is not true, and a still later time, t3, at which the proposition expressed is again true.

In examples (1) and (2) the interpretation of *baa* involves iteration or repetition of the action described by the verb. However *baa*, like *again* in English, may in some cases not involve true repetition, but merely indicate the restitution of a former state of affairs. Rothkegel (1979) refers to this as 'restitutive use', and Dowty (1979) calls it 'internal interpretation'. Consider an English example:

(3)   John opened the window again.

On an iterative or external interpretation of (3), John opened the window twice; on a restitutive or internal interpretation, John restored the window to its former state of being open. There are similar examples in Sissala:

(4)   Ɓa hé náŋá   mé va   mʊɔ́ ká baa cakse.
      they add together at walk a-little and again separate
      'They come together, stay together for a little while and separate again.'

On an iterative interpretation, (4) would describe two acts of separation. However, this was not in fact the intended interpretation. The hearer was intended to understand merely that the animals, after coming together, returned to their former state of separation. That is, the intended interpretation was not iterative but restitutive.

Rothkegel (1979) draws attention to the fact that verbs often have iterative or restitutive content. Thus the prefix *re-* in French often marks this, as in *revenir, retomber*. In German, prefixes as well as verbal compounds with *wieder* fulfil this role, and restitutive suffixes such as -sɛ and -nɛ perform the same role in Sissala:

(5)	a.	kommen	'to come'	wiederkommen	'to return'
	b.	leben	'to live'	beleben	'to revive'
(6)	a.	ceŋ	'to meet'	caksɛ	'to separate'
	b.	lúŋ	'to heat'	lúnsέ	'to reheat'

These verbs, with iterative or restitutive morphology, are often used with *again* or *baa*, as example (4) above, with 'separate', shows.

Besides these restitutive suffixes, there is also a verb *bɪrɛ* 'return' in Sissala, which indicates restoration of an earlier state. It is often used with non-resultative verbs. Consider (7):

(7) Ba siέ gɔ gɔala ná nέ ko tenni ká lɔɔléwa ná
     they so dance dance DEF SDM come finish and lorries DEF
     baa bɪrɛ pá wɔ́.
     again return collect them
     'So they finished dancing and the lorries collected them again.'

Bɪrɛ in this case helps to indicate that the lorries took the people back to where they had come from. Because of *bɪrɛ*, an interpretation in which the people were collected twice in the same place is ruled out.

Bɪrɛ (or its alternative form *bɪr*) may also be used without *baa*, as the next example shows. *Baa* is used iteratively in the first conjunct; in the second conjunct, the same happening is viewed restitutively.

(8) Daŋgáná baa wɪ pómé ri, a bɪr ko?
     Dangana again NEG come-out IM and return come
     'Is Dangana not born again and returned?'

According to Sissala belief, the dead may come back via normal birth. Dangana is believed to be reincarnated, therefore *pómé* with *baa* describes a repeated happening. However, if somebody has returned, this can also be seen as the restoration of a former state, and this is what is described in the second conjunct.

5.2.1.2. The durative use

In addition to its iterative and restitutive use, *baa* has a durative interpretation similar to that of *still* in English. Consider (9), which is taken from a description of fishing practices amongst the Sissala. Fishing at night is worthwhile after or during heavy rain, which brings new water and fish from the rivers to the dam:

(9) Ká náŋwúɓʊʊra a ɓɪdíílé di
     then fishermen make food eat

ka   baa dɪdɛllɛ   tɔɔ nɔ́ŋɔ́ pʋlɛ.
and still IPF-wait   day next   light
'The fishermen make food for themselves, eat, and still wait until the next day.'

In the above case, the use of *baa* suggests the amount of extra time the fishermen might stay after having eaten. Thus, if a fisherman was lucky during the night and caught a lot of fish, he might go home. If he was not so lucky, he would stay *baa* (on) until the morning.

The length of time involved with this use of *baa* varies from context to context. Consider (10):

(Previous discourse: 'After some time, another car came. The people were all looking. The Fulani griots and the members of the CDR (political party) of Boura had come.')

(10)   Mʋɔɔ, rí   lɔɔlɛ nɔ́ŋɔ́ má   né   dɔ́mɛ   a-á   ko.
       little COMP lorry other also SDM make-noise and-IPF come
       Nɪɛ   wuu baa bí-bel.
       People all still IPF-watch.
       'After a little while, another lorry was coming and made a noise. The people were still watching.'

The timespan involved here is the time from the arrival of the Fulani griots and the members of the CDR until the arrival of the new lorry. While in (9) the 'more' time has to do with an extension into the future, in (10) *baa* 'more' has to do with a prolongation of time in the past. More specifically, what is conveyed by generalised implicature is that the people had been waiting when the first lorry came, and were still waiting when the second lorry came. The latter use would typically be translated into German with *immer noch*.

There has been some discussion in the literature about whether it is part of the meaning of *still* or *noch* that the states of affairs described in the proposition expressed are expected to come to an end (see for example Doherty 1973). I agree with König (1977) that this is not part of the meaning of *noch* in German, since there are clear examples where the state of affairs described is not expected to end. Similarly, in Sissala, although the state of affairs described in (9) and (10) is clearly expected to end, it is not expected to end in (11):

(11)   a. Ɛ né lɛl ná   baa tóó,
          now war DEF more is-not,
       b. ká nʋɔ ná   má baa.
          but vow DEF also still

c. Ba wı   lísέ.
   they NEG lifted
   'The war is no more, but the vow still (holds). It has not been lifted.'

There is no indication at all that the 'vow' should ever come to an end. In fact, it is expected that it will not, since the legendary vow – that the people should be stung by mosquitos in order to stay awake at night during wars – is merely an explanation of a state of affairs, which everybody knows cannot be changed. Hence, *baa* like *noch* carries no implication about whether the state of affairs described will or will not come to an end.

Baa in its durative interpretation is also used in the negative, as example (11) shows, and it means 'not any more' as in English, rather than 'not yet' or 'noch nicht', as in German. Consider (12):

(12) ı   zizaamɔ nέ   kué   a-á   tɔwı   paarʊ ɓa-á   bʊl
      when mimosa SDM comes and-IPF sprouts leaves they-IPF say
      rí   tɔ́ɔ́ liɔ́   nέ.   Duɔ́ŋ baa   tó.
      COMP dry season SDM rain   more not-is
      'When the mimosa begins to sprout leaves, they say that the dry season begins, and there are no more rains.'

Without *baa*, (12) would merely express that there are no rains in the dry season. The addition of *baa* implies that there have been rains before.

Or consider a further example:

(13) ŋ há   bɔ́sέ ʊ́: ŋ sέ, 'í   baa   kaŋjaa mʊ́?'
      I when asked him I said you no more school go
      Rí   'kai!'
      COMP never
      'I asked him and said: "Are you not going to school any more?" (He said) "Never!"'[1]

Without *baa*, (13) conveys merely that the person in question does not go to school. The addition of *baa* implies that he did go to school at one stage.

So far, all the examples we have seen have had temporal interpretations. As with German *noch*, *baa* can also be used non-temporally. Its non-temporal uses are described and illustrated in the next section.

5.2.2   Non-temporal uses

5.2.2.1   Baa *with VP scope*

Syntactically, non-temporal *baa* may occur as a constituent of the VP, either preceding the verb or in VP-final position. Corresponding to this narrowing of syntactic scope comes a narrowing of semantic scope. Consider (14) where *baa* is positioned VP-finally:

(14)   Háála   má   ŋmíŋmɔwɛ hányɛ́ baa.
        women too IPF-beat   Hanhɛ́ as-well
        'The women too were beating "Hanhɛ" as well.'

Má, which has the subject noun phrase in its scope, indicates that the women acted in parallel to someone (in fact, the men). *Baa* indicates that they performed an action which was 'more' (rather than parallel) to some other action, and it implies that there was playing involved besides the playing of *Hanhɛ*. If the verb phrase of (14) was negated with *baa*, this implication would still hold.

In the next example, *baa* also has VP scope:

        (If you drink coffee are you then able to sleep?)
(15)   Má á keno rí   á bɪ   bɪsɛ né   yá? A baa   ja
        also we sit   COMP we speak talk SDM or   we as-well want
        dóŋ má rɛ-ɛ́.
        sleep also IM-Q
        'We are together talking, or not?
        Do we need sleep as well?'
        'Brauchen wir dann auch noch Schlaf?'

The use of *baa* in this example implies that they wanted something else besides sleep. This implication would persist if the sentence were negated. *Baa* also conveys that this 'something else' is viewed as 'more' rather than a mere addition.

Sentence (16) is an example of *baa* with negation:

(16)   Bakakoo baa wɪ   oŋ   nɔŋ   wuu fá.
        warthog add NEG thing other all   fear
        'The warthog doesn't fear anything else.'

The use of *baa* in (16) implies that the warthog did fear something. Indeed in the previous discourse, the speaker had indicated that the warthog fears humans. Without *baa* the utterance would convey that the warthog fears nothing.

5.2.2.2 Baa *with full sentential scope*

It is striking that the temporal and non-temporal uses of *baa* substantially coincide with those of *noch* in German. In each case some form of addition is involved.

Consider (17): the background to this example is that someone had just been asked to comment on the reaction of the women at a particular meeting:

(17)   (N: Luc, did you see them? How were they?
        L: They were happy and smiled.)
        M: Ba mómó ká baa bɔsɛ́ wɪɛ́   má.
              they smiled and more asked matters also
              'They smiled and what is more, they also asked questions'.

M provides further evidence for L's claim that the women were happy. On the one hand he confirms that the women smiled, and on the other hand he mentions that the women asked questions, as further evidence for the conclusion that the women were happy. *Baa* gives the hearer a clue that the proposition it introduces is supposed to be seen as further evidence for this conclusion.

A similar case is (18):

(18)   Ɔŋ   ɛ̃   tuu zíné   kɪŋkáŋ.
        monkey knows tree climbing well
        'The monkey is good at climbing trees.'
        Ɔŋ   sɪɛ́ baa lúmɔ́ má weri.
        Monkey so more quick also very
        'What is more the monkey is also very quick.'

Here again, *baa* has the sense of 'moreover, what is more'. It provides additional evidence for some conclusion already derivable, at least in part from the immediately preceding clause.

The next example is interesting because extensive use of contextual assumptions is needed to see the force of *baa*.

(19)   l   vɔwɛ omo, í baa   zʊʊ bɔ́sí-ŋ kɔsɛ bɔsɛ   né
        you tie thing you on-top enter ask-me bad ' question this
        í   kokume miŋ nɛ́ɛ́?
        COMP donkey be-in where
        'You tie the thing up yourself (the donkey, which pulled itself free),
        and on top of that you ask the stupid question where the donkey is?'
        'Du bindest etwas selbst an und dann stellst Du (auch) noch die blöde
        Frage nach dem Esel?'

The point of the utterance is that the hearer has made one mistake in tying up the donkey badly, and is now compounding his stupidity by asking where the donkey is.

In all these cases, where *baa* has the force of a sentence adverbial 'moreover, what is more, on top of that', it is reasonable to assume that it takes the whole proposition expressed in its semantic scope.

5.2.3   The standard-comparative use

In this section I will discuss a use of *baa* which does not obviously belong with either the temporal or the non-temporal uses so far discussed. Syntactically, *baa* is a constituent of the sentence as a whole, and the best translations are 'still' or 'anymore'; however, as I will show, the sense is not the standard durative one. Like *baa* with its interpretation 'moreover' and 'what is more', *baa* in this use has the force of a sentence adverbial. Since there is always a comparison to a standard involved, I will call this use 'the standard-comparative use'.

In (20) the speaker is describing a distance between a certain location and two end-points – two standards.

(20)   Rɛwa né é baa   to   Hamale. Lʋʋ mɛ́ né   ʋ dé-é
        here this F more is-NEG Hamale Léo at   SDM it INT-IPF
        miŋ ɛ́ ná.
        in   that
        'Here, this is no longer Hamale, it is already Léo.'
        'Das ist nicht mehr Hamale hier, das ist schon Léo.'

The speaker has reason to believe that the hearer does not know where Léo starts and Hamale ends. For similar cases in German, see König (1977), and in Dutch Rombouts (1979). Despite the translation 'no longer', no obvious temporal sense is involved.

The following example is taken from a description of the guava tree. No temporal interpretation is possible here:

(21)   Goyaavʋr paarʋ jɛ́l rí wɔ́ gbesi ni kɛ   lum6uri
        Guava   leaves big and their length SDM surpass lemon
        paarʋ, ká baa   wı mɔ́ŋgó paarʋ má mɔhĩ.
        leaves and any-more NEG mango leaves also reach
        'The width and length of the guava leaf surpass those of the lemon tree leaf, and are "no longer" as big as the mango leaf.'
        ' . . . und ist noch nicht so groß wie das Mangoblatt.'

The implication of this example is that the guava leaf is bigger than the lemon leaf, but not as big as the mango leaf.

It is interesting to note that in Sissala the utterance literally says that the guava leaf is no longer as big as the mango leaf, while in German and English the correct translation would be 'not yet'.[2] In other words, the Sissala sees the mango as the norm from which the guava diverges, whereas the European sees it as the norm to which the guava aspires.

I would like to introduce one more example of this kind, where an actual object is compared to a prototype. Consider (22):

(22)   Dıcaka rá   baa   to   ŋne.
        dicaka NEG more is-NEG this
        'That is "no longer" a "dicaka".'

A *dıcaka* is a Sissala chair, similar to a stool with low legs, but with a long back. The person who uttered (22) was asked to judge whether a stool with a hint of a back was a *dıcaka* or not. In his opinion it was not. But since the conversation was about *dıcaka* he compared the object with it, using *baa to* 'no longer'.

In this section, I have illustrated a variety of uses of *baa*, with many different translations. However, the fact that a word has many different translations does not make it ambiguous. I will argue that much of the apparent 'ambiguity' of *baa* results from the interaction of a single, general core meaning with variations in the content and context of utterances in which it occurs.

Closer examination of the translations of *baa* – that is, words like *again, still, more, moreover* and *in addition* – shows that they fall into two classes. Some directly affect the truth-conditions of the utterances in which they occur, while others merely affect non-truth-conditional aspects of utterance interpretation: presuppositions, conventional implicatures, or processing strategies. I will argue that this is a genuine and irreducible ambiguity, of a type that, though quite common, has not often been remarked on in the literature.

In the next section, I will show that the uses of *baa* fall into two distinct types: truth-conditional and non-truth-conditional. In the following section, I will argue that the truth-conditional uses can be reduced to a single, general core meaning. In the final section I will show that there is a further range of uses which might be seen as intermediate between truth-conditional and non-truth-conditional senses. I will use these as the basis for some speculation about how such ambiguities between truth-conditional and non-truth-conditional senses arise.

5.3   The problem

5.3.1   Distinguishing truth-conditional from non-truth-conditional phenomena

Words like *also*, *again*, *more*, *another*, which imply the existence of an object, event or quantity additional to the one explicitly mentioned, raise an interesting theoretical question: how, if at all, do they affect the explicit truth-conditional content of utterances in which they occur? These words are standardly analysed as affecting not explicit truth-conditional content but presuppositions, conventional implicatures or semantic constraints on relevance. In chapter 4, I adopted this approach in analysing *also* and its Sissala counterpart *má*.

In chapter 4, I followed Blakemore (1987) in analysing *also* in English (and hence *má* in Sissala) as affecting not the explicit truth-conditional content of utterances but the way in which they are processed. In Blakemore's terms, *also* carries not a truth-condition but a semantic constraint on relevance. Thus (23) and (24), for example, are analysed as entailing simply that John left: what *also* does is indicate that (23) should be processed in a context containing the information in (24), and (25) should be processed in a context containing the information in (26):

(23)   John **also** left.
(24)   Someone other than John left.
(25)   John also **left**.
(26)   John did something other than leave.

However, this is not the only possible analysis of *also*. An alternative would be to analyse (23) and (25) as explicitly expressing the propositions in (27) and (28), or the logical forms in (29) and (30), which would be pragmatically enriched in context by specifying the reference of x:

(27)   John, in addition to someone other than John, left.
(28)   John left, in addition to doing something other than leaving.
(29)   John, in addition to x, left.
(30)   John left in addition to doing x.

In this case, the information in (24) and (26) would be entailed by (23) and (25), rather than merely being part of the context.

Another alternative would be to analyse *also* as carrying what Wilson and Sperber (1979) and Sperber and Wilson (1986a) call a low-ordered entailment: that is, an entailment which does not normally contribute to the point of utterance, and hence is perceived as in some sense 'background'. On either of these last two alternatives, *also* would directly affect the explicit truth-conditional content of utterances in which it occurred. How do we decide which of all these semantic analyses is the best one to adopt?

In the case of *also*, there seem to be good arguments against the truth-conditional alternatives and in favour of an account in terms of semantic constraints on relevance. In the first place, a truth-condition should be able, in at least some circumstances, to fall within the scope of negation, questions and other logical operators. This is one of the reasons why Wilson (1975) and Kempson (1975) argued that many so-called 'presuppositions' are in fact regular entailments, capable of affecting truth-conditions in regular ways. For example, they argue that (31) must be analysed as entailing, rather than presupposing (32), because the so-called 'presupposition' can fall within the scope of negation, as in (33):

(31)   Jane regrets that Steven resigned.
(32)   Steven resigned.
(33)   Jane doesn't regret that Steven resigned, because Steven **didn't** resign.

That is, the fact that (32) is false is enough on its own to make (31) false too – which is just what we would suspect if (31) entailed (32).

However, it is hard to construct examples in which the 'presupposition' of *also* falls within the scope of negation – either alone or in combination with other aspects of the truth-conditional content of the utterance. Thus (34)–(37) all sound very odd:

(34)   ?John didn't leave **also**: he just left.
(35)   ?John didn't leave **also**: he left, but he didn't do anything else.
(36)   ?John didn't leave **also**: he didn't do anything at all.
(37)   ?John didn't do anything, so he didn't **also** leave.

In the second place, it is hard to construct examples in which the 'presupposition' of *also* constitutes part of the main point of the utterance. Thus (38) and (39) sound very odd:

(38)   John left, and he left **also**.
(39)   A: I know John left, but did he do anything else?
        B: ?Yes, he left **also**.

The resistance of the 'presupposition' to incorporation within the main point of the utterance or the scope of negation, suggests strongly that it does not contribute at all to the explicit truth-conditional content of the utterance. This is why I have treated its equivalent in Sissala as a semantic constraint on relevance (see chapter 4).

There are other words in this class, however, where the arguments point in the opposite direction. Thus, *other* in (40) could be analysed either as having the explicit truth-conditional content (41a) and carrying the 'presupposition' in (41b), or as having the explicit truth-conditional content (42) or the logical form (43):

(40)   (Mother, introducing her child.) This is my other child.
(41)   a. This is my child.
        b. The speaker has another child than the one being introduced.
(42)   This is my other child than the one you know of.
(43)   This is my other child than x.

However, there seem to be decisive arguments against the analysis in (41) and in favour of the analyses along the lines of (42) and (43).

The main argument is that an analysis in terms of presuppositions would predict pragmatic oddness or anomaly when it does not occur. Thus (44) is an acceptable utterance, but on the presuppositional analysis it would be predicted to express the contradiction in (45):

(44)   This is my child. I have no other children.
(45)   ?This is my child. I have no children.

It would be more sensible here to see *other* as contributing to the truth-conditions of the utterance, so that (44) would express something like the proposition in (46):

(46)   This is my child. I have no other children than this.

Moreover, it is easy to see that the content of *other* can contribute to the main point of the utterance as in (47a), and can fall within the scope of negation, as in (47b):

(47)   a. I like African violets, but I like other plants better.
        b. I like African violets, but I don't like other plants.

Here, if the content of *other* were removed, the intended interpretation of both utterances would be lost.

Having established that some particles make a contribution to truth-conditions, while others are more fruitfully analysable as carrying conventional implicatures or semantic constraints on relevance, I would now like to take a closer look at the uses of *baa* and its translations, to see into which category they fall.

5.3.2 Truth-conditional and non-truth-conditional uses of *baa*

In this section, I will argue that the uses of *baa* and its translations fall into two distinct classes with respect to those tests outlined in the last section: some appear to be straightforwardly truth-conditional; others do not.

Consider the interpretation of *still* and *again* in the following two utterances:

(48)   John is still happy.
(49)   John is happy again.

Do these utterances differ in their truth-conditions, or merely in their conventional implicatures? That is, could (48) and (49) be, strictly speaking, true if John was happy at the time of utterance, but had never been happy before? It is clear that the answer is 'No'. Examples (50) and (51) are not just pragmatically odd: they are genuine contradictions:

(50)   ?John was never happy before, but he is still happy today.
(51)   ?John, who was never happy before, is happy again today.

That is, *still* and *again* make genuine contributions to the truth-conditions of utterances in which they occur.

This conclusion is confirmed by the fact that the contribution of *still* and *again* may be part of the main point of an utterance. Consider (52):

(52)   a. John left.
        b. He left today.

In (52a), the speaker gives some information which is repeated in (52b). The main point of (52b) is made by the addition of *today*, a word which is clearly truth-conditional. Examples (53b) and (54b) below can be interpreted along similar lines, with the main point being made by the addition of *still* and *again*:

(53)   a. John's happy.
        b. He's **still** happy.
(54)   a. John's resigned.
        b. He's resigned **again**.

By contrast, phrases like *what is more, on top of that* and *also* contribute nothing to the truth-conditional content of utterances in which they occur:

(55)   John is in England. What is more, he is happy.
(56)   John is in England. On top of that, he is happy.

By the same token *what is more*, which is the translation of the use of *baa* in (17) and (18), and *on top of that*, which is like the use of *baa* in (19), cannot fall within the scope of negation or questions:

(57)   ?? John isn't happy **what is more**: he's just happy.
(58)   ?? Is John happy **on top of that**, or is he just happy?

The only way (57) and (58) could be marginally acceptable is in their 'metalinguistic' or interpretive use, which is of course not the way the test is to be understood. Nor can these words constitute part of the main point of an utterance. Examples (59b) and (60b) are appropriate (if at all) only as repairs or rephrasings, not as repetitions with additional information, along the lines of (52)–(54):

(59)   a. John's happy.
         b. ?He's happy, what is more.
(60)   a. John's happy.
         b. ?On top of that, he's happy.

I shall follow Blakemore (1987) in treating these phrases as determining not the truth-conditions of an utterance but the way it is processed; in her terms, they impose 'semantic constraints on relevance'.

It seems, then, that the uses of *baa*, like the words which translate them, fall mainly into two classes, one truth-conditional and the other non-truth-conditional. Thus (1)–(4), (7)–(16), are truth-conditional, while (17)–(19) are non-truth-conditional. I will return to examples (20)–(22) later.

It seems that all temporal uses of *baa* are truth-conditional, but not all non-temporal examples are non-truth-conditional. As we know from German *noch*, there are cases, especially with stressed *noch*, where a non-temporal use can make a contribution to truth-conditions. Consider (61) and (62):

(61)   Ich habe **noch** einen Bruder.
         'I have another brother.'
(62)   Herr Ober, **noch** ein Bier.
         'Waiter, another beer.'

Without *noch*, (61) suggests the existence of only one brother; *noch* implies that there is another, which changes the truth-conditions. Likewise in (62), without *noch*, the speaker is not committed to the claim that he has already had a beer; with *noch*, he is. Again, the truth-conditions of the utterance are affected.

In Sissala too, the non-temporal use of *baa* may contribute to the truth-conditions of the utterance. In (14)–(16) *baa* does make a contribution to truth-conditions, since in (14) under negation it would still hold that something was played, in (15) that they needed something and in (16) that the warthog fears something. These positive assumptions are not there without *baa*.

In the next section I want to look more closely at the truth-conditional uses of *baa*.

5.4   Truth-conditional uses of *baa*

5.4.1   Ambiguity or vagueness between the temporal interpretations?

Again in English implies that there is a t1 at which the proposition (P) expressed is true, a t2 at which it is not true, and a t3 at which it is true again. *Still* on the other hand does not imply that there is an intermediate period at which P does not hold. If *baa* is to have one common meaning covering both 'again' and 'still', then the iterative and durative interpretations cannot be seen as part of the strict semantic content of *baa*. There must be some single, more general meaning, of which these two interpretations are special cases.

What then could be the one common meaning of truth-conditional *baa*? What is common to all the more specific meanings is that the proposition expressed is true at t1, and that there is an additional t at which P holds. Its meaning is therefore in some sense equivalent to 'more'. *Baa* is very similar to French *encore* in this respect, which can also be interpreted as 'again' and 'still'. *Encore* also implies that the proposition expressed is true at t1, and that it is true at some additional t.

Here, someone might object as follows. Clearly, there is a truth-conditional difference between 'still' and 'again'. Would it therefore not be more sensible to consider *baa* as having not one sense but two, so that there is ambiguity between the durative and iterative readings? I would respond to this objection as follows.

The objection takes the line that linguists have sometimes taken in the analysis of *and*, which has often been claimed to be multiply ambiguous between truth-functional, temporal, causal and additional meanings. However, Carston (1984) argues convincingly that the difference in meaning is not part of the linguistic semantic content of *and*, nor is it a matter of implicature, as Grice (1975) claims. Implicatures are distinct from the proposition expressed by the utterance, its truth-conditional content, or in Grice's terms, what has been said. What Carston shows is that pragmatic considerations can affect not only the implicatures of an utterance containing *and*, but also the proposition expressed. The point has been made more generally in a number of works by Sperber and Wilson and has been touched on in chapter 2, section 3.1.

In line with Carston's analysis of *and*, I reject the view that *baa* and *encore* are ambiguous between the 'still' and 'again' readings; nor are those readings achieved by implicature in the Gricean sense. I follow Sperber and Wilson in claiming that pragmatic considerations can play a major role in determining the proposition expressed by an utterance, and therefore its truth-conditional content.

My claim is that *baa* and *encore* have a core meaning 'more', which is vague rather than ambiguous between the repetitive and durative interpretations. However, this vague meaning interacts with other semantic, pragmatic and contextual considerations to determine much more precisely the proposition that the utterance will express. Which interpretation is chosen at any given time is determined by considerations of relevance. The hearer will take the first plausible set of contextual assumptions and enrich the proposition expressed to either the 'still' or the 'again' interpretation. For instance, in example (1) the speaker expects the hearer to have a context available in which the people referred to as 'we' will be temporarily separated from each other. Because of this available context, the hearer interprets *baa* as 'again' rather than 'still'. According to Sperber and Wilson (1986a), the result is a richer, more specific set of truth-conditions than those determined by the strict semantic content of the sentence uttered.

5.4.2   Enrichment

A further reason for rejecting the ambiguity solution is that there are not only repetitive and durative interpretations of *baa*, but also a variety of others. I have already introduced the restitutive interpretation, which results only in certain types of context. In (63),

(63)   Bob sold his house again,

for example, the hearer should already know, or be able to infer, whether Bob had already sold his house once, in which case an iterative interpretation would be intended, or whether he had not sold his house before, so that a restitutive reading must be intended. In choosing between these interpretations, he should, as always, be guided by considerations of relevance. The difference between the iterative and restitutive use is thus a matter of pragmatic enrichment of a single core meaning, and not a matter of semantics, as Dowty (1979) and Rothkegel (1979) would suggest.

In example (4), the hearer must already know, or be able to infer, that the animals referred to had not undergone an act of separation before, but had merely been separate. If this is the most accessible assumption, then a restitutive interpretation will result. On the other hand, if the animals had manifestly separated a number of times, then an iterative interpretation would result.

In (7) the hearer must have access to assumptions to the effect that there are two states of affairs in which the people went by lorry, not two states of affairs in which the people were collected in the same place to go by lorry in the same direction. Again the appropriate assumptions are chosen by considerations of relevance.

These are not the only cases which would cause a problem in a strictly semantic account. There are a number of examples where context is needed to decide which actions or events are to be considered as repeated when *baa* or *again* is used. Consider (64):

(64) ɩ   baa nɛ́   fafalí   ná-á.
      you still understand old-time-speech DEF-Q
      'Do you still understand the old way of speaking?'

The point of this utterance is not to ask whether the hearer once understood the old ways of speaking and still remembers them. The question is rather whether he remembers the old ways of speaking which others of his group once knew long, long ago. Clearly, to arrive at this interpretation, a substantial amount of contextual inference is required. It would be sad, on the basis of this example, to have to appeal to an extra *sense* of *baa*.

A similar case is (65):

(65) Ba baa wɪ   wɔ   ana   tɔɔ   dɪhí ɛ̄   rí
      they more NEG their father village place know COMP
      wɔ́   ko.
      they come
      'They don't know anymore where their father's village is, in order to
      go there.'

The above utterance is taken from an account of the slave trade, and refers to the descendants of the slaves. The utterance does not imply that the same people once knew where their father's village was. Rather it has to be understood that other people once knew their village and had to leave, and because of this their descendants are in this abnormal position of not knowing the village of their fathers. Thus 'they' has to refer to the nation as a whole and not only the particular people living there now. Again, a substantial amount of context-based inference is needed to arrive at the appropriate interpretation.

A different type of problem is (66):

(66)   a. Amá ɪ-ɪ   taŋa pii bɪɪ ná   rí   du,
           but if-you really take seed DEF COMP plant,
       b. ʊ baa wɪ   móŋgó fere   nɔŋ
           it again NEG mango grafted bear
       c. ʊ-ʊ́   nɔŋ   móŋgó tɪɪ nɔna né.
           it-IPF bears mango self fruits SDM
           'But if one plants its (the grafted mango's) stone, it will not bear grafted mangoes again (but normal mangoes).'

The speaker of (66) expects the hearer not to know that grafted mangoes do not grow automatically from a seed but that their trees have to be grafted again first. It is clear that the utterance does not indicate that the stone itself bore mangoes before. By a process of context-based inference, the hearer should be able to arrive at the interpretation that the stone of the tree which produced the grafted mango will not automatically produce grafted mangoes, unless it is grafted again. It is hard to see how this could all be specified in an extra sense of *baa*.

Neither an analysis in terms of ambiguity, one in terms of implicature (Grice), one in terms of semantic decomposition (Rothkegel) nor one in terms of different scope (Dowty) can adequately account for the full range of facts. It seems that Sperber and Wilson's suggestion that pragmatic enrichment is often necessary to determine the truth-conditions of a proposition is the most fruitful way to deal with these cases.

5.4.3   Is expectation part of the meaning of *baa*?

Some linguists have assumed that an expectation is part of the meaning of *noch* in German in the sense that it means 'more than expected' rather than just 'more' (e.g. Hoepelman and Rohrer 1981). Let us consider (67)–(69) and see whether this interpretation of 'more than expected' applies to every example:

(67)   Bill is still eating his dinner.
(68)   The milk in England is still brought to the door.
(69)   I'm going to buy medicine for Bill, he's still got these chest pains.

Sentence (67) implies that Bill is eating his dinner longer than expected, and it also implies that he is expected to finish his dinner. Sentence (68) implies that it is against expectation (to a continental European for instance) that milk should still be brought to the door. Unlike (67), it does not imply that there is an expectation to the effect that this practice will stop in England. So there are two types of expectation which one could argue are part of the meaning of *still*, *noch* and *baa* in (67) and (68).

I have already argued that the second type of expectation, which implies that (67) will come to an end and (68) not, is not part of the meaning of *still*, *noch* and *baa*, but arises from general implicatures. What about the other consideration that 'still' in English, German and Sissala means 'more than expected'? Let us consider (69). If there is an implicature that the hearer might have expected the chest pains to have stopped, then this implicature is much weaker than the implicature of expectation in (67) and (68). In fact, it could be argued that all the speaker wants to convey is simply that there was a further time than the one the hearer knew about – more time – in which Bill had chest pains.

It is clear that in Sissala in some of the examples given, there is expectation involved in the sense of 'more than expected' as, for example, in the case of (11). However, there are other cases where no expectation is involved: for example, in (2), with the translation 'again', where no expectation in the sense of 'more than expected' is reported. Thus expectation cannot be part of the core meaning of *baa*. Should we say that there is an ambiguity between the cases which convey expectation and the cases which do not? For the reasons given above, it seems that an alternative solution would be preferable.

Let us take a concrete example. In the case of (11), the use of 'but' suggests that (11b) is intended to contradict an expectation created by (11a). Given the background assumption in (11'a), (11a) might contextually imply the conclusion in (11'b):

(11')   a. If the war is no more, then the vow does not hold any more.
        b. The vow does not hold any more.

Example (11b) would then contradict an expectation created by (11a) – but not because of the meaning of *baa*.

More generally, it appears to be true that an utterance containing durative *baa* would in most cases not be optimally relevant unless the hearer had some expectation that the state of affairs described would already have come to an end. For example, while it might be quite *true* to say 'I went to work at 9.00 and was still there five minutes later', it would hardly be relevant to say so, since the standard expectation is that one's working day lasts longer than five minutes. It is quite generally irrelevant to draw one's hearer's attention to information he is quite capable of inferring for himself. The often conveyed expectations in utterances with *still* are thus satisfactorily explained on pragmatic grounds alone.

5.5   The relation between truth-conditional and non-truth-conditional uses of *baa*

In the last two sections I drew a distinction between truth-conditional and non-truth-conditional uses of *baa*. I suggested earlier that while there is no ambiguity but merely vagueness within the truth-conditional uses, there is genuine ambiguity between the truth-conditional and non-truth-conditional uses of *baa*. The reason is that there is a sharp distinction between the functions of truth-conditional particles and semantic constraints on relevance. The former determine aspects of conceptual representations; the latter determine the way such conceptual representations will be processed. It is hard to think of some core 'meaning' which is neutral between two such different functions. There seems to be a genuine ambiguity involved.

It is clear, however, that there is a relation in meaning between the truth-conditional and non-truth-conditional uses. In both cases, some notion of addition is involved. Let us review the analysis of *moreover* as first introduced by Blakemore (1987:91–7) and already mentioned in chapter 4. Consider (70):

(70)   a. John must be English.
        b. He never turns his fork over.
        c. Moreover, he has an RP accent.

Moreover in this case encourages the hearer to *add* the premise contained in (70c) to the premise in (70b) in order to provide further evidence for the same conclusion (70a) 'John must be English'. This notion of addition is clearly related to the notion of addition involved in the truth-conditional uses of *baa*.

I have so far ignored examples (20)–(22). König (1977, 1981) analyses *noch* in examples parallel to these cases as a scalar particle indicating a scale of typicality. He claims that these cases are non-truth-conditional but that there are Gricean conventional implicatures, as interpreted by Karttunen and Peters (1975) – see chapter 4 – involved. I do not see these cases in exactly the same way as König does: for one thing, I do not think that they are truly non-truth-conditional, though they may be on their way to becoming so.

To explain what I mean, let us first look at an English use of 'again':

(71)   John's polite. But then again, he's English.

This could be paraphrased as (72):

(72)   John's polite. But then when I think again, he's English.

If *again* is understood as modifying an implicit higher predicate 'think', it has the same temporal function that it has in normal temporal cases.

Likewise *baa* and *noch* could be seen as functioning in a similar way in these comparative cases. Let us speculate on how *noch* and *baa* might have come to be used that way in the first place. Let us consider again example (20), which is ambiguous between two interpretations: one is a straightforward temporal interpretation, in which the speaker implies that at an earlier time the location where she was, was indeed Hamale; the other interpretation suggests that the speaker concentrates on the spatial aspect of the journey – the speaker imagines herself thinking over time at different points of the journey between Hamale and Léo where she is located. In that case *baa* modifies a higher predicate, to convey something like (20′):

(20′)   I no longer think that this is still Hamale.

Alternatively, one could imagine the range of stools, or guava leaves, actually growing or shrinking through time. Clearly these examples are the most abstract uses of *noch* and *baa* – but it is none the less fairly easy to see how they might have developed out of more concrete, temporal uses. I thus suggest that in the case of (20)–(22) implicit matrix clauses (of the proposition expressed) such as 'I still think that' or 'it still seems to me that' – themselves supplied by pragmatic enrichment – may be posited, which are modified by *noch* and *baa*. *Baa* and *noch* are, then, truth-conditional, though what they modify cannot be established on the basis of linguistic analysis alone.

The idea is, then, that a word that starts by contributing to the truth-conditional content of the proposition expressed by an utterance may come, as for example in (20)–(22), to modify implicit predicates which are not linguistically expressed. Many adverbs, like *frankly*, as in *Frankly, he's a fool*, can be handled in this way. As a final stage in their development, they become semantic constraints on relevance, contributing no longer to truth-conditions, but helping to determine the way the utterance is processed. Notice that *more* in English can work that way. It has an obvious truth-conditional use, but can also be used as a semantic constraint on relevance:

(73)   a. Tom's a cook.
        b. More (= Moreover), he's a good cook.

And *still*, *noch* and *baa* may be analysable along these lines.

5.6   Conclusion

In this chapter I have shown how one particle which has a number of different temporal and non-temporal interpretations can be ambiguous between a truth-conditional and non-truth-conditional use, and vague between different truth-conditional uses. I have suggested that truth-conditional phenomena may become non-truth-conditional via an intermediate stage where they modify implicit predicates supplied by pragmatic enrichment.

There is a lot of work to be done in this area, but it seems that the notion of pragmatic enrichment derived from relevance theory might enable us to achieve much simpler analyses on the purely linguistic level, which, when combined with content, context and considerations of relevance, might be flexible enough to deal with the rich diversity of data which analyses based on multiple ambiguity must necessarily ignore.[3]

6 *Defining in Sissala*

6.1 Introduction

Every language with referential expressions seems to have some means of indicating to hearers not only *that* a referent of a certain type is required, but also where to search for appropriate referents, and how easily accessible they are. Within the framework of relevance theory, such expressions, in at least some of their uses, should be analysable as semantic constraints on relevance, contributing not to truth-conditional content but to reducing the hearer's processing load. In this chapter, I will look briefly at some Sissala data of this general type.

It has long been thought that defining expressions – determiners – play an important role in this aspect of processing (see Clark and Clark 1977:466–7; Clark and Marshall 1981; Hawkins 1978; Nunberg 1977). Thus, according to Hawkins a speaker using a definite article has the following in mind:

a. He introduces a referent (or referents) to the hearer.
b. He instructs the hearer to locate the referent in some shared set of objects.
c. He refers to the totality of the objects or mass within this set that satisfy the referring expression. (1978:125)

In English, a noun phrase containing the indefinite article *a(n)* can be used with specific or non-specific reference. Either can be the basis for further definite reference. Thus in an example like (1)

(1)   A colleague of mine has just given me a call,

the speaker might have wanted either to introduce a specific colleague or just to introduce the referent in a non-specific way. As Lyons (1977:189) points out, regardless of whether the speaker had a specific person in mind, he can subsequently refer to the same person by means of the expression *the colleague* or *my colleague*. Lyons comments (p. 189),

'Once any information at all has been supplied about an indefinite referent, it can then be treated by the participants as an individual that is known to them both and identifiable within the universe-of-discourse by means of a definite referring expression.'

I shall not review the vast literature on 'defining' in English here. I will merely introduce the Sissala defining expressions, compare them with their English counterparts and explain their possible functions within relevance theory. In section 6.2 I discuss specific and non-specific determination, and in 6.3 the use of the definite marker *ná*. In 6.4. I show that determiners in Sissala have a deictic origin. I examine and dismiss the claim that the deictic origin of determiners proves the necessity for mutual knowledge in processing definite NPs. My claim is that determiners are devices used by the speaker to facilitate access to certain conceptual addresses, and in some cases establish new addresses. My conclusion will be that determiners play an important role in processing, by guiding the hearer towards the intended interpretation with a minimum of processing effort.

6.2   Specific and non-specific determination

There are three different non-deictic determining devices in Sissala, involving on the one hand the morphology and/or tonology of the noun and on the other hand a variety of determining particles; for reasons I will discuss later, I do not want to call these particles 'determiners'. The morphology/tonology distinguishes between specific and non-specific: the particles are *ré* 'non-specific'; *né* 'specific'; and *ná* 'known' or 'easily predictable'. Consider (2a–c):

(2)   a. Bál ré.
          'It is a man.'
       b. Bááló né.
          'It is a man.'
       c. Báálɔ ná.
          'It is the man.'

Example (2a) might be an answer to the question 'What is it?', where the expected answer concerns a stereotypical object/person, with no specific reference. It is often used to describe the qualities of a particular man, meaning 'he has all the characteristics of a real man – being courageous, strong, etc.' Examples (2b) and (2c) might be answers to the question 'What is it?' or 'Who is coming?' In (2b) the hearer is encouraged to consider the man as a specific individual, unknown, and in (2c) the man is a specific individual, whose existence is either known or easily predictable.

It is important to note that the specific/non-specific distinction is primarily to be found in the morphology/tonology of the noun. In the above case, *bál* is non-specific and *báálɔ́* is specific. In most cases this distinction is only indicated by tone: high tone on the last syllable for non-specific, as in *yɔwɔ́* 'market' non-specific, and *yɔwɔ* 'market', specific. However, the tonal distinction between specific and non-specific is often neutralised when the basic tone of the noun is high anyway, and 'specific' is basically tonally unmarked, i.e. a high tone on a noun does not become low because of specific marking. There are a few words referring to humans – e.g. 'man', 'child' and occupational terms such as 'blacksmith' – where the morphology itself is affected.

I will concentrate initially on the use of *ré* and *né*, deferring discussion of *ná* until 6.3.

Notice first that the specific/non-specific ambiguity which is inherent in the English indefinite article – see example (1) – is resolved in Sissala by the use of two different morphological/tonological markers: *né* for specific and *ré* for non-specific.[1] To give a comparable example to (1), consider (3) and (4):

(3)   Ʊ mʊ yɔwɔ́ ré.
        'He went to a market.' (non-specific)
(4)   Ʊ mʊ yɔwɔ né.
        'He went to a market.' (specific)

In (3) the speaker has no specific market in mind. The purpose of mentioning the market is not for subsequent reference, but merely as part of a characterisation of the sort of place he went to. In (4) the purpose of mentioning the market is to make possible subsequent reference to the place he went to.

What exactly is the nature of the specific/non-specific distinction? Clark and Clark (1977:466), basing their insights on Slobin (1979), claim that a hearer who is asked to decide whether an utterance like (5) is true,

(5)   A robin is a bird,

'uses the semantic procedure for *robin* to create an object in memory that has all the defining and characteristic features of robin. It is the prototype *robin*. The task then is to examine this object to see whether it passes all the necessary tests in the semantic procedure for "bird".' Suppose, now, that a hearer does not know what a robin is, but is told that a robin is a bird. He will process that utterance by working out its analytic and contextual implications, using the logical and encyclopaedic entries for 'bird'. He may conclude, for example, that robins have all the prototypical properties of birds: wings, feathers, beak, ability to fly, etc.

It seems that non-specific devices in Sissala encourage this sort of prototypical or stereotypical processing, using schemas associated with the encyclopaedic entry of the concept to which these devices are attached.

Consider (6) and (7) (where TDM = typicality discourse marker):

(6)   Bala   ká títúr   rí.
        monitor-lizard is reptile TDM
        'The monitor lizard is a reptile.'

(7)   Abijan   ká tɔɔjɛ́lɛ́   rɛ́.
        Abidjan is town-big TDM
        'Abidjan is a big town.'

In (6) the hearer is encouraged by the use of *rɛ́* to look up the prototype or schema for 'reptile', and to use it as part of the context; in (7) the use of *rɛ́* encourages him to do the same with the prototype or schema for 'big town'. The use of *rɛ́* thus encourages the hearer to draw on his knowledge of reptiles in (6) and his knowledge of big towns in (7) in working out the contextual implications of the utterances. For instance, if the schema for 'big town' contains the information that big towns have many cars, wide roads and so on, then the contextual implications can be drawn that Abidjan has many cars, Abidjan has wide roads and so on. In the case where the hearer has no prior knowledge of Abidjan or monitor lizards, he will be encouraged to assume that they have the typical properties of big towns and reptiles, respectively. Through this process of comparison the hearer can start to construct entries for concepts of 'Abidjan' and 'monitor lizard' themselves.

In the case of *nɛ́* I want to argue that the hearer is encouraged to pick out a specific individual rather than merely accessing a stereotype or schema, and that this often involves opening a new conceptual address. For example, a discourse may start with utterances (8)–(10) (where SDM = specific discourse marker):

(8)   Oŋ   ní   ise   a   gʋɔrɛ . . .
        monkey SDM got-up and roamed
        'A monkey got up and roamed . . . '

(9)   Losú   ní   zʋɛ́.
        hunger SDM entered
        'There was a famine.'
(10)   Yibiŋ   ní   zʋɛ.
        Rainy-season SDM entered
        'There was a rainy season.'

In each case the use of *nɛ́* encourages the hearer to create a new conceptual address for the subject NP, an address under which information about a new specific individual may be stored.

Examples (8)–(10) could create the impression that *nɛ́* only occurs in subject NPs or discourse-initial utterances. This is not the case: for example if in a procedural discourse the speaker has to answer the question 'How do you build a house?', he may reply as in (11):

(11)   ι   já   a   6á dole ní . . .
        you look-for and cut beam SDM
        'You look for a beam and cut it . . . '

In (11) the hearer is not merely encouraged to use an existing encyclopaedic schema for beams: rather the use of *nɛ́* indicates that a specific beam is needed, for which a new conceptual address should be set up.

Both *nɛ́* and *rɛ́* can be used in the plural. In the case of *rɛ́* this has very much the same effect as *des* has in French. Consider (12)–(14):

(12)   Elle a apporté des fleurs.
        She has brought flowers.
(13)   Ʋ   tɛŋ   púná pɛ́ biɛ́llɛ́ rɛ́.
        his body fur   has stripes TDM
        'His fur has stripes.'
(14)   Bakla   wuu ní   yírɛ́   náŋá.
        Bush-animals all   SDM called others
        'All the bush animals called each other.'

In the French example in (12) and the Sissala example in (13) the NPs are non-specific, while in (14) the NP is specific.

The specific/non-specific distinction in Sissala also falls in with Donnellan's (1966) referential and attributive distinction, though this distinction has mainly been drawn with definite NPs. Consider (15):

(15)   The loving mother picks her child up when it cries.

Constructions like (15) are said to be typically ambiguous (or vague) between a referential interpretation, where *the loving mother* is a directly referring expression, and an attributive use, where the noun phrase is a description which is used to locate possible referents. It seems that specific marking and *né* in Sissala are quite well adapted to the referential use, and non-specific marking and *ré* to attributive use. Lyons (1977:191) points out that the referential/attributive distinction applies to indefinite expressions, and may indeed be more 'to the point' than the specific/non-specific distinction.

Although in English the specific/non-specific distinction is not morphologically marked, it interacts in well-known ways with verbs of propositional attitude to create genuine truth-conditional ambiguities. Contexts inducing such ambiguities are traditionally called 'opaque' (see Quine 1960:14ff.). An example of ambiguity in an opaque context is (16):

(16)   Jane wants to marry a doctor.

On one interpretation, there is a specific doctor that Jane wants to marry; on the other interpretation, Jane wants to marry someone, but not a specific person, who has the property of being a doctor. In Sissala, because of the morphological distinction between specific and non-specific, this ambiguity should not arise.

However, in the negative the difference between specific and non-specific appears to be neutralised. Consider (17) and (18):

(17)   Bál ra.
        'He is not a man' (a typical one)
        'It is not a man' (What you have identified is not a man.)
(18)   Ʊ to bal.
        'He is not a man' (a typical one)
        (What you have identified is not a man.)

In (17) the morphology of the noun is non-specific, and the determining particle is replaced by *ra*, a constituent negation which is also used in cleft constructions of the kind: '[woman *ra* (not)] did it'; *ra* is the negative counterpart of both *ré* and *né*. In (18) there is a negative copula and no determining particle at all.

The non-occurrence of specific negation is not, of course, peculiar to Sissala. It is hard to think of circumstances in which it would be relevant to make a negative statement about a specific but indefinite man. In colloquial English, where *this* is a specific indefinite marker (see Maclaran 1982), (19a) is acceptable, but (19b) is pragmatically odd:

(19)   a. I saw this beautiful vase in a shop yesterday.
       b. I didn't see this beautiful vase in a shop yesterday.

By contrast, negation with definite NPs is possible in Sissala, as in English.

When the definite determining particle *ná* is used, the existence of a referent is not in question and therefore *ná* occurs with specific morphological marking:

(20)   ʊ tó   báálɔ́   ná.
       it is-not man-SPEC DEF
       'It is not the man.'

The question I would like to consider is why Sissala has both specific/non-specific morphology and a range of determining particles. My answer will be that the particles, on further investigation, turn out to perform primarily a discourse or processing function. Consider a typical use of *rɛ́* in a descriptive discourse:

(21)   a. Baka koo ká ballɛ   duó   rí
          warthog is animal strong TDM
          'The warthog is a strong animal'
       b. nyúú gʊra   gʊra,
          head tubal tubal
          '(with) a tubal head,'
       c. nyiduoru bɛllɛ nyɪɪsɛ,
          teeth   two solid
          '(with) two solid teeth,'
       d. múdʊ́ŋ ɓikúl,
          tail   short
          '(with) a short tail,'
       e. ká   nacíkí cakɛ.
          and feet   compressed
          'and compressed feet.'

Points to notice about this example are that conjuncts (21b), (21d) and (21e) contain non-specific NPs, which are appropriately tonologically marked, but that only the first non-specific NP, in (21a), is marked with the particle *rɛ́*. My hypothesis is that the use of *rɛ́* accounts for the phenomena noticed above: that the hearer will typically use schematic or stereotypical information from the encyclopaedic entry of the associated NP, in processing the utterance as a whole. *Rɛ́*, on this account, would be a marker of typicality, rather than merely non-specificity.

In the case of *nɛ́*, the argument for a discourse or processing function seems equally strong. If we assume that there is a distinction between specific and general concepts in the language of thought, then the distinction between specific and non-specific morphology or tonology would guide the hearer towards the appropriate type of concept. However, a specific individual may need to be mentioned, even though it will not necessarily play any role in subsequent discourse. My hypothesis is that *né* is used to indicate to the hearer that the individual in question *will* play a subsequent role, and that it is thus worth opening an encyclopaedic entry where subsequent information about the individual can be stored. Hence the many discourse-initial occurrences of *né*.

Support for the view that *ré* has primarily a discourse or processing function, and is not merely a marker of non-specificity, comes from its co-occurrence with so-called ideophones. Ideophones occur in abundance in African languages. They are not a grammatical category; typically they are expressions with adjectival or adverbial grammatical function, which share phonologically distinct (often idiosyncratic within the language) structurally repetitive forms; they also include onomatopoeia. These forms are not nominal, and therefore the term 'non-specific' no longer applies. None the less, they may be associated with *ré*:

(22)   Bala   tɛŋ   to   sólósóló,
        monitor-lizard's body   is-NEG   smooth
        ʋ́ taŋa   ká hʋrahʋra ré.
        it really is rough   TDM
        'The body of the monitor lizard is not smooth, rather it is rough.'
(23)   Betúni   va   búkbúkwa ré.
        elephants walk in-groups TDM
        'Elephants walk in groups.'

In (22) the ideophonic expressions are adjectival, and only the affirmative is marked with *ré*. In (23) the ideophonic expression is adverbial. Although in these cases it is no longer possible to talk about non-specificity, there is a description involved, and cognitively *ré* has the same function as before: it encourages the use of stereotypical information from the encyclopaedic entries for 'rough' and 'walk in groups' in deriving the contextual implications of the utterance. In cognitive terms the use of *ré* in all these cases makes sense.[2]

It is perhaps worth mentioning that *ré* and *né* are obligatory in some cases: for instance, in an answer to a question (descriptively used). In a one-word sentence, where there is no overt copula, the determining particle might be seen as performing the function of a copula. Certainly, some linguists have thought that such particles are verbs or defective verbs (Givón 1976; Crozier 1984).

Further uses of these markers are discussed in chapter 7. My conclusion about the uses discussed in this chapter is that though *ré* and *né* fall in with the specific/non-specific distinction, their primary use is not to mark this.

In the next section I will discuss the use of *ná*.

6.3   Definite determination

The particle *ná* is typically used when a subject has already been introduced with *ré* or *né* earlier on in the discourse. Consider (24):

(24)   a. Abijan jɪsɛ   náŋá ká **jɪtukni**   **ni.**
           Abidjan houses some are storey-houses SDM
           'Some of the houses of Abidjan are storey houses' (i.e. houses
           with more than one floor).
        b. **Jɪtúkní**   **ná**   naŋa keŋ jɪsɛ   fi   arí botorowa.
           storey-houses DEF some have houses ten and three
           'Some of the storey houses have thirteen floors.'

In (24a), 'storey houses' is introduced with *né*. The houses are mentioned for the first time and the use of *né* suggests that it is worth opening an individual concept 'the storey-houses of Abidjan', for subsequent reference. The subsequent mention of 'storey houses' is then marked with *ná*, the definite marker.

However, *ná* is not only used in cases where an individual concept has just been introduced. Whenever the speaker thinks that the hearer can access an individual concept with the appropriate reference, she may also use *ná*. In other words, *ná* behaves pretty much like the definite determiner *the* in English.

Before I introduce more Sissala data, it is worth pointing out that in recent years pragmatic analysis of definite noun phrases has generally been conducted within the terms of the mutual-knowledge framework introduced by Clark and Marshall (1981). Clark and Marshall claim that definite reference cannot be adequately handled without appeal to the notion of mutual knowledge. It is worth mentioning here that I follow Sperber and Wilson (1982b, 1986a) in rejecting the mutual-knowledge framework on the grounds that it is not only not necessary but also insufficient.

Clark and Marshall (1981:22) claim that successful reference can be guaranteed only on the basis of mutual knowledge, which can be assumed to exist on four main grounds: community membership, universality of knowledge, physical co-presence and linguistic co-presence (pp. 35–44). My claim will be, following Sperber and Wilson, that definite reference can be achieved in the absence of mutual knowledge, and that, moreover, the existence of mutual knowledge would rarely be enough to identify the intended referent.

What is needed for successful reference is not mutual knowledge but the ability to access the appropriate individual concept, and the criterion of consistency with the principle of relevance. As will be seen, the Sissala data fit more naturally into a relevance-theoretic framework than into a framework of mutual knowledge.

Example (24) above illustrated the linguistically anaphoric use of a definite NP, in which reference is assigned on the basis of a conceptual address recently established in the discourse. How is the correct referent selected? According to the mutual-knowledge framework, speaker and hearer must have mutual knowledge of a set of storey-houses. But for all we know, they may have mutual knowledge of many such sets, in Abidjan and elsewhere. The mutual-knowledge framework says nothing about how the appropriate set is selected. According to relevance theory, reference assignment involves taking the most accessible concept referring to a set of storey houses – in this case, the concept just introduced into the discourse, and testing the resulting interpretation for consistency with the principle of relevance. Could a speaker aiming at optimal relevance have intended that interpretation: that is, could she have thought it would achieve adequate contextual effects for the minimum justifiable processing effort? If so, then that is the only interpretation consistent with the principle of relevance, and the one the hearer should choose.

Example (25) illustrates the use of *ná* on the basis of what Clark and Marshall call physical co-presence:

The woman is physically present.
(25)   Ŋ   pá   háálɔ́   ná   die.
         I   give lady   DEF   yesterday
         'I say "hello" to the lady.'

In this case the hearer will have to realise that he should not search in memory for the referent of 'the lady' but that the one who is visually identifiable is the one the speaker had intended. As in the previous example, speaker and hearer may have mutual knowledge of many potential referents, and it is only by the criterion of consistency with the principle of relevance that the hearer is able to make the right choice. The mutual-knowledge framework fails to describe how the choice is made.

Ná may also occur in cases where the appropriate concept is accessible via the encyclopaedic entry of another concept used in the discourse. Consider (26):

(Talking about the sea.)
(26)   Kal wuu wɔhɔ, gbaŋ, nasaarawa   arí wɔ   háálá arí wɔ
        day every noon evening white-people and their wives and their
        bɛlɛ   miŋ nyii ná mɛ.
        children in   water DEF in.
        'Every day, noon and evening, the white people, their wives and
        children are in the water.'

Example (26) is taken from a description of Abidjan, which includes a description of the seaside. Though the concept for 'sea' (Sissala *mʋʋ*) had been introduced before, the concept for 'water' (Sissala *nyii*) had not. However, the encyclopaedic entry for 'sea' should include the information that the sea is composed of water. Since the concept of water is easily accessible via the encyclopaedic entry for 'sea' the speaker can introduce it with *ná*.

Very similar to this is the next example, in which a funeral is described by a close relative of the deceased. After the concept 'corpse' had been introduced, the following expression is used:

(27)   . . . laarɛ   teŋ ná
        . . . caressing body DEF
        '. . . caressing the body'

From his knowledge of the scenario for funerals, the hearer can infer, via considerations of relevance, that the body referred to is the body of the dead person.

In the next example, the speaker had just described how people were caught in the past and brought to Niamey, the capital of Niger:

(28)   Ba dʋnɔ né   dé ká ráŋ, kapital, yosi ná   né.
        they only SDM INT are there capital   slaves DEF SDM
        'Only they (the population of Niamey) make up the capital, the
        slaves.'

The speaker never explicitly used the word 'slaves' in the preceding utterances. He was, however, describing slaves. It is possible that the hearers had already made the mental connection between the lexical item *yosi* 'slave' and a description of the fate of the people who had been caught. In this case the mention of 'slaves' would act as a confirmation that the connection was the intended one. However, the younger audience may not have known what these people were called; in that case the mention of 'slave' provides the missing lexical entry for the conceptual address which had most likely been established. Because *yosi ná* refers to a conceptually established entity, the speaker can use *ná*.[3]

Ná may also be used when the hearer has access to the associated concept through the encyclopaedic entry of a more general concept. Consider (29) and (30):

(29)   . . . a   laalɛ siigoru, tokowiwa ná.
          . . . and wore knives swords   DEF
          ' . . . and wore knives, the swords.'

(30)   Bee   duo bísɛ́? Sınsʋɔ́lá ná   nɛ́   yá-á?
          which kind talk   proverbs DEF SDM P–Q
          'Which kind of talk? The proverbs?'

In (29) the hearer has the referent of 'sword' easily accessible through the encyclopaedic entry for 'knives', and it is therefore introduced with *ná*; in (30) the hearer has the referent of 'proverbs' easily accessible through the encyclopaedic entry for 'talk'.

Another example of the use of *ná* on the basis of encyclopaedic information involves inference based on stereotypes or schemas. For example, in European culture it is typical for a kitchen to have a stove, a room to have a window, etc. Consider (31) and (32):

(31)   ʊ sɪɛ́ ke sʋʋwie   ná   mʋbʋɔ.
          he so sit dawa-dawa DEF under
          'So he sat down under the dawa dawa tree.'

(32)   Mʋ gʋvɛrnɛman biiro ná.
          go government office DEF
          'Go to the government office.'

In (31) the speaker did not know about the particular dawa dawa tree that the person was sitting under; however, he knows that there is always at least one tree in the centre of the village, under which people meet in the shade. *Ná* helps the hearer to access a typical village-centre schema, which contains 'the tree which gives shade and provides a meeting place'.

Example (32) is taken from a text about the slave trade. When the audience shows some disbelief of the speaker's account, the speaker tells them to go to *the* government office, where there is a picture on the wall, showing the slave traders. The hearers most probably did not know the particular government office referred to. However, their encyclopaedic entry for 'government offices' contains enough information to imagine the speaker's account, and to accept his evidence. Therefore *ná* is appropriate.

Sometimes the speaker introduces a referent which the hearer might not have known, but which he may be able to access on the basis of the utterance together with his prior knowledge. Such cases are referred to by Clark (1977) as 'bridging' implicatures. For example, (33) follows a description of the boats in the harbour of Abidjan:

(33)   Nyiidaborbɪnɛ́wa   ná . . .
        old-boats   the
        'The old boats . . . '

Since the speaker had been talking about 'boats', the knowledge that boats get old was easily accessible. The speaker mentions those old boats because he himself sees it as extraordinary that the old boats should be kept in the harbour rather than be destroyed and removed. It is not to be expected that the hearer actually had a concept 'old, unusable boats in Abidjan harbour' already accessible, when (33) was uttered. This shows that mutual knowledge of the referent does not need to be established prior to the utterance. A definite expression such as *ná* may be used when it is easy to see that its existence is required to yield an interpretation consistent with the principle of relevance. 'Bridging' implicatures are analysed in the framework of relevance theory in Wilson and Sperber (1986a).

Unlike in English, in Sissala names may also be marked with *ná*. An example is (34):

(34)   Ba sísɛ́nyɛ sɪɛ yiki ʋ   yo   ká siɛ́ la   a   pá
        they now   so   push him throw and so   take and give
        Sénu Kuncé ná.
        Sanon Kountie DEF
        'Now they have dethroned him, and have given it (the chieftancy) to (the) Sanon Kountie.'

There are similar uses of the definite article with proper names in German, French and many other languages. In German, the point of marking a name with the definite article is sometimes to emphasise the fact that the person in question is already known to both speaker and hearer. This is also the case in Sissala. The point of adding the definite article is to remind the hearer that he already has an encyclopaedic entry for Sanon Kountie, which he can use in working out the contextual implications of the utterance. Omission of the definite article might suggest that the name of the new chief is being given merely because it might be useful in the future to know it, and not because the hearer already has knowledge of this person and is expected to use it in processing the utterance. In German, definiteness may also be used to express a negative attitude, especially if the form *Herr* or *Frau* is replaced by the definite marker, e.g. *die Müller, der Schneider*. It is possible that the use of *ná* with names in Sissala has similar attitudinal purposes.

In a number of recent works (see Kempson 1988 and references therein), Kempson has drawn attention to a use of definite NPs which bears some similarities to so-called 'bound variable anaphora'. In such cases, the definite NP does not have a single, definite referent but a variety of possible referents depending on the interpretation of a prior expression with variable reference. Similar cases occur in Sissala. The background to the following example is a discussion of marriage practices in the 'olden days', when a man had to share his girlfriend with his unmarried older brother, if the older brother so wished. Most participants in the discussion felt these practices could no longer be followed, and the following rhetorical question gives one reason why:

(35)   Eské tolwie ná   má tɪ saŋŋʋ é ri-i?
       is-it girl   DEF also self agree F IM–Q
       'Would the girl herself be in agreement?'

The hearer knows that most Sissala girls would not agree to this practice any more. Of course, 'the girl' is no particular girl, it stands generically for any girl whose boyfriend has an unmarried older brother. By considerations of relevance the hearer can infer that *ná* does not refer to any specific person, but that for each potential boyfriend there will be one potential referent of 'the girl'. Kempson shows how these examples can be analysed in terms of relevance theory, and draws detailed parallels to the relevance-theoretic analysis of bound-variable pronouns.

In the next example there is a typical attributive use of the description marked with *ná*:

(36)   Tʋtʋmɛ ná   má háála há   mɪŋ wɔ́ mɛ.
       works DEF also women which in   they in
       'The works in which the women are involved.'

In (36) the definite NP 'the works' is the head of the relative clause. This creates a problem for the mutual-knowledge framework, since before the utterance the hearer may not have known that any such works existed. Clark and Marshall (1981:23) refer to such clauses as 'reference-establishing relative clauses'. They explain the presence of this quite 'unknown' referential expression in terms of a transformational approach on which the definite NP was moved from a deep-structure position in which it was indefinite. Thus *Bill is amazed by **the fact** that there is so much life on earth* could be said to have been derived from *That there is so much life on earth is **a fact** which Bill is amazed by*.

Similarly, (36) would be derived from something like 'the women are involved in work', where 'work' would be indefinite. Such transformational structures are no longer as popular as they once were. My point is that in this case, the transformational solution proposed by Clark and Marshall is motivated solely by their desire to save the mutual-knowledge framework. In the framework of relevance theory, an utterance such as (36) would be appropriate as long as the idea that the women were involved in work was easy for the hearer to accept on the basis of his encyclopaedic knowledge. Example (36) falls in with the examples of 'bridging implicatures' discussed on page 195.

6.4 Origin of determiners

A number of linguists have made the observation that non-deictic determiners have developed from deixis (see, for example Clark and Marshall 1981; Lyons 1975; Thorne 1972, 1974). In Sissala both *ré* and *ná* are still used deictically, and according to Sissala speakers *nɛ́* could be used interchangeably with *né* 'this', though it is rarely used that way these days.[4] I have found no evidence of its deictic use in the recorded texts.

Rɛ́ is used as a locative and can mean 'here', as in (37):

(37)   Ʋ mɪŋ rɛ́.
       he is-in here
       'He is here.'

It can also be used in an instruction accompanied by pointing:

(38)   Mʋ ré   wa.
       go here PL
       'Go this way.'

However, the locative/demonstrative *rɛ́* is phonologically invariant and is different in this respect from the particle *rɛ́*, which is sensitive to its phonetic environment and may change its vowel quality in the same way as discussed for the interpretive-use marker *ré*, discussed in chapter 3.

The particle *ná* is derived from the verb 'to see':

(39)   ʊ   ná   háálɔ́   ná.
       he   saw   woman   DEF
       'He saw the woman.'

It is assumed that the two forms are related, because *ná* is frequently used in what Lyons (1977:648) calls a 'quasi-referential' way – very much like French *voici* and *voilà*. According to Lyons, it can be called 'quasi-referential' because it is not clear whether it is used to draw attention to an entity or to the location of the entity. Consider (40) and (41):

(40)   Gbaŋ   bínbílí baná há   péré.
       evening hour   four   which reached
       Ná! Buuné   pí   wó   zensi.
       see Boura-people take their xylophones
       'It is four o'clock. See (*voici*)! The people of Boura take their xylophones.'

(41)   Ná   cɔlmɔ . . .
       see spear . . .
       'See (*voici*) the spear . . . '

In (40) the informant was asked to observe a funeral celebration and write down immediately what was happening. The *ná* is meant to draw attention to what is happening at that moment in the real world. However, it is not clear whether *ná* is meant to be referential or locative.

In (41) the speaker is describing a picture of the slave trade which is in a government office. He describes the picture as if the hearer could see it. One of the things he describes is the spear, mentioned in (41). It is not clear in this case either whether the *ná* is referential or locative.

Ná in the 'voilà' sense may also be used as what Blakemore (1987) would call an inferential constraint on relevance, first mentioned as example (15) in chapter 4, repeated here for convenience as (42):

(42)   a. Vaa cʋʋlé   né   ɓiɛ́na.
          dog stupid SDM really
          'It is really a stupid dog.'
       b. Ná, tɔ́ɔ́biri ŋ lɪsɛ,   ʋ   lɛ   ziŋbal.
          see night   I loosen he leave courtyard
          'You see (*voilà*), at night, I let him loose outside the courtyard.'
          (English translation of continuation: 'He comes and pulls and pulls at the door, in order to enter. He tries in vain, and then sleeps in

the middle of the doorway. And I sleep in the courtyard and hear the howling of all the dogs, but I never hear his howling, never, never. I don't see him.)

Ná in this case prefaces a series of premises meant to justify the claim in (42a). Its use is very much like English *you see* (see chapter 4).

The above examples illustrate how the use of *ná* has shifted from verbal to deictic semi-referential use, then to inferential use as in (42), before becoming a definiteness marker. However, *ná* in some cases clearly picks out a space rather than an individual object as referent. This is so in the following example, where there is a separate demonstrative marker other than *ná*:

(43) Ɗné   rí   ŋné   ná . . .
this-one and that-one there
'This one and that one there . . . '

Example (43) is a recording of an utterance accompanied by a gesture pointing out certain unripe fruits. There is no separate distal demonstrative in Sissala: *né* is used for 'this' as well as 'that'. However, to indicate spatial distance he may add *ná* (cf. French *celà* 'this there' = 'that').

When *ná* is used temporally, it is either anaphoric to a previously mentioned time or it indicates a distant time in the past. Consider (44) and (45):

(44) Tɛŋ ná mé háálɔ́, rı u bɔ́mɔ́ ri ʋ wero, ɓaá   ja.
time that at woman if she bad if she good they-IPF marry
'At that time, whether a woman was good or bad, they would marry.'

(45) Zaa né ɓa bɛ́llɔ́, daarɛ né   ká jíja   ya.
today this they admire think SDM then IPF-marry P
'Today, they admire each other, think about it and then marry.'

While in (44) the determiner is *ná*, indicating time long ago, in (45) it is *né*, which is otherwise strictly deictic, meaning 'this' (in this age).

This section has shown how determiners have developed from deixis. Clark and Marshall (1981) take the fact that definite markers may develop from deixis as strong support for the mutual-knowledge framework. Deixis is based on mutually visible phenomena, thus Clark and Marshall argue that non-deictic definite expressions point to mutually known entities. If Clark and Marshall are right, then the other determiners in Sissala, the *né* and *rɛ́*, which also have their roots in deixis, should also pick out mutually known entities when used non-deictically. However, this is not the case, since both are used to introduce unknown or non-established material. Also, as some of the above examples show, the speaker does not always care whether the hearer actually knew of the entity marked with *ná* before the utterance took place. In example (41) he describes a picture as if the hearer was seeing it, but in fact, what is described is completely new to the hearer. In that case, as in other examples, the speaker had already made a context accessible to the hearer, into which the new entity was easily integratable. The use of *ná* does not presuppose mutual knowledge: it only presupposes certain possibilities of interaction between utterance, cognitive abilities and considerations of relevance. The mutual-knowledge framework is empirically as well as psychologically inadequate.

As far as the development of determiners and particles from deixis is concerned, it seems natural that this should happen. Our most basic and earliest communicative experiences have to do with visual perception and pointing. It is not surprising that events are often reported as if pointing into the real world was taking place. Thus, even markers which are reserved in the language for deictic use may occasionally be used non-deictically. Consider (46) and (47):

(46)   ɩ   ná omo né   a   bɪɪnɛ
       you see thing this and think
       rú-ʋ   né   were kɛ   ʋ ná.
       COMP-it SDM pretty surpasses it that
       'You see this thing and think that **this** one surpasses the beauty of that one.'

(47)   Abijan jɪɪsɛ,   ʋ   mʋʋ, ʋ   yɔwɔ,   ɓa   nyáŋ wuu to
       Abidjan houses its sea   its market they these all   are-NEG
       oŋ-béllé-tenné.
       thing-admire-finish
       'The houses of Abidjan, the sea, its market, all of those, are always admirable.'

In (46), the speaker visualises the market situation while describing it. He uses the deictic *né*, although he knows that the hearer cannot see its referent. Then he picks out the same thing with a pronoun and marks it with *né*. He then refers to another thing with a pronoun and *ná*. By considerations of relevance the hearer should be able to work out that the thing referred to by *ʋ ná* is something else he has already seen. It is not clear whether *ná* refers just to a thing, or a thing seen some distance away (spatially), or seen earlier on (temporally). Likewise the deictic *nyáŋ* 'these' is used anaphorically in (47). This illustrates how deictic markers may gradually acquire non-deictic uses.

6.5   Conclusion

In this chapter I have introduced three different defining particles, *ré*, *né* and *ná*. I have claimed that the typicality marker *ré* is a constraint on relevance or processing aid, guiding the hearer to access encyclopaedic entries with stereotypical or schematic information, while *né* encourages the hearer to open a new specific address. These 'discourse markers', which help the hearer to save processing effort, make good sense in a relevance-theoretic approach.

The definite marker *ná* is used with known or easily predictable concepts. I have shown that the Sissala data, especially where bridging implicatures are involved, is more easily explainable in terms of relevance theory than the mutual-knowledge framework, since within relevance theory the hearer is able to determine the right referent via considerations of relevance, while the mutual-knowledge framework provides no means of determining a unique referent.

I showed with Sissala data how definite, specific and non-specific defining devices develop from deictic expressions, and that the development of definiteness from deixis is no evidence of the need for mutual knowledge in processing definite expressions.

The reader may have wondered whether the interpretive-use marker *ré* and the typicality marker *ré* have something in common, or whether they are just homophonic and have different senses. Since one is a constraint on relevance and the other a truth-conditional particle, there is no processing mode which could make them synchronically related. When compared with *né*, the two uses of *ré* may have a negative factor in common – they never lead the hearer to access specific descriptively used referents. However, whether *ré* could actually have this as part of its overall meaning is a decision I would not like to make without further investigation. For one thing, more research has to be done on other devices, especially *né*. Since there is, after all, quite a difference between the typicality-defining device and interpretive use, I have chosen to treat them completely separately in this book without, however, committing myself to the claim that the two uses of *ré* are purely accidental.

7 Meanings and domains of universal quantification

7.1 Introduction

In chapter 5 I showed how a particle can be ambiguous between truth-conditional and non-truth-conditional uses, and vague between different truth-conditional uses. In some respects *wuu*, which can mean 'all', 'every', 'each', 'any', 'whole', 'very' and 'always' raises similar issues. What makes it interesting to raise the question of vagueness versus ambiguity again is the fact that while some of the truth-conditional uses can be represented within predicate calculus, others cannot – which underlines the inadequacy of a purely predicate-calculus treatment of truth-conditional quantificational phenomena.

Though there is no question that all the quantificational (non-idiomatic) uses of *wuu* make a contribution to truth conditions, the question arises how the differences between the 'all', 'every' and 'each' interpretations are to be represented. They cannot be represented in terms of differences in quantifier, or in quantifier scope: rather, they appear to involve differences in the way the given quantifier is viewed: collectively or distributionally; 'one by one' or 'one amongst many'. I will argue that these differences in interpretation are genuinely truth-conditional, and cannot be seen as involving constraints on relevance, as discussed in chapters 4 and 5. Since such differences cannot be captured in predicate-calculus terms, this provides further confirmation of the inadequacy of predicate calculus for natural-language semantics.

A related issue has to do with the domains of *wuu* – that is, the sets of individuals quantified over – how they are established and how they are interrelated in discourse. I shall discuss the fact that they seem to be indeterminate in some cases, and that speakers and hearers may not have the same assumptions about a domain; I shall also discuss the case where domains are 'loosely' fixed. On the basis of these cases, I shall examine Morton's (1986:105) claim that 'there is an anaphora of quantifiers'. As

202

in chapters 1 and 2, my conclusion will be that in accounting for such 'anaphora', it is not coherence relations but relevance relations that provide the best explanation of the facts.

In section 7.4 I shall explain and illustrate with Sissala examples the similarity between generic determination and quantification. I shall show how the two may be interchanged in discourse, depending on which contextual effects are to be achieved. I shall end this section by showing that there is a crucial difference between generic determination and quantification.

7.2   Meanings of *wuu*

7.2.1   Uses of *wuu*

In this subsection I will introduce the different uses of *wuu* and in 7.2.2 I will draw some conclusions.

7.2.1.1   Wuu *as a quantifier*
In most of its uses *wuu* occurs as a quantifier, and, as examples (1)–(5) will show, it covers a range of uses which have different forms in English. This means that form does not guide the Sissala speaker to more precise quantificational interpretations, as is the case in English.

(1)   Nɪɛ̀   wuu   sɪɛrʋ   tɔrɛ.
       people all   inside happy
       'Everybody was happy.'

(2)   Nɪɛ̀   ná   náŋá wuu fa   há   bíɾɛ́ mú jɪɪsɛ ɓa
       people DEF   others all   PAST which return go   houses they
       há   ná   lɔɔ́lɛ́, ɓa   wuu bíɾɔ́ fá   ko.
       when saw   lorry they all   return run come
       'All the people who had gone home, when they saw the lorry, they all ran back again.'

(3)   Nɛŋ   wuu   ɪɔ   rí   wííɾɛ́   losu sí   kíllɛ́
       person every knows COMP   next-year famine will surpass
       dʋla.
       this-year
       'Everybody knows that next year's famine will be worse than this year's.'

(4)   ɪ   pɪɛ́ ná   nɛ́   sɪɛ́ kué rɪ   nyʋ,   ɪ   baa
       when yams DEF SDM   then come when germinate you add

ja   daasɛ a   cɔ́ŋsɛ́ yıı   wuu daa   bala.
fetch wood and plant mound each wood one
'When the yams have germinated, you also fetch wood, and you place
one piece of wood on each mound.'

(5)   Rí-í   cén   nɛ́ŋ   wuu ʋ   wíbʋlí nɛ   ka ...
      if-you meet person any his speech SDM is
      'Anybody you meet will say ... '

As will be seen from these examples, *wuu* can occur with either a plural
or a singular noun: in (1) and (2) it occurs with a plural noun. In (1) the
translation is 'everybody', and in (2) it is 'all'. In examples (3), (4) and (5)
it occurs with a singular noun. In (3) the translation is 'every', in (4) it is
'each' and in (5) it is 'any'.

It is clear that the NP in each case refers to more than one person;
however, there are differences in how this 'group' is seen. In (1) and (2) it
is seen collectively and in (3) and (4) it is seen distributionally: that is, the
group may be regarded as a unit, or its members may be picked out for
individual attention in various ways. While (1) and (2) answer the
question 'How many members of the group?', (3) and (4) answer the
question 'Which members of the group?' (For the distinction between
collective and distributive see Vendler 1967.)

As far as the distributional interpretation is concerned, English
distinguishes between *every* and *each*. Vendler (1967) describes this
difference informally as follows: '*Every* is distributional by considering
individuals amongst others, and *each* is distributional by considering
them one by one.' That is, (3) picks out the individual members
simultaneously, whereas (4) suggests that some sort of temporal ordering
in the selection process is involved.

In example (5) it is clear that the speaker does not intend that *every*
person has to be met in order to make the proposition expressed true;
rather the suggestion seems to be: 'Pick out a person you like and she will
say ... ' However, the translation 'if you meet someone ... ' would not
be entirely adequate. The use of *wuu*, like the use of *any*, suggests that it
is true of *every* person that if you meet her she will say ...

In one sense it is not surprising that Sissala should have only one form
for all four cases, since in predicate calculus they can all be represented
with the universal quantifier $\forall$. However, within predicate calculus the
representation for *all*, *every* and *each* differs from that of *any*. Consider
(6) and (7):

(6) $\forall x \, \forall y \, (M(y,x) \rightarrow S(x))$
(7) $\forall y \, ([\forall x \, M(y,x)] \rightarrow \forall x \, S(x))$

In (6), where the universal quantifiers are outside the scope of '$\rightarrow$' the notation has to be understood as 'for all x and for all y, if y meets x then x will say . . . '; while (7), where the second universal quantifier is within the scope of 'if', has to be read as 'for all y, if for all x, y meets x, then every x will say . . . '. These two different interpretations have different truth-conditions: (6) corresponding to 'if you meet anyone', and (7) to 'if you meet everyone'.

Since Sissala, like English, uses a singular noun for the 'every' as well as the 'any' interpretation, the intended meaning of the quantifier cannot be detected here by purely linguistic means. Before I make some suggestions about how the intended interpretation is identified, let us consider some further uses of *wuu*.

Wuu is also used with the negative and can mean 'no', and with certain nouns 'nothing', 'nobody' and so on. Consider (8) and (9):

(8)   Mʋɔsı kuoro há búl wíí   ré.   ɪ   nέŋ   wuu wı   híísέ
        Mossi chief   as say word TDM COMP person no   NEG shame
        kέ.
        above
        'As the Mossi chief says: there is nobody above shame.'
(9)   Bakakoo baa   wı   oŋ   nɔŋ   wuu fá.
        warthog again NEG thing other any fear
        'The warthog doesn't fear anything else.'

What is interesting about these examples is that, semantically, the universal quantifier is outside the scope of negation: the examples can only have wide scope quantifier readings. Thus (8) corresponds to $\forall x$ $^{-}S(x)$ in predicate calculus and not to $^{-}\forall x\ S(x)$, which is the translation of 'Not everyone is above shame'. This latter reading would be indicated with constituent negation and optionally with a sentential negation marker as well, as in (8'):

(8')   [[Nεŋ   wuu ra]   (wı)   [híísέ ke.]]
        person every NEG NEG shame above
        'Not everyone is above shame.'

Ra indicates that the subject NP is within the scope of constituent negation.

Similarly in (9) (ignoring *baa*), the utterance can only be interpreted with wide scope quantifier, corresponding to the predicate-calculus translation: $\forall x\ \forall y(W(x) \rightarrow {}^{-}F(x,y))$ 'for all x and for all y, if x is a warthog, then he does not fear y'. The translation $\forall x\ (W(x) \rightarrow {}^{-}\forall y$

(F(x,y)) 'for all x, if x is a warthog, then it is not the case that for all y, x fears y' would be represented in Sissala as in (9′):

(9′)   [Oŋ nɔŋ   wuu   ra]   [[bakakoo] (wɪ)   [fá]].
       thing other every NEG warthog   (NEG) fear
       'The warthog doesn't fear everything.'

In (9′) the front shifted object is syntactically in the scope of constituent negation, indicated with *ra*, while *wɪ* indicates sentential negation.

Examples (8′) and (9′) show that differences in scope are linguistically encoded in Sissala in negative sentences, while differences between the 'every' and 'any' interpretations in positive sentences are not linguistically encoded, as we have seen.

7.2.1.2   Non-quantificational uses of wuu

Wuu in Sissala can also be used in ways which do not correspond to the universal quantifier in predicate calculus. Some of these uses coincide with the English use of *all*. Consider (10) and (11):

(10)   Tié   wuu   hɪl.
       earth all   dry
       'All the earth was dry.'

(11)   . . . aá   de   daarɛ vok   wuu   mi.
              and INT cross brook all   in
       ' . . . and were crossing the whole brook'

While *wuu* in (10) is translatable into English with *all*, *wuu* in (11) is only translatable with *whole*. Although the earth and the brook are wholes, they are divisible into parts; it is possible for part of the earth to be dry or part of the brook to be crossed. The use of *wuu* here indicates that every part of the earth was dry, and every part of the brook was crossed.

There are more abstract examples involving a similar use of *wuu*. Consider (12):

(12)   Ba súllɛ́   wɔ   cícuɔ   bɔk   ná wuu wɪɛ́.
       they forgot their morning tiredness the all   matters
       'They forgot all the tiredness of the morning.'

Although tiredness is not physically divisible into parts, it is possible to remember it in full or only in part. Here *wuu* indicates that it is being remembered in full.

The 'whole' interpretation of *wuu* occurs only with singular nouns. It is not an interpretation adequately represented in terms of the universal quantifier of predicate calculus. As we have seen, the universal quantifier answers the question 'how many?' (of a group), or 'which members?' (of a group). *Wuu* in (10)–(12) answers a rather different question: 'how much?' (of an object divisible into parts). Hence, its occurrence (like that of English *all*) with singular and non-count nouns.

Notice that in (11), where 'brook' is a count noun, *wuu* could also be interpreted as *every* or *each*; on this interpretation, the truth-conditions of (11) would be completely different. While in the case of the 'whole' reading there is only one brook, in the case of the 'every' and 'each' reading there are many. Again we have a case where different interpretations of *wuu* have different truth-conditions. This difference, however, is not representable with predicate calculus, since the 'whole' interpretation does not correspond to either a universal or an existential quantifier.

In some cases the hearer has to resolve vagueness or ambiguity of a noun before finding the right interpretation of *wuu*. Consider (13):

(13)   dılla ɓıcέllέ   a   tɔ   síέ   wuu mi

      ears thing-big and cover $\left\{\begin{matrix} \text{eyes} \\ \text{face} \end{matrix}\right\}$ all at

      'having big ears which cover $\left\{\begin{matrix} \text{both his eyes'} \\ \text{the whole face'} \end{matrix}\right\}$

The word *síέ* is used in Sissala for 'eyes' and 'face'. There is therefore ambiguity between those two interpretations. Depending on which interpretation is chosen, *wuu* is either a quantifier or an indicator of wholeness. The 'eye' reading calls for a 'both' or 'all' interpretation, which is collective; the 'face' reading calls for a 'whole' interpretation. The 'face' reading was the intended one in this case. The speaker expected the hearer to have enough knowledge about elephants to be able to resolve the ambiguity, and assign the right interpretation to *wuu*.

7.2.1.3   Wuu *and scalarity*
The 'whole' interpretation of *wuu* may be extended to indicate extremeness on a scale, for example of distance. Consider (14):

(14)   Ʊ mıŋ sıɛrı   wuu.
      he is-in distance whole
      'He is very far (away).'

Without *wuu*, the distance involved could be small or big; *wuu* indicates that the 'whole' (possible) distance is to be considered. Here the addition of *wuu* narrows down the truth-conditions of the proposition that would otherwise be expressed.

Consider (15) and (16) with quantificational expressions:

(15)   Ɓa má wuu de   koŋi ka   kááné kɛnɔ ɾɪ   heŋgbele ká
   they also all   INT lean and leave   skin   and bones   and
   ɓa   dɪkáŋ   wuu sʊsɛ.
   their big-part all   dead
   'They also became all lean and were only skin and bones, and almost
   all of them died.'

(16)   Gɪrmɛ́ mʊɔ́   wuu há toó   ʊ   wíɛ́   mɛ́.
   wrong a-little all   P   is-not his words in
   'There is not even a bit wrong in his speech.'

The use of *wuu* in (15) and (16) is clearly similar to that in (14), in that it
has an 'extremeness' or scalar effect. Here, though, the addition of *wuu*
does not alter the truth-conditions of the utterance, it merely expresses
them more explicitly. This increase in explicitness contributes to optimal
relevance. By adding *wuu*, and thus increasing the hearer's processing
effort, the speaker suggests that the hearer would not otherwise of his
own accord have accessed this interpretation, or that he would have
been inclined to dispute it and ask for confirmation. Hence the implication of unexpectedness or surprise: compare *All my friends have
come*, which conveys surprise, with *My friends have come*, which is
neutral.[1]

All the uses of *wuu* so far discussed have been truth-conditional.
However, there is one more use conveying 'extremeness' which is truly
non-truth-conditional: here *wuu* combines with *má*, and the two particles
together have the interpretation 'even' or 'at all' (see chapter 4).
Consider (17):

(17)   Siwie   paarʊ wuu gunni, ká pɪ́ɛ́   é dé   wɪ
   groundnuts leaves all   bent   and yams F INT NEG
   nyʊɛ́   má wuu.
   germinate even
   'All the leaves of the groundnuts were hanging down. As for the
   yams, they did not even germinate.'

Wuu in *má wuu*, like *all* in *at all*, has to be seen as an idiom, and appears
to be non-truth-conditional, with no close relation to the quantificational
use.

The examples discussed so far represent the major uses of *wuu*, which
are all truth-conditional. The question of how differences among these
truth-conditional interpretations are to be represented, and whether
they involve vagueness or genuine ambiguity or polysemy, will be
discussed in the next section.

7.2.2   *Wuu* and truth-conditions

I have tried to show that as far as predicate-calculus representations are concerned, *wuu* must be assigned the same representation when it has the interpretation 'all', 'every' or 'each', and that this representation must be distinct in quantifier scope from the one assigned when it has the interpretation 'any'; there is no standard predicate-calculus representation when it has the interpretation 'whole'. If we treat *wuu* the same way as *baa* in chapter 5, then we can say that all the four quantifier interpretations, 'all', 'every', 'each' and 'any', have as their common meaning universal quantification, and that there is vagueness between the different scope readings as illustrated with examples (6) and (7).

There has been some discussion in the literature (see Kempson and Cormack 1980) of whether the so-called 'scope ambiguities' exhibited by (18) are really a matter of ambiguity or vagueness:

(18)   Everyone loves someone.
      a. $\forall x\ \exists y$ (Loves xy)
         'Everyone has someone they love.'
      b. $\exists y\ \forall x$ (Loves xy).
         'There is one particular person who is loved by everyone.'

The same question arises in Sissala over whether *wuu* on its quantifier interpretations is really vague or ambiguous. Resolving these questions satisfactorily would take one well beyond the scope of this book. Here I shall simply assume – following Grice's principle of Modified Occam's Razor: senses are not to be multiplied beyond necessity – that an account in terms of vagueness is to be preferred to one in terms of ambiguity as long as both are possible. An account in terms of vagueness would involve specifying that a universal quantifier was involved in each case, but allowing its scope to be determined on partly pragmatic grounds. This, then, is the sort of account I propose to adopt.

The next question is how the 'whole' interpretation should be handled. This interpretation has no standard translation into predicate calculus, where quantifiers apply only to countable objects and not to mass terms. How should it be dealt with? And is there vagueness or ambiguity between the quantificational and non-quantificational uses?

Example (11), which has the two possible interpretations 'every river' and 'the whole river' (or 'all the river'), might lead us to the conclusion that a case of genuine ambiguity is involved. However, within a relevance-based framework, these interpretations could just as well be handled by a vagueness account. Moreover, if ambiguity is involved, is it *wuu* itself which is responsible for the 'ambiguity' in (11)? Finally, are there not good reasons for treating *whole* as in some sense related to the clear cases of quantification?

As mentioned before, *whole* implies that the referent of the associated noun must be divisible into parts. This accounts for the oddness of cases where no partition is possible. Compare (19) and (20):

(19)   ?The whole body died.
(20)   The whole body shook.

While it is common to speak of body parts shaking, one usually uses *die* only in the case of the death of a (complete) body. In some sense therefore, *whole* has a quantificational meaning: think of a whole cake cut into twelve pieces. It is therefore not surprising that a language like Sissala uses exactly the same word for 'whole' and universal quantification.

I propose therefore to treat *wuu* as vague between quantificational and wholeness uses. Wholeness might be treated as involving universal quantification over parts. The quantificational interpretation is usually found with count nouns, while the 'whole' interpretation is found with mass nouns, thus making the intended interpretation obvious.

However, as we have seen, count nouns such as *river*, *person*, *cake*, may also be seen as having parts, and as in the case of (11), genuine truth-conditional differences may arise between the collective/distributional interpretation and the part/whole interpretation. The 'ambiguity' in (11) is not directly due to the quantifier, but to the possible count noun and part/whole interpretations of the noun.

Further support for an analysis involving vagueness between the 'whole' and quantificational interpretations is provided by the fact that in some cases, especially in some temporal uses, it is impossible to decide whether a collective/distributional or 'whole' interpretation is intended. Even a native speaker would find it hard to say how *wuu* should be understood.

Consider first two temporal uses of *wuu* which are clearly quantificational, followed by three examples which are not clear at all:

(21)   . . . a   puure paaru có   a   di tápúl wuu.
        and pluck leaves cook and eat day   every
        ' . . . and they pluck leaves and cook them, and eat them every day.'
(22)   . Binsε baná wuu ní   betuu   kaa lul
        years four all   SDM elephant takes give-birth
        betuwie   bala.
        elephant-baby one
        'Every fourth year the elephant gives birth to one baby.'

Here the correct – quantificational – interpretations are selected on pragmatic grounds. In (21), it is unlikely that people would eat leaves all day. In (22), again for pragmatic reasons, the four-year periods must be seen as countable units; this is similar to German *Alle vier Jahre hat der Elefant ein Junges.*

In the following case, however, it is not clear at all whether *wuu* is meant to indicate wholeness or quantification:

(23)   Nyii   ná ko   ri   wuu.
        water the come IM   all
        'The water is coming all the time.'

The hearer of (23) is expected to interpret *wuu* in a temporal way. Syntactically, *wuu* is in a position where adverbial phrases and temporals may occur. Due to the absence of any noun *wuu* could be seen as fulfilling the function of a temporal adverb, similar to 'always' or 'continuously'. However, let us consider two more examples before we make a final decision on that.

In order to know whether *wuu* functions as a quantifier or as an indicator of wholeness in this case, we would have to know how a Sissala views time – as a whole or as countable moments which pass by. English uses *all* in 'all the time', with the singular which occurs with wholeness. As we see, in Sissala there is no linguistic clue. If we were insisting on an ambiguity between the 'whole' and 'quantifier' interpretation then this case would leave us with a serious problem: it would force us to assign *wuu* to one of the two meanings. Assuming vagueness, we can just leave this use unspecified without having to commit ourselves further.

Sissala may also use *wuu* to indicate a stretch of time where only the beginning is explicitly referred to. Consider (24) and (25):

(24)   Bamma ré die   wuu sié   mıŋ re-ε.
        others IM yesterday all then in IM-Q
        'Have some been here since yesterday?'
(25)   Nεrɔ há ko   ré cícʊɔ   ná wuu, losu   kánʊ́.
        person which come here morning the all   hunger catch-him
        'The person who has been here since the morning is hungry.'

The 'since' interpretation in this case is due to the literal translation 'all the time from this morning, he is hungry'. Again it is not clear whether *wuu* represents 'wholeness' or 'countable moments', and it seems not very important to know, either. The very existence of such indeterminacy is strong support for treating *wuu* in all its truth-conditional uses as 'vague'.

Returning to the question of whether *wuu* in (23) should be regarded as an adverb or a quantifier with an implicit noun, let us consider (24) and (25). The scope of *wuu* is not only the stretch of time explicitly mentioned in the preceding NP – yesterday, morning – but includes the whole stretch of time from that explicitly mentioned up to the time of utterance. The domain of *wuu* is determined on partly pragmatic grounds. It could therefore be argued that *wuu* in (23), too, has an implicit noun, 'time', in its scope, which makes *wuu* a quantifier without an explicit domain.

My conclusion on this point is that by assuming vagueness rather than ambiguity between all these truth-conditional uses of *wuu*, combined with pragmatic determination of scope and quantificational domains, complexity on the linguistic level can be largely avoided. This, then, is the account that I propose to adopt.

Now let us consider the question of whether the difference between the collective versus distributional interpretations, and 'one-by-one' versus 'one-amongst-many' interpretations of *wuu*, is genuinely truth-conditional. As was mentioned above, the difference between 'all', 'each' and 'every' is that they provide answers to different questions. I shall argue that because they provide answers to different questions, they make different contributions to truth-conditions. Thus the whole range of uses of *wuu* (apart from the idiomatic use in *maa wuu* discussed above) can be analysed in truth-conditional terms, with *wuu* being vague among all these possible uses. Consider (26) and (27):

(26)   a. Jean and Duncan are married.
        b. Jean and Duncan are both married.
(27)   a. Susan, Mary and Jill are sisters.
        b. Susan, Mary and Jill are all sisters.

Example (26a) has two possible interpretations: one equivalent to (26b), and one – a more natural one – on which Jean and Duncan are married to each other. Example (26b), unlike (26a), rules out the possibility that Jean and Duncan are married to each other. Example (27a) similarly has two possibilities of interpretation: whereas (27b), unlike (27a), rules out the possibility that Susan, Mary and Jill are sisters of each other. This suggests that (26a) and (26b), (27a) and (27b) are not fully truth-conditionally equivalent, and that *all* and *both* do affect truth-conditions. This is confirmed by the fact that (26a) and (26b), (27a) and (27b) provide answers to different questions. Example (26a), unlike (26b), can be an appropriate answer to the question 'Which people are married to each other?' Example (27a), unlike (27b), can be an appropriate answer to the question 'Which people are sisters of each other?'

Each and *every* answer questions with *which*: which members of a group? They differ in the way these members are viewed: individually or as part of a group. The individual reading imposes a temporal sequence or some more abstract ordering on the interpretation, which makes it truth-conditionally different from the group reading. Consider (28) and (29):

(28)   He poured the water over the flower bed in one go, and watered every violet.

(29)   ?He poured the water over the flower bed in one go, and watered each violet.

Example (29) is odd because the watering of 'each' violet implies that each one was watered separately or after the other, thus 'watering in one go' and 'watering each violet' are incompatible. Thus the collective versus distributional interpretation and the 'one-by-one' versus 'one-amongst-others' interpretation also result in different truth-conditions.

How is it possible, then, that different languages may make different choices of quantifiers when trying to express the same propositions? For instance, Sissala uses *all* in (1) while English uses *every*: in (22) English uses *every* while German and Sissala (as indicated by the plural) may use *all*. The answer to this is that some languages may idiomatise certain quantificational uses, which other languages may not. Thus in English *everybody* may occur in an answer to the question *how many?* as well as *which members of the group?* In the case of (22) the same truth-conditions result when the four-year period is seen distributionally, as in English, and when 'all four-year periods' are seen collectively, as in German and Sissala. Again, the fact that the difference between collectivity and distribution can be neutralised in some languages, as with *everybody* in English, suggests that a vagueness analysis of the differences between 'all', 'each' and 'every' makes sense.

I have now considered all the uses of *wuu*, and argued that every use makes a contribution to the truth-conditional content of the proposition expressed, with the exception of *wuu* in *má wuu*, which was analysed as an idiom and treated as a constraint on relevance (see chapter 4).

7.2.3   Concluding remarks

What this section has shown in theoretical terms, is that a language can choose one form, with one semantic meaning, which can then be enriched into a multitude of more specific meanings for pragmatic reasons, and in particular for reasons of relevance. My suggestion is that an account in terms of vagueness between different truth-conditional meanings provides simpler and more explanatory solutions than one in terms of ambiguity or polysemy, which would pose problems in indeterminate cases.

One result that is perhaps worth emphasising is that the fact that two expressions differ in truth-conditions may not always be obvious at first sight. For example, most people would say that *John and Bill left* is truth-conditionally equivalent to *Both John and Bill left*. I have argued that, none the less, 'both' does make a contribution to truth-conditions, as is shown by the difference in interpretation between (26a) and (26b) above. I have suggested that similar truth-conditional differences can be found between 'each' and 'every', as shown by (28) and (29) above. It is important to remember, then, that many truth-conditional differences may not be representable in standard first-order predicate calculus – but they are truth-conditional differences none the less.

In the next section I shall examine the function of *wuu* in discourse by considering its various domains.

7.3   Domains of *wuu*

7.3.1   Nature and role of domains

In the last section I pointed out that quantifiers have domains, and that the exact interpretation of a quantifier depends on the kind of domain involved. Thus count nouns require an 'all', 'every', 'each' or 'any' interpretation of *wuu*, while mass nouns require a 'whole' interpretation. What was not mentioned, but implicitly assumed, is the fact that certain nouns or kinds of nouns provide a delimitation of domains. Nor was the role of domains in the connectivity of discourse discussed. These aspects are the subject of this section.

Quantifiers necessarily range over a certain domain. A domain is a set of objects quantified over. The largest possible domain is the universe. Consider (30):

(30)   All tortoises are toothless.

The domain of *all* in (30) is the set of tortoises in the whole world, provided that no more restricted domain has been mentioned or is implied.

In discourse, quantifiers usually range over more restricted domains: the total domain under consideration is what model theory calls 'a universe of discourse'. In model theory, a function F assigns a subset of the domain of discourse to each predicate symbol in the formal language; thus truth and falsity can be determined by seeing which objects fall within the domain of a given predicate and which do not. However, though model theory demonstrates nicely the character of quantificational application, it is inadequate for dealing with the complexity of its use in communication.

Morton (1986:105) starts his paper on 'domains of discourse' by mentioning that 'hidden and hard to express assumptions are involved in the anaphoric relations which tie individual assertions into coherent stretches of discourse'. Since his paper is about quantification, these 'hidden and hard to express assumptions' apply to the fixation and interrelationship of domains of quantifiers.

I pointed out in chapter 1 that linguistic semantics is too impoverished to yield full propositional forms, with fully determinate truth-conditions for every utterance. In the last section I pointed out that the logical forms linguistically encoded by quantifiers have to be pragmatically enriched in order to derive fully propositional forms. In this section I will argue that enrichment of logical forms also plays a substantial role in the fixation of domains.

As far as the interrelationship of domains is concerned Morton comes to the following three conclusions:

1   The domain of the quantifier depends on the predicates, in particular the sortal nouns, which have appeared earlier in the discourse.
2   The domain of a quantifier in the body of a discourse is not automatically determined by the predicates in previous sentences.
3   There must be a coherence to the domains of quantifiers in a discourse. To a first approximation: a common discourse needs a common domain. (1986:112)

Morton continues:

There is a tension between these conclusions. If all the quantifiers in a discourse are to have the same domain, or even if their domains are to be related in systematic ways, then it seems that the initial sentences of the discourse cannot set the domain, for this will set the domains of later quantifiers more than seems to be the case. There seem to be two alternatives: either the initial sentences set a domain which is then stuck to, or the domain can only be set, and the quantifiers only understood, after the whole discourse is over. Certainly the first of these sometimes occurs, particularly when there is a domain of discourse clearly set by particular common nouns ('we're talking about cars: ... '). And certainly the second occasionally occurs. But it seems very implausible that these are the only alternatives.

Morton goes on to say that 'there is some kind of anaphora between quantifiers'. He admits, though, that what exactly the 'intermediate' domains are is an open question.

Morton mentions a special problem case where speaker and hearer may agree on a certain domain, but not have the same beliefs about it. Another problem is the fact that a quantified proposition has 'presuppositions', which might turn out to be untrue in subsequent discourse. Consider (31):

(31)   All John's children are asleep, but then John doesn't have any children.

Although, in predicate calculus, universal quantification, as in (30'),

(30') $\forall x$ (Tortoise $(x) \rightarrow$ toothless (x))

does not require that the domain actually has members, in normal conversation one would expect that (30) makes a claim about existing animals. How then can sentences like (31), which may indeed occur in natural conversation, be justified? Also, how can it be justified that a full set is introduced, but continuation in discourse reveals that the set was not really full? Are these cases where the hearer has to 'repair' his assumptions? Morton argues that some of these 'denials' in discourse make the presupposition-carrying proposition untrue and the utterance unacceptable, while others do not make the propositions untrue and the utterance is acceptable.

Morton (1986:124) ends his paper with a number of open questions:

What is the exact form of the rules which equip discourses with assumptions about the extent of their domains of quantification and their relation to the predicates occurring in them? What is required to block such assumptions? These are large questions, and all I can hope to have done in this chapter is to have made it plausible that they are real questions, and potentially answerable.

While Morton's paper indeed raises some interesting questions about natural-language discourse domains, it admittedly also leaves many of them unanswered. I will try to answer some of them by showing, using Sissala data, how discourse-initial and -medial domains are established, and how quantifiers may interact: what is made explicit and what is assumed. As will be seen, there is a great similarity to English and other languages in the way domains are fixed, though the way quantifiers are made explicit and left implicit is language-specific. However, the main claims of this section are not about language-specific phenomena. The section could have taken almost any language as a basis. I will consider the way domains are identified in general, by looking afresh at attested natural data from a hitherto unanalysed language. My claim will be that relevance theory provides the basis for the identification of domains, and a solution to Morton's problem cases.

7.3.2   Establishment of domains in Sissala

How important the fixation of a domain is, becomes clear when isolated utterances like (32) have to be interpreted:

(32)   Ba dé   cɔŋsɛ ninni ní   a   culli   ŋmɛ́sɛ́ ná   wuu
        they INT placed lights SDM and overarch streets DEF all
        ní   ká   jนsɛ   má wuu a   ninni.
        SDM and houses also all   have lights
        'Lights are placed in all the streets, and all the houses also have lights.'

The question that immediately arises is 'The streets and the houses of what?' When uttering (32), the speaker must have assumed that the hearer would have a domain accessible, either because that domain had been mentioned before, or because it was otherwise manifest to him which domain was intended.

In the above case the domain had been mentioned before. The utterance is taken from a description of the town Abidjan, which was mentioned in the introductory remark: 'Abidjan is a big town'. Further on, 'Abidjan' is again mentioned in a more restricted context – the town of Abidjan by night. Consider (33):

(33)   Abijan tɔɔ́ sıɛrʋ títaŋ má dé .   né wɔhɔ né.
        Abidjan town inside night also exactly like day   SDM
        'The night of the town of Abidjan is just like the day.'

Example (32) immediately follows this utterance. The speaker assumes that the proposition expressed by (33) is optimally relevant in a context made accessible by his previous utterances. To achieve an optimally relevant interpretation, the linguistically encoded logical form of (32) has to be enriched to something like the propositional form in (32'):

(32')   At night, lights are placed in all the streets of Abidjan, and all the houses of Abidjan have lights.

Given the previous discourse, this is the first interpretation consistent with the principle of relevance.

Another way of establishing a domain is by taking into account the participants in the conversation and other people explicitly or implicitly introduced. Consider (34):

(34) ι   ɾɪ   Sɪzanɪ wuu ní   dié   kué   έ   ná?
      you and Susanne all   SDM yesterday came like that
      'You and Suzanne, you both came yesterday?'

Example (34) is the beginning of a conversation, and therefore 'you and Suzanne' introduces two participants into the domain of discourse. In interpreting the domain of *wuu*, the easiest assumption for the hearer to make – and the only one consistent with the principle of relevance – is that the domain consists of the two people just mentioned. *Wuu* has to be translated into English with *both*. *Both* is often regarded (see Allan 1986) as another form of universal quantification; Sissala confirms this view.

In (35) the initial domain of discourse is people in Léo wanting to celebrate the arrival of the president of Burkina Faso:

(35) Ba   ja   lɔɔlεwa. Nɔ́ŋɔ́ mʊ Hamɪl a   pa   fol-gɔkε,
      they fetched lorries   some go Hamale and collect Fulani-griots
      nɔ́ŋɔ́   má mʊ   Bʊzʊ a   pa   Kiélé   gɔgɔara. Ba
      another also went Bozo and collected Dagaati dancers they
      káŋwɔ́   wuu kaa ko   mʊ́ Lʊʊ.
      take-them all   take come go Léo
      'They fetched two lorries. One went to Hamale and fetched the
      Fulani griots. The other went to Bozo in order to fetch the Dagaati
      dancers. They took them all and brought them to Léo.'

'They' in 'they fetched lorries', is probably impersonal; the impersonal in Sissala is often used in cases where other languages use a passive. It would thus mean 'the people who were there', though it is clear that only a few actually did the fetching. The initial domain is then widened to include the Fulani griots and the Dagaati dancers. The natural assumption is that 'them all' in this case refers to the Fulani griots, the Dagaati dancers and the people who fetched them; therefore the domain of *wuu* is the union of these various 'groups'.

Domains of discourse, and domains of quantification in particular, may include not only people and objects but also activities, as (36) shows. The speaker may refer to a series of activities which he has introduced earlier on in the discourse with '*έ wuu*' 'all that'.

(36) a. (If a human being sees the hare he kills it for food. At night the cats
and big snakes look for the hare in order to kill it for food.)

  b. Arí έ wuu cuoŋsi ha púló.
    with that all   hares   still   multiply
    'In spite of all that hares multiply.'

The initial domain is established by 'the hare', which is intended to be
generic; and it could therefore be said that the initial domain is the set of
all hares. In (36a) certain activities are added to the domain. These are
then quantified over in (36b), with the expression 'all that'.

The purpose of this section was to show informally how domains can
be introduced in discourse, and how domains in non-initial position are
influenced by the initial domains. The question is, of course, how does
the hearer know that 'all that' in (36b) is meant to quantify over the
activities mentioned in the preceding proposition, and not over anything
else. The answer will be given in the next section.

7.3.3   Choice of domains and relevance

In 7.3.2 I showed how domains of quantification can be introduced: by
description ('all the streets of Abidjan') or by lists ('you and Suzanne'),
and how a domain can be influenced by preceding domains ('They took
them all'). In this section I would like to discuss further the interrelationship of domains, and how the hearer is able to discover the intended
delimitation of the domain of *wuu*. Before returning to examples (32),
(33) and (36), I would like to discuss first the interrelationship of domains
and quantifier, in a complex sentence. Consider (37):

(37) Paara wuu isi dahá a dú wo baksɛ wuu.
    farmers all   rise stand and plant their farms all
    'All the farmers decided to plant all their farms.'

This example is like one of the artificial examples taken from a logic
book. The different possible interpretations are well known. What has,
however, hardly been attempted yet is an explanation of what the hearer
actually does in order to derive the intended interpretation at any given
time.

'All the farmers', of course, quantifies over a restricted domain,
namely the set of Sissala farmers; and the domain of 'all their farms' is
established by reference to this initial domain. However, what exactly
the domain of 'all their farms' is depends on the referent of *wo* 'their'.

Example (37) can be interpreted in at least three different ways: (a) 'all farmers planted all farms (their own and each other's)'; (b) 'every farmer planted all his own farms'; (c) 'every farmer planted other people's farms', in which case *wo* is not co-referential with 'every farmer'. Predicate calculus helps to distinguish between these three readings:

(37')   a. All farmers planted all farms.
$$\forall x \, \forall y \, ((\text{farmer } (x) \land \text{farm } (y)) \rightarrow (\text{plant } (x,y)))$$
   b. Every farmer planted all his farms.
$$\forall x \, \forall y \, ((\text{farmer } (x) \land \text{farm } (y) \land \text{own } (x,y)) \rightarrow (\text{plant } (x,y)))$$
   c. All farmers planted all their farms.
$$\forall x \, \forall y \, ((\text{farmer } (x) \land \text{farm } (y) \land \text{own } (x,y)) \rightarrow (\text{plant } (x,y)))$$

The domain of the quantifier in 'all farms' differs in each case. In (37'a) 'all the farms' refers to all the Sissala farmers' farms; in (37'b) 'all the farms' refers to all those owned by a given farmer; and in (37'c) it refers to all those *not* owned by a given farmer.

Notice that each of these three readings has different truth-conditions. It is therefore important that the hearer is able to choose the intended interpretation of (37), which may represent at least three different propositions. In fact, the speaker intended interpretation (37'b). According to relevance theory, for this interpretation to be chosen the hearer must have the right context available, allowing him to make the right choice of domain.

What, then, is contextually different in the three possible interpretations? In interpretation (a), 'all farmers planted all their farms', the initial mention of farmers provides access to the encyclopaedic information that farmers have farms. This interpretation is achieved by taking the domain of *wuu* to be the total set of farms, so that all the farmers worked on all the farms. In interpretation (b), 'every farmer planted all his farms', the initial mention of a farmer must provide access to the encyclopaedic information that a farmer may own more than one farm, which will in turn open up the possibility that each farmer planted all his own farms. Interpretation (c), 'all farmers worked on some other people's farms', would depend on accessing the encyclopaedic information that farmers may work on each other's farms – an assumption which would be highly accessible on some occasions in Sissala culture.

How does the hearer know which context to choose and how to delimit the intended domain of the quantifier? The answer is, as always, by the criterion of consistency with the principle of relevance. He should take the first interpretation which a speaker aiming at optimal relevance – that is, adequate effects for the minimum necessary effort – might have intended to convey. As we have seen, of the two possible interpretations, one highly plausible, one less so, the more plausible should be the more accessible, and hence the only one consistent with the principle of relevance. In this way, plausibility and hearer's expectations can affect interpretation via the criterion of consistency with the principle of relevance.

However, before I go on to other examples, let us return to Morton's claim that there is an anaphora of quantifiers and that there has to be coherence between quantifiers in a discourse. It is clear that there is anaphora between quantifiers in interpretations (a) and (b) above, but not in (c). Likewise there is coherence (as defined in chapter 1) between quantifiers in (a) and (b) above but not in (c). I have already demonstrated the inadequacy of coherence as a criterion of textuality, and this is just one more example of it. What makes a unit of text 'connected' is not the interrelationship of domains but relevance relations between text and context.

In example (32) the speaker establishes an initial context, providing access to encyclopaedic information about the town of Abidjan: let us call this (CO); he then introduces a subcontext (SCO) consisting of information drawn from the 'chunk' 'Abidjan' and describing 'Abidjan at night'. This is then enriched with the information that the night is like the day, hence always light. The speaker then introduces further subcontexts, again drawn from the same overall entries, and describing 'the streets of Abidjan' and 'the houses of Abidjan'.

As was mentioned in chapter 2, in constructing a context for interpreting an utterance, the hearer is likely to take into account information derived from the most recently processed utterance, which will still be in short-term memory and therefore easily accessible. The hearer will thus have the subcontext (SCO) immediately accessible when processing 'all the streets' and 'all the houses' and will naturally assume that the domain of the quantifier is 'Abidjan', or 'Abidjan by night'.

In the case of example (36) things are very similar. As mentioned, the initial domain of discourse is the set of all hares. The aim of the subsequent description is to introduce encyclopaedic information about the hare. Thus with every new characteristic the context expands. Probably only some of the information is still in short-term memory (see chapter 2) and provides the initial and some expanded context for immediate processing, other information has probably already been dismantled and filed at appropriate encyclopaedic addresses. What can safely be said is that by the time the hearer has processed (36b) the encyclopaedic entry for 'hare' will consist of a 'chunk' that includes most of the information provided by propositions mentioned earlier on in the discourse.

7.3.4　Characterisation of domains and indeterminacy

In all the cases mentioned so far, the domains of *wuu* were determinate and the hearer was able to characterise them in the same terms as the speaker. In many cases, however, the domain of the quantifier may not be characterised in the same way by speaker and hearer, and in most of these cases it is not intended to be either.

In the following example the speaker gives a rough indication of what the domain of *wuu* is meant to be, but he leaves it to the hearer to fill in the exact details. Although the speaker might have some idea of what these details are, it is unlikely that the speaker's and hearer's characterisations are identical. In fact, it is most likely that they are not. This means that as far as communication is concerned the domain of *wuu* is indeterminate, and there is a discrepancy between what speaker and hearer may take the domain to be:

(38)　ɪ　há　co　ŋ, ɛ　wuu a.
　　　you what want me that all　do
　　　'All that you want to do to me, do it.'

Here, the speaker does not know exactly what the hearer wants to do. The domain of *wuu* is the union of everything that the hearer wants to do, whatever that may be. However, the utterance would be irrelevant if the *hearer* did not know either what he wanted to do. Therefore, though the speaker may not be able to list the objects in the domain, but merely characterises them by a description, he expects the hearer to be able to supply a list. This means that if there are implicatures, they are highly indeterminate – the speaker merely has general expectations as to the type of thing the hearer may want to do.

This example supports Sperber and Wilson's claim that communication, and in particular the recovery of implicatures, cannot be achieved solely by decoding. As Sperber and Wilson (1986a:56) indicate, the speaker may have a very vague informative intention, made manifest, say, by simply sniffing appreciatively at the seaside, thus motivating the addressee to think along certain general lines. In this case the resemblance between the speaker's and hearer's thoughts may be correspondingly loose.

The following example is the beginning of a discourse. Let us consider how the hearer is able to fix the domain of *wuu* in the third utterance:

(39)   a. Févrié   cana   tápʋlɛ mɛré   né   zaa.
           February month day   twenty SDM today
        b. Ɛzʋmmɛ súwɔ́.
           Ezummè dead
        c. Yútʋmɛ   peri   dɪhī   wuu.
           funeral-news reach place every
        d. Buuné   púl   ko   híhé náŋá   mɛ́.
           Boura-people start come put   others at
           'Today is the 20th of February. Ezummè is dead. The funeral news
           has reached everywhere. The people of Boura begin to assemble.'

As we see, the discourse-initial utterances (39a) and (39b) do not provide any overt indication of the domain of 'all places' introduced in (39c). In (39d) the speaker mentions 'the people of Boura' and therefore the town where the funeral took place. Does this mean that the places in Boura are the domain of *wuu*, and that the speaker intended to delay the exact mention of the domain? Very text-bound discourse analysts would probably have to come to this conclusion, because no other domain is explicitly mentioned in the text.

It is clear, though, that the speaker expected the hearer to have assumptions available about where the funeral would take place right from the beginning. The discourse was delivered at Boura, and that is where Ezummè came from. Did the speaker then mean to convey that the funeral message arrived in every place in Boura? Only those familiar with Sissala customs and who have appropriate assumptions accessible would know that he wanted to indicate that announcements had been made in Boura and the village or villages where the relatives of the dead live. Here the domain is fixed implicitly, by reference to encyclopaedic information.

A further question is whether the speaker expects the hearer to know exactly what the places in the domain will be: that is, whether he should be able to list them. This is most definitely not the case. While in the case of (38) the hearer was expected to supply a list of the domains, all the speaker of (39) wanted the hearer to understand was that the funeral was announced in all the places whose residents a Sissala person would normally expect to have been informed. He was not particularly concerned about the exact identity of those places.

It is, of course, possible that some of the people addressed with this discourse were able to list the places in the domain of *wuu*. As always, the assumptions that people have access to, and the contextual implications they draw may differ from person to person. However, if this extra information is not needed to establish consistency with the principle of relevance it cannot be shown to be part of the speaker's intentions, and the resulting contextual implications would not be implicatures.

This example shows that the hearer is meant to look for consistency with the presumption of 'optimal' and not 'maximal' relevance. Once the hearer knows that people in all the relevant places have been informed, he may well have derived enough effects for the utterance to be worth his attention. He could go on processing by supplying a list of those places, but does not *have* to do so in order to achieve an interpretation consistent with the principle of relevance. The risk and responsibility of doing so are his alone.

In this section we have seen that Morton is right about the existence of possible discrepancies between the speaker's and hearer's thoughts in the case of quantification and domains. What he failed to note is that these discrepancies might be quite deliberate, and are, in fact, very common in communication. Relevance theory, which is based on an inferential model and not a semiotic model, can handle these cases without difficulty.

In the next section I would like to consider further Morton's claim that there is an 'anaphora of quantifiers'.

7.3.5   Anaphora of quantifiers?

There is no doubt that domains of quantifiers are sometimes interrelated. However, is this necessarily the case? Does it mean that, whenever a quantifier does not interact with anything that has been said before, a new discourse is beginning, as Morton seems to suggest? Consider example (40):

(40) a. l-í kan-ı bio
    if-you have-your child
  b. ı wʊ-ʊ dıɛ́sɛ́ weri
    you not-him raise well

c. ká í   dé   dıεsɛ a   wıέ   wuu ní
   and you INT raise do things all   SDM
d. ká gul   ká ʊ   wıέ   wuu a   bɔn bɔn,
   and go-wrong and his things all   become bad bad
e. omo   wuu fíísέ   nέ.
   things all   innate SDM
   'If you have a son and he is not well brought up, but you have
   done everything to bring him up well, and failed and all his ways
   become bad, (know that) all things are already there at birth (not
   learned).'

There are three *wuu*'s in this text, ranging over three different domains.
Suppose we were the addressees of this piece of discourse and had to
assign more specific domains to these quantifiers. Which domains would
we choose?

For quantifier 1, 'you have done everything to bring him up well', we
might assume that the addressee had, for example, tried to teach him
high moral standards (to be honest, to work hard, be responsible for his
family, etc.) and given time and money for this 'teaching'.

For quantifier 2, 'all his ways become bad', we might assume that he
does not reach adequate moral standards (is lazy, perhaps, steals, lies, is
irresponsible). However indeterminate this second domain is, it is clear
that it is completely different from the first domain.

For quantifier 3, 'all things are already there at birth', we might
assume that everything (good and bad) that happens to a person is
predestined at birth. In this case it seems clear that *no* anaphora of
quantifiers is involved, although there is a certain amount of overlap in
the way these domains are characterised: moral standards are the
common element in 1 and 2, and bad things are a common element in 2
and 3.

What Morton calls 'anaphora', therefore, does not always exist, even
when there is more than one quantifier. There is no obvious semantic
relationship between the domains of the first and second quantifier.
There is, however, coherence in the discourse, which is about a hypothetical son. Thus the absence of a coherence relationship among
quantificational domains may not have any effect on the overall coherence of the discourse.

Morton touches on another problem which a coherence-based discourse model cannot handle: he mentions the case of presuppositions or
second-order implications, which sometimes seem to be cancelled in
discourse, or which have to be understood as satisfied in a certain way.

How does the hearer go about interpreting these utterances in the right way? Before looking at a Sissala example let us consider one of Morton's examples (1986:122–3) which does not have a universal quantifier, but which is nevertheless relevant to the discussion:

(41)   a. A: Is there anything which could
                loosen this bolt?
         b. B: A number five wrench could do the
                job, but we have none.
         c. B: A spanner from the green box might
                well work too.

Morton makes the interesting point that (41b) would be conversationally acceptable even if there was no number five wrench, and in fact none had ever been produced, whereas (41c) would be conversationally unacceptable if it was found out that the green box contained nails and not spanners. He comments that 'this particular conversation makes assumptions which tie the user of "spanner in the green box" to a claim that there are such things, though, and does not require a similar tie for "number five wrench". What is the difference between them?'

Surely the acceptability of (41b) and (41c) hinges on considerations of optimal relevance. It would be quite relevant to point out that if there *were* a number five wrench, it would do the job, or if we *had* a spanner, it would do the job. But it would clearly be pointless to specify that the spanner had to come from a particular green box in order to work. Hence the reference to a green box in (41c) detracts from the relevance of the utterance and makes it conversationally unacceptable if the box contains no spanners. Given a scenario in which the provenance of spanners affected their usefulness, (41c) would become as acceptable as (41b).

The answer to Morton's problem is that as long as there is a context available in which (41c) would be optimally relevant, the utterance will be acceptable. If the speaker has achieved optimal relevance, it follows that the hearer should have an appropriate domain accessible for every quantifier in the discourse. Repair is only necessary when the speaker fails to achieve optimal relevance, and the hearer has to reinterpret the preceding utterance; or in the case of a joke, where the speaker deliberately leads the hearer astray before he makes the context available for the right interpretation.

There are many examples in the language of spontaneous discourse which require a loose or figurative interpretation to achieve optimal relevance. The following Sissala example shows how a claim involving quantification turns out to be false if taken literally, but where the hearer would have been expected to reinterpret the utterance in such a way that explicit repair was not necessary afterwards:

(42) a. Bidi-fólwa ná   há   la   nıbiine   mí wuu zɔ́kɔ́.
         food-early DEF which take humans at all   spoilt
      b. Bándáwá wı ɔ́sɛ́   weri.
         beans   not given well
      c. Lɛɛmıɛ́ wuu zɔ́kɔ́.
         corn   all   spoilt
      d. Pıɛ́   má tóó.
         yams also not-there
         'All the early crops which sustain man (during the time of hunger) are spoilt. The beans have not yielded well, the corn is all spoilt and there are no yams.'

In (42a) the speaker claims that *all* the crops were spoilt, while in (42b) he says that the beans had not produced well. Literally there is an inconsistency, and an automatic 'anaphora' of quantifiers would break down at this point. Example (42a) makes a claim about the non-existence of food, which is contradicted by a literal interpretation of (42b). However, as Sperber and Wilson (1986a, 1986b) point out, a literal interpretation is not always the optimally relevant one. Thus, when asked by a friend *How much do you earn?*, it is often adequate to give a rough approximation of the real figure, while on a tax form it is crucial to give the exact figure. The figure given to the friend yields adequate effects for less processing effort than would be needed for the exact figure.

Similarly, in the above Sissala example, the implication is that the few available beans did not make the situation significantly different; in fact they amounted to nothing, taking all the other losses into account. To go into great detail and explain that the crops were spoilt except for a few – a very few – beans would have caused the hearer unnecessary processing effort. Here the looseness may reside in the quantifier, or in the use of the verb 'spoilt'. In either case, the utterance, on a loose interpretation, will have adequate effects for minimal effort, and hence achieve optimal relevance.

This text can be compared with Morton's example (1) (1986:108)

(43)   When I arrived at the house the burglars must have just left.
        Everything was gone: the furniture, the curtains, even the ashtrays.

As Morton points out, *everything* does not really mean 'everything' in the strict sense. There might still have been door knobs and light switches, etc. Again *everything* may be seen as loosely used; here, however, there is an alternative strictly literal interpretation, on which the domain of 'everything' is the set of 'easily takable things of some value to burglars' (Morton's solution). There are thus a variety of ways in which an effect of looseness or indeterminacy may be achieved.

In this section I have pointed out that though in some cases there may be something like an anaphora of quantifiers and coherence between quantifier domains, this is not always so. When it exists, it is relevance relations, relations between text and context, which best explain it.

7.3.6   Implicit and explicit quantification

In Sissala, as in English, quantification may be implicit in the second conjunct of a co-ordinate sentence. Consider (44) and (45):

(44)   Nιέ   wuu fá   ko   ciki
        people all   run come crowd
        a   bél   wó   má haá gɔ   έ.
        and watch them also how dance like-that
        'All the people ran and were crowding together in order to watch also their style of dancing.'

(45)   Ba   gʋɔrɛ dıhī   wuu
        they roam place every
        ní   a   suki   já   wɔ́   namıέ didi.
        SDM and together look-for their meat   to-eat
        'They roam everywhere and look together for their meat to eat.'

In (44) the quantified subject of the first conjunct is also the quantified subject of the second conjunct; *a* conjoins VPs, guaranteeing the same subject for the two conjuncts.

In (45) the location is quantified with *wuu* in the first conjunct and it is clear that the same quantified location also holds for the second conjunct, though this interpretation is not imposed by the syntax, as it is with (44). Basically the same processing principles apply here as with the processing of all non-coordinate structures. The content of the first utterance supplies the context for interpreting the second. Thus non-explicit information needed to establish a propositional form can be taken from the context set up by the preceding proposition. In the case of (45) this is the location 'everywhere'. (For discussion of the role of contextual information in the enrichment of co-ordinate structure, see Carston (1984) and chapter 8.)

The next examples show how a quantified direct object is implicitly understood in a whole series of conjuncts:

(46)   ı   kúsέ wɔ́   wuu.
        you cut them (rice plants) all
        ı   kúsέ
        you cut
        a   hé
        and put
        a   vɔwɛ guumé,
        and bind bunch
        a   hé kúré mí,
        and put basket in
        a   ka
        and take
        a   ko   jaa,
        and come house
        a   ka
        and take
        a   ko   bil
        and come put
        a   dáánέ mʊɔɔ,
        and last a-bit,
        ká pí ŋmɔwɛ,
        and take beat,
        a   sıέ máŋsέ
        and now measure
        a   ná έ   ná ı   muì há   ɔsέ
        and see manner the your rice how produce
        a   mú peri.
        and go reach

        'You cut them (rice plants) all. You cut them and bind them into bunches. You put them in a basket and go home. You leave them for a little while and then you beat them. You measure them in order to see how much rice you have produced.'

The quantifier *wuu*, which is given only in the first VP, is then implied in every single conjunct, and, as we see, this can be a considerable stretch of speech in Sissala. While in the case of VP conjunction with *a*, naturally no subject can occur in the second conjunct, it is syntactically permissible, and a stylistic requirement in Sissala, not to mention an object again, for some period after it has been introduced. This is demonstrated in (46). The only reason for breaking this stylistic convention is for focal purposes.

Knowing that subject NPs cannot occur with *a* constructions, it is puzzling why the speaker should choose to make the quantifier explicit in the second conjunct, as is done in (47):

(47) Nɪɛ́   wuu sɪɛ́ dé   miŋ wɪhálá   sɪɛrʋ a   wuu koŋi.
      people all   now INT in   suffering in   and all   lean
      'Everybody was suffering and (everybody) was lean.'

The only explanation for this quantifier repetition can be that the speaker wants to highlight the quantity for a purpose. There are always some people suffering, but it is an extreme situation when everybody is suffering and lean, as happened during the time of famine. As always, this information would be left implicit unless there was some reason for explicitly directing the hearer's attention to it – the most obvious reason being that he would otherwise have interpreted the quantifier rather loosely.

The following example has a front-shifted object with the *wuu* quantifier. The utterance has three conjuncts. The object and quantifier are implicit in the second conjunct, and represented with a resumptive pronoun and explicit quantifier in the third conjunct:

(48)   Ɔmɛŋsɛ wuu ní
          streets all   SDM
          6a   bil
          they put
          a   jɛllɛ
          and widen
          ká   hé wo   wuu rɪ   kootal.
          and put them all   with tar
          'The streets are all widened and tarmacked.'

As in (48), it is redundant from a strictly truth-conditional point of view to repeat the quantifier in the last conjunct. Again this repetition, which costs the hearer extra processing effort, can only be explained in terms of extra-contextual effects. The above utterance was produced by some-body from a small village for villagers for whom it is quite extraordinary that *all* the streets should be tarmacked. Since 'tarmacked streets' is the most extraordinary aspect of the whole utterance, only the last conjunct exhibits the repeated quantifier, which is designed to guarantee strict rather than loose interpretation, which might otherwise have been chosen.

As we have seen, although it is impossible to make a subject referent explicit and still use *a* as the 'and' marker, it is nevertheless possible to make the quantifier explicit, in order to lead the hearer to further contextual effects. Syntactically, this is only possible where quantifier floating can take place. These examples thus provide evidence for quantifier floating in Sissala.

7.3.7   Concluding remarks

I have shown how at the beginning of the text domains of discourse and quantifiers are fixed by considerations of relevance, i.e. are not necessarily explicitly introduced in the text. I have also shown how at any given stage in discourse the hearer is able to fix a domain for the quantifier he is just processing. I have argued that domains are never determined by the text alone; context, background knowledge and considerations of relevance play a crucial role at every point in processing a stretch of discourse, in initial, medial and final positions.

I have also shown that domains can be more or less determinate and that there may be a discrepancy between the speaker's and hearer's characterisation of them. It is important to note that this is not an imperfection, but may be fully intended by the speaker.

Just to say that there is 'anaphora of quantifiers' is not saying very much at all. Not only is such 'anaphora' not possible without support from the context, certain surface 'anaphoric' phenomena, as, for instance, explicit quantifiers which range over the same domain, are not there primarily for truth-conditional reasons, but to achieve contextual effects which would not otherwise be achieved.

7.4   *Wuu* in relation to determination

In order to have a complete view of the function of *wuu*, it is also necessary to look at determination. This section will therefore discuss the relation between quantification and determination.

7.4.1   Nature and role of determination versus quantification

Vendler (1967) and Lyons (1977) have stressed the great similarity between determination and quantification. As Vendler indicates, utterances such as (49) and (50) would generally be interpreted in terms of universal quantifiers:

(49)   Bala   ká títúr   rí.
        monitor-lizard is reptile TDM
        'The monitor lizard is a reptile.'

(50)   Abijan ŋmɛŋsɛ ná   daha lɔ́léwa né   kán̄ɛ́.
        Abidjan roads DEF on   cars SDM   many
        'There are lots of cars on the roads of Abidjan.'

To a first approximation, (49) is equivalent to (49'), and (50) to (50'):

(49')   All monitor lizards are reptiles.

(50')   There are lots of cars on all the roads of Abidjan.

The question is, what exactly is determination and why should quantifier interpretation sometimes be assigned to what are syntactically determiners, as in (49) and (50).

The term 'determiner' is normally used for definite and indefinite articles and demonstratives. According to Lyons (1977:452) 'Their primary semantic function is that of determining (i.e. restricting or making more precise) the reference of the noun-phrases in which they occur: hence the term "determiner".' He describes the difference between determiners and quantifiers as follows (1977:454–5):

> Determiners are modifiers which combine with nouns to produce expressions whose reference is thereby determined in terms of the identity of the referent; quantifiers are modifiers which combine with nouns to produce expressions whose reference is thereby determined in terms of the size of the set of individuals or in terms of the amount of substance that is being referred to. In other words, a determiner tells us which members of which subset of a set of entities are being referred to; a quantifier tells us how many entities or how much substance is being referred to. With respect to this distinction, imprecise though it is, 'this' is clearly a determiner in the phrase 'this man'; and 'many' and 'much' are clearly quantifiers in the phrases 'many men' and 'much bread'.

However, Lyons also points out (p. 456), that the borderline between determination and quantification is not always clear. There are cases both in English and in Sissala, where quantifiers may also perform the function of determination. Compare (51) and (52):

(51)   A: Which sweets do you want?
        B: All of them.
        (Example from Lyons (1977:456))

(52)   Bee   ká balleduó   rí   a   mɪŋ nibíbísí   tíé
        panther is animal-strong TDM and is-in people-black earth
        wuu.
        all
        'The panther is a strong animal and is found all over Africa (black man's land)

All in (51) is as much an answer to *which*, and therefore a determiner, as an indicator of quantity, and therefore a quantifier. In (51) the utterance is as much an answer to the question 'In *how many places* in Africa is the panther to be found', as to 'Where is the panther to be found'. Therefore *wuu*, too, may serve as a determiner as well as a quantifier. And, as I indicated earlier in this chapter (pages 203–13), the difference between the quantifiers 'every', 'each' and 'all' may have to be analysed in much the same way as Lyons is proposing to analyse the differences between quantifiers and determiners. It seems clear, then, that the analyses I have given, and those that Lyons has given, must be regarded as preliminary at best.

Of course, determiners which are related to quantification are of a special kind; they are generally referred to as 'generic' determiners. Dahl (1975:99) defines 'generic' in the following way: 'The common semantic property of all generic expressions is that they are used to express law-like, or gnomic, statements.'

Allan (1986:136) points out that there are three different types of generic NPs in English: the definite generic, which occurs only in countable NPs; the *a(n)*-generic; and the unmarked indefinite generic, which occurs both with plurals and with uncountables. Sentences (53a), (53b) and (53c) are examples:

(53)   a. The tortoise is toothless.
        b. A tortoise is toothless.
        c. Tortoises are toothless.

In English, as in Sissala, there is no special marking for 'generic' within the NP; therefore it can only be interpreted as such for pragmatic reasons.

Sissala definite and indefinite marking is different from the English defining system, as outlined in chapter 6.

All the different indicators of specificity, non-specificity (typicality) and definiteness, are also used generically.

Allan (1986:137) sees definite generics as 'abstracting from individuals to genera, species, kinds, and suchlike; thus are they aptly named "generic".' He comments:

These abstract generic sets are denoted holistically by definite NPs because each is unique: for instance the abstract generic set labelled 'the African elephant' is unique in that there may be other species of elephants but, according to the implication of S's description, they do not warrant the description 'African elephant'. Definite generics are also referential NPs. Neither type of indefinite generic denotes abstract generic sets, and in fact 'generic' is a somewhat misleading label for such NPs. The so-called a(n)-generic denotes an unspecified, but typical individual from the set (or genus), and the NP is nonreferential. The unmarked generic, however, refers to a subset of individuals from the universal set of such individuals.

In example (52), definiteness is expressed with the unmarked low-tone on *ɓee* 'panther' and non-specificity with high-tone on *ballɛduó* 'strong animal' and the typicality marker *rɛ́*. There are no special verbs which help to identify the generic interpretation. This is in line with Smith's claim (1975) that the generic is universally not determined by types of verbs. In a case like (52) the hearer will interpret the utterance generically if no interpretation based on a more restricted domain and specific individual referent comes immediately to mind.

The generic definite interpretation leads the hearer to think that being a strong animal is a property of all panthers; however, the non-specific marking on 'is a strong animal' does not make the hearer believe that panthers alone are strong animals; it leaves the possibility open that other animal kinds are also strong. Thus the interpretation of the definite and non-specific marking in (52) is in line with Allan's predictions. It is also clear that it is definiteness which is like universal quantification and not indefiniteness.

That definite generics are intimately related to universal quantification is frequently noted. I will discuss this in more detail in section 7.4.2

7.4.2   Interrelationship between determination and quantification in discourse

According to Allan, quoted above, generics are abstractions from individuals, and in discourses which describe generic kinds, they are sometimes represented with normal plural pronouns, and sometimes quantified. Consider (54):

(54)   Betúú   ɓidíílé ní   ká: nyɔ́ɔ, paarʊ rí   ɓinyʊ́ʊ́lɛ́. Rɪ
      Elephant food   SDM is   grass leaves and shoots   if
      betúúní   ní   múɛ le   baka rɪ   píɛ   rí   boŋbúó mɪŋ
      elephants SDM go   leave farm and yams and manioc is-in
      ráŋ. Baá dé   jɛrɛ   yɪla   wuu ní   ka tuŋ wɔ.
      there they INT destroy heaps all   SDM and eat all.
      'The elephant's food is grass, leaves and shoots. When the elephants go to the fields and there are yams and manioc, they destroy all the heaps and eat them (the crops).'

In this example the text starts with the mention of 'the elephant's food', which is in the singular and will be interpreted generically, if there is no other interpretation more accessible and consistent with the principle of relevance.

Then the narrator proceeds by extending the context – the elephant searches for food on the farms – and switches to the plural form of 'elephant' as if he were referring non-generically to a restricted domain of elephants. From the interpretation of the immediately preceding utterance the hearer knows, of course, that elephants in general are being referred to; the speaker can therefore afford the change from generic to non-generic representation.

The question remains, though, why the speaker bothers to change from singular to plural. Does this not increase processing effort? It is likely that he does this in order to facilitate processing of the following universal quantifier: it is individual elephants that are responsible for destroying all the yam heaps.

Consider also (55), which is also taken from a description of a particular kind of antelope.

(55) Rı kuó   ní   né   dɔ́mɛ ʋ   ŋmɔ́wɛ́ ʋ   mıısɛ né   ʋ
      if   antelope SDM hears noise he beats   his nose SDM his
      vállɛ́ náŋá   ná   né   ɓa   wuu gim.
      companions DEF hear they all   flee
      'If the antelope hears a noise he makes a noise with his nose. When his companions hear, they all flee.'

From the preceding utterances the hearer knows that *kuó ní* is meant to refer to the whole class of this type of antelope. Therefore he will also assign the pronouns to the generic set.

Although it can be said that it is typical of all antelopes that they tap their noses when they hear a noise, it is not expected that at any given occasion this is what *all* antelopes will be involved in. Thus, it seems that the corresponding quantifier in this case is rather 'any' than 'all', since any antelope one might pick out may behave in this way, but it is unlikely that all antelopes would do exactly the same thing collectively.

There is again a change from generic to non-generic interpretation which is expressed with the pronoun *ɓa* and the quantifier *wuu*. Since the quantifier cannot go with the generic determiner, the speaker has to change to a non-generic expression. The quantifier is in this case more appropriate than generic determination, because the speaker wants to talk about a certain quantity of antelopes.

What these interchanging uses of generic determination and quantification show is that though they have distinctly different functions, as outlined under 7.4.1, it must be part of the hearer's conceptual knowledge that generic refers to a full set, and is therefore equivalent to universal quantification. Because of this, the speaker can change from generic determination, introduced in one utterance, to plural nouns and/or universal quantification in the next. He knows that the hearer has all the necessary assumptions for appropriate interpretation immediately accessible.

7.4.3   Generics and restricted domains

In example (52) 'the panther' is introduced generically; in the second VP, following *a* 'and', it is said that it 'is all over Africa'. What is interesting in this case is that the property predicated in the first VP conjunct, 'being a strong animal', is a property of all panthers in the world, but the predication of the second conjunct, 'being all over Africa', is not a property of all panthers – yet both conjuncts have the same subject. Thus the determination and quantification of the first conjunct is not identical to that of the second conjunct. Should we conclude from this that the speaker was mistaken about the facts; that he did not know that there are panthers somewhere else? Or is the referent in the second conjunct not to be interpreted as generic? This assumption would be troublesome for Allan's claim that generic definiteness refers to a whole unit of a kind. From the syntactic point of view alone this seems unlikely, since the subject is the same for both VPs.

In the last section I claimed that the speaker can afford to switch freely from generic representation to quantification, because in his logical entry for generic concepts it will be stated that a generic refers to a full set. Does example (52) not cause problems in that the first conjunct suggests a universally quantified interpretation which, if carried over to the second conjunct, would be literally false?

What this example seems to me to show is that generic determination is not exactly equivalent to universal quantification. It may be that 'typicality' is more relevant in certain contexts than the fact that 'universal quantification' is involved. Thus, it could be said that it is typical of the panther to be found in any part of Africa, as it is typical for it to be found in Asia, though not *all* panthers live in Africa nor do *all* of them live in Asia.

It seems that if a certain property applies to a large enough number of the generic kind, the generic form is still appropriate; this is not possible for idiosyncratic predication. Consider (56)–(58):

(56)   The fir tree is found all over Germany.
(57)   ?The fir tree is found in my back garden.
(58)   The fir tree is found in many back gardens.

While it could be said that it is typical of fir trees that they are found in all parts of Germany, it cannot be said that it is typical of fir trees to be in my back garden. However, the generic form seems appropriate again when fir trees are found in many back gardens, because in that case it can be said to be typical of fir trees to be found in back gardens. Therefore (57) is odd, but (56) and (58) are not.

When the hearer interprets an utterance with a generic NP, he must decide whether to interpret it in terms of universal quantification, or of some weaker notion of 'typicality'. These decisions are made for pragmatic reasons. In (52) it would just be inconsistent with other assumptions which the hearer may have about panthers that 'all' of them are living in Africa.

These considerations suggest that Allan is indeed wrong in claiming that definite 'generics' always correspond to the universal quantifier literally used. The problem is that they sometimes do and sometimes do not. One possible answer would be to say that in some generics the universal quantifier is loosely used. Whether or not this solution is correct, the fact that the hearer can nevertheless interpret utterances properly is clearly a matter for pragmatics rather than semantics to explain.

7.4.4   Concluding remarks

This section has shown how generic determination is related to universal quantification, but is not identical to it, and how the speaker may exploit the relation between the two in discourse. From a purely 'surface' point of view, the change from generics to non-generics seems odd. However, the hearer knows that these various representations are not just arbitrary, but are intended to guide him towards different contextual effects.

8 *Co-ordination and stylistic effects*

8.1 Introduction

Sissala has three different forms of 'and', whose use is syntactically conditioned: *ká* is used to conjoin Ss, *a* is used to conjoin VPs, and *rí*, or *arí*, is used elsewhere. The different co-ordination constructions also differ in their pragmatic effects: for example, sentential co-ordination with *ká* might be analysed as suggesting that the event described in the second conjunct was unexpected, whereas non-sentential co-ordinations carry connotations of stereotypicality. The question I shall consider in this chapter is how these pragmatic differences can be explained.

In principle, such differences in pragmatic effect might be traced to any of three sources. First, the various co-ordinating conjunctions might differ in their truth-conditional meaning: use of *ká*, for example, might *entail* that the event described in the second conjunct was unexpected. Second, the co-ordinating conjunctions might have a common truth-conditional meaning but differ in their non-truth-conditional meaning: *ká*, for example, might carry a constraint on relevance (as discussed in chapter 4), specialising it for use in contexts in which an element of unexpectedness was presupposed. Third, the pragmatic differences among conjoined structures might arise not from the lexical meanings of the co-ordinating conjunctions, but from syntactic factors. This is the idea I shall pursue.

My claim will be that where the speaker has a choice between the co-ordination of non-verbal constituents (NVCs), VP co-ordination and S co-ordination; the form he chooses will follow from considerations of relevance. Since S co-ordination requires more linguistic processing effort, it will only be chosen to achieve some extra effect; i.e. some effect that could not have been achieved by the less costly NVC or VP co-ordination. If processing effort were ignored, there would be various theoretical options for dealing with the pragmatic effects of co-

238

ordination. However, on the basis of the principle of relevance, and especially considerations of least effort, only one solution is psychologically plausible.

8.2   The syntax of 'and' in Sissala

In this section, I will briefly sketch the syntax of *rí* (*arí*), *a* and *ká*, and show how their use is syntactically conditioned. In later sections, I will illustrate and discuss their pragmatic effects.

8.2.1   Co-ordination of non-verbal constituents

The co-ordinating conjunction *rí* and its variant *arí* connect NPs, PPs, numerals and adjectives.[1] I will call these 'non-verbal constituents'. In principle, as in English, any number of conjuncts can be used, and *rí* prefaces every conjunct but the first, or it is used only in the last conjunct. The following examples will illustrate this.

Sentences (1) and (2) are examples of NP conjunction: in (1) the conjoined NP is in subject position; and in (2) it is in object position:

(1)   [Pɪlɛ́kɛ́   rí   wɔ́wʋlɛ́nɛ́rɛ́ nɛ́]   mʋɛ́ hɛ́ baksɛ . . .
       [chameleon and spider   SDM] went put farms
       'The chameleon and the spider went and made their farms . . . '
(2)   ʋ ɓidíílé ní   ká [náŋwʋlɛ́ rí   fiŋfiili wɪɛla].
       his food   SDM is [fish   and flying things]
       'His food is fish and flying animals.'

Sentence (3) is an example of PP conjunction; (4) illustrates the conjunction of a series of PPs.

(3)   [Ballɛduoru   wuu sɪɛrʋ rí   ɓiwɪɛla   wuu sɪɛrʋ] lʋ́m   é
       [strong-animals all   in   and small-animals all   in]   speed F
       mʋ́lmɛ́ ɔŋ   kɛ   dɪkáŋ   wuu ní.
       concerning monkey surpasses big-part all   SDM
       'Amongst all the strong animals and amongst all the small animals, as far as speed is concerned, the monkey surpasses most of them.'
(4)   Háálá náŋá de   fɔ́kɛ́ kokísí ná   tá   ká pii   hé
       women other INT shell shells DEF throw-away and take put
       [gbaŋsɛ mɛ́ arí gáráwa nyuu, rí   bɔ́tɔ́wa mʋl   má tɪɪ].
       [calabash into and tins   on-top and sacks   under even]
       'Some women shell them and throw the shells away and put them into calabashes, on top of tins, and even under sacks.'

Sentence (5) is an example of conjoined numerals: 'fifteen' in Sissala is a compound of 'ten' and 'five', and the two numerals are conjoined with *rí*:

(5) ɩ wa-á   a rí-í   nó wó rí   wɔ hé naŋá
     you NEG-IPF do COMP-you see them COMP they put others
     mɛ́ fí, [fi   rí   bɔmmʋɔ].
     at ten [ten and five]
     'You will not see them except in groups of ten to fifteen.'

Finally, (6) is an example containing conjoined adjectives:

(6) Góyáá tuu dé   ká [mʋlá mʋlá rí   sóló sóló].
     guava tree INT is [even   and smooth]
     'The guava tree is even and smooth.'

In none of the above examples could *rí* be replaced by either *a* or *ká*. Examples (7)–(10) are ungrammatical:

(7) (Compare with (1))

     *[Pɩlɛ́kɛ́ $\begin{Bmatrix} a \\ ká \end{Bmatrix}$ wɔ́wʋlɛ́nɛ́rɛ́ nɛ́] mʋɛ́ hé baksɛ.

(8) (Compare with (3))

     *[Ballɛduoru wuu sɩɛrʋ $\begin{Bmatrix} a \\ ká \end{Bmatrix}$ ɓiwɩela wuu sɩɛrʋ] lúm é mʋlmɛ́ ɔŋ kɛ

     dɩkáŋ wuu ní.

(9) (Compare with (5))

     *ɩ wa-á a rí-í nó wó rí wɔ hé náŋá mɛ́ fí, [fi $\begin{Bmatrix} a \\ ká \end{Bmatrix}$ bɔmmʋɔ].

(10) (Compare with (6))

     *Góyáá tuu dé ká [mʋlá mʋlá $\begin{Bmatrix} a \\ ká \end{Bmatrix}$ sóló sóló].

Thus *rí* can occur in these NVC phrases.

8.2.2   Co-ordination of VPs

VPs in Sissala are either conjoined with the co-ordinate marker *a* or are paratactically connected without a marker. Thus, *a* is optional syntactically. The pragmatic effects of its presence or absence are discussed below.

There are certain restrictions on the formation of VP co-ordination or parataxis. All conjuncts are governed by the temporal indication of the first conjunct: thus, if the first conjunct is marked for past tense, then all the other conjuncts are in the past.[2] The following examples will illustrate.

Sentences (11) and (12) are examples of VP co-ordination:

(11)   Ʊ [túmɔ́   (a)   pá   Bʊkɛ́rɛ́].
        she [worked (and) give Bʊkɛ́rɛ́]
        'She worked for Bʊkɛ́rɛ́.'

(12)   l   sɪsɛ́nyɛ́ sɪɛ́ [tɔk   nɪ́ŋ   (a)   mʊ́, (a)   coki yɪ6ʊʊ́   ná,
        you now   so [take fire (and) go (and) cut mound DEF
        (a)   nyɪkɛ   (a)   6a yɪla   viva].
        (and) lighten (and) cut mound IMP-walk]
        'You now take fire. You clear the mound place there and burn (the place). You now form the mounds while walking.'

Example (12) has a series of conjoined VPs, all optionally connected with *a*. 'Optionally', of course, means syntactically optional. In the text from which the example was taken, *a* had to be there for pragmatic reasons. I will discuss this further below.

VP co-ordination is not possible with *rí* or *ká*: (13) and (14) are ungrammatical.

(Compare with (11))

(13)   *Ʊ [túmɔ́ $\begin{Bmatrix} rí \\ ká \end{Bmatrix}$ pá Bʊkɛ́rɛ́].

(Compare with (12))

(14)   *l sɪsɛ́nyɛ́ sɪɛ́ [tɔk nɪ́ŋ $\begin{Bmatrix} rí \\ ká \end{Bmatrix}$ mʊ́, $\begin{Bmatrix} rí \\ ká \end{Bmatrix}$ coki yɪ6ʊʊ́ ná, $\begin{Bmatrix} rí \\ ká \end{Bmatrix}$ nyɪkɛ . . .]

Thus VP and NVC co-ordination have their own special co-ordinating conjunctions in Sissala.

8.2.3   Co-ordination of Ss

Sentential co-ordination is marked with *ká*, which may conjoin two sentences with different subjects and with different tenses. Where there are more than two conjuncts, *ká* like *a*, and like *and* in English, may recur, or it may occur only in the last conjunct. The following example will illustrate: (15) is an example of sentence co-ordination:

(15)   [Betʊ́ʊ́   coŋoroŋ pérí   mɛ́ɛ́trɛ́ bɛllɛ ká   ʊ́   ziŋ   má
        [elephant height   reach meters two   and his weight also
        peri   kíílʊ́   bʊ́í-ammʊɔ.]
        reach kilos thousand-five.]
        'The height of the elephant reaches two meters and his weight reaches five thousand kilos.'

Here, neither *rí* nor *a* is possible. (16) is ungrammatical:

(16)   *[Bétúú coŋgoroŋ pérí méétré bɛllɛ $\begin{Bmatrix} \text{rí} \\ \text{a} \end{Bmatrix}$ ú zíŋ má peri kíílό
búí-ammʋɔ.]

Sometimes, as in (17), the identical subject of the second clause is omitted:

(17)   [ʋ wɪ cáná   pere   ká   [e] lɛ.]
       [she not month reach and [e] left]
       'She did not stay a month, and left.'

That this is sentence rather than VP co-ordination is evidenced by the ungrammaticality of (18) with *a* and *rí*.

(18)   *[ʋ wɪ cáná pere $\begin{Bmatrix} \text{a} \\ \text{rí} \end{Bmatrix}$ [e] lɛ.]

In some cases it is not clear at first sight why the speaker chose sentential co-ordination rather than VP co-ordination with *a*. Consider (19):

(19)   [A lɪsɔ́   ré   ká   [e] tá.]
       [we taken IM and [e] left]
       'We have taken (some) and left (some).'

In this example, the interpretive-use marker, *ré*, is the clue to the choice of *ká*. The whole of the first conjunct is presented as a report of speech, and the scope of *ré* must therefore be the sentence as a whole – making VP conjunction impossible. Thus (20) is ungrammatical:

(20)   *[A lɪsɔ́ ré $\begin{Bmatrix} \text{a} \\ \text{rí} \end{Bmatrix}$ [e] tá.]

In other cases, however, either sentential co-ordination or VP co-ordination would be grammatical, and the choice between them must be made on non-syntactic grounds. Consider (21), for example:

(21)   [Rɪ kɪŋkáná nɛ́   [ɓú óŋ   a   dí]   ká   [e] kááné],
       if lion   SDM [kills a-thing and eats] and [e] leave-over
       ʋ má [mú pú-ú   ní   a   dí.]
       he also [go take-it SDM and eat]
       'If the lion kills something, eats and leaves some, then he (hyena)
       also takes some and eats.'

Here the sentential conjunction *ká* has been chosen at a point where the VP conjunction *a* would not only be grammatical but has, in fact, just been used. Here the speaker must have had pragmatic reasons for choosing S co-ordination with *ká*. I will discuss this case further below (see pages 253–8).

This section was designed to show that there are grammatical restrictions on the use of *rí*, *a* and *ká* and that the three different co-ordinating conjunctions mark NVC co-ordination, VP co-ordination and S co-ordination respectively. The question arises, why does a language have such distinctions, and why does a speaker sometimes use S co-ordination when grammatically he could have used the more economical VP co-ordination? I will discuss these issues in section 8.5.3. First I will briefly review some recent work on pragmatic effects of co-ordination in English.

8.3   Pragmatic effects of *and* in English

The pragmatic effects of co-ordination in English have been well studied in recent years, and it is interesting to note that these studies have tended to discredit lexical explanations. The fact that similar effects are found in all types of Sissala co-ordinate structures provides additional disconfirmation of the lexical approach, since systematic ambiguity would have to be postulated not just in a single co-ordinating conjunction, but in each of three distinct conjunctions. I will briefly outline the results of such studies here.

In formal logic 'and' is truth-functional: if P is true and Q is true then 'P and Q' is also true, whereas, if either P or Q is false, 'P and Q' is false. According to this analysis, 'P and Q' and 'Q and P' are logically equivalent. However, in natural language, as was pointed out by Grice (1967), the order in which the conjuncts are stated may have significant pragmatic effects. Consider (22) and (23):

(22)   Peter went to the shops and bought some wine.
(23)   Peter bought some wine and went to the shops.

Example (22) would normally be construed as conveying that Peter went to the shops in order to buy wine; in (23) this interpretation is not possible. In both cases, an interpretation based on a temporal ordering of the events described is natural, in the absence of further contextual information. Whereas in (22) Peter is understood as having gone to the shops at time t and bought wine at time t+1, in (23) he is understood as having bought the wine at t and gone to the shops at t+1. However, non-temporally ordered interpretations are also possible: for example, as partial answers to the question 'What activities did Peter perform today?'

Grice argues that the temporal, additional, purposive and causative interpretations of co-ordinate constructions in English are not part of the meaning of *and*; he proposes to analyse them as implicatures conveyed by conformity to the maxim 'Be orderly.' Carston (1985, 1988a) argues that they are not implicatures but part of what Grice calls 'what is said', i.e. of the proposition expressed by the utterance, of its explicit truth-conditional content. They are not implicatures, she shows, because like other aspects of truth-conditional content, they fall within the scope of negation and other logical operators.

In saying that these temporal, additive, etc. connotations are not part of the meaning of *and*, we endorse the view that these connotations are due to pragmatic factors. More specifically: Carston (1988a) argues that 'the meanings are the result of the way our minds organise information into connected scenarios or scripts, making a variety of connections amongst events and states of affairs in the world (that variety doubtless determined by innate constraints on our powers of conceptualisation). So we relate events temporally, causally and for that matter spatially.' Thus she claims that these pragmatic effects of co-ordination are the outcome of an interaction between pragmatic principles and general properties of the mind, rather than the meaning of *and*. It is an explanation of this general type that I propose to offer for a rather different range of effects in Sissala.

Blakemore (1987:111–20) makes a rather different point about the pragmatic effects of co-ordination in English. She argues that co-ordinate utterances are not processed in exactly the same way as independent utterances, since a sentential co-ordination is consistent with the principle of relevance only if it has contextual effects not carried by the conjuncts in isolation. On the assumption of relevance theory, the extra processing effort caused by the co-ordinate structure and the conjunction must be compensated for by extra contextual effects. Thus, compare (24) and (25):

(24)   John plays the clarinet. Mary sings.
(25)   John plays the clarinet and Mary sings.

In (24) each of the two propositions is presented as relevant in its own right; in (25), what is presented as relevant is the conjoined proposition as a whole. The hearer of (25) is thus encouraged to look for implications of the proposition as a whole, which could not have been obtained by considering each conjunct in isolation: he might conclude, for example, that John accompanies Mary on the clarinet while she sings – a conclusion which is less clearly warranted by (24).

Here again the pragmatic effects of co-ordination are seen as arising from some non-lexical source. What is particularly interesting about Blakemore's account is that it emphasises the importance of processing effort in the creation of such effects. Within the framework of relevance theory, processing effort is seen as a major influence on pragmatic interpretation (see, for example, Sperber and Wilson 1986a, chapter 4, section 6). This is an idea that I want to pursue.

8.4   Pragmatic effects of co-ordination in Sissala

In general, Sissala co-ordinate structures have the same possibilities of pragmatic interpretation as equivalent structures in English. For example (26) is naturally understood as instrumental ('the pig was beaten with the stick' mentioned in the first conjunct):

(26)   ʊ pí   daa (a)   ŋmɔwɛ koo.
         he took stick (and) beat   pig
         'He beat the pig with a stick.'

However, there is no reason to think that this is due to the lexical meaning of the conjunction *a*. As Carston points out for English *and*, differences among temporal, causal, instrumental, etc. interpretations are the result of an interaction between linguistic structure, pragmatic principles and the way our minds organise information into connected scenarios. Exactly the same arguments apply to Sissala. There is therefore no reason, on the basis of the phenomena so far considered, to postulate anything more than a single truth-conditional sense for the three Sissala words for 'and'.

As mentioned above, the pragmatic effects of co-ordination that concern me in this chapter lie elsewhere. Sometimes a speaker who would have chosen NVC or VP co-ordination uses S co-ordination instead. The effect is generally to suggest that there is something unusual, unexpected or particularly significant about the events described in the second conjunct. For instance, in the case of example (21) above, while it is expected that the lion would eat what he has killed, it is not so much expected that he would leave left-overs. Or consider another example, which has both *a* and *ká*:

(27)   a. ʊ tɔ́ɔ́sɪɛrʊ   jɪsɛ   náŋá,
            its town-inside houses some
        b. 6a   pí   simiti   ni
            they take cement SDM
        c. a   sɔ́   wɔ́
            and build them
        d. ká   6ásɛ́ wɔ́   wuu arí   céŋsé.
            and nail them all   with zinc
            'Some of the houses (of Abidjan) are made with cement and they all have zinc (roofs).'
        e. ʊ jɪsɛ   wɪ jɪɲolli   kéné.
            its houses not mud-roofs have
            'Its houses don't have mud roofs.'

Here the fact that *all* the houses have zinc roofs is unusual, and this conjunct is introduced with *ká* rather than *a*.

One possible account would be to say that *ká*, in addition to its truth-conditional meaning, carries a semantic constraint on relevance, indicating that the proposition it introduces is to be processed in a context which would make it unexpected, unusual or particularly remarkable. The use of *ká* would then be designed to get the hearer's special attention for this information which goes against his expectation. This is similar to the account developed in Carlson's (1987:2–19) analysis of the co-ordinate conjunctions *ká* and *má* in Súpyíré, a language of Mali. According to Carlson's data, the use of these two markers coincides with the uses of *a* and *ká* in Sissala. However, Carlson does not comment on the obvious grammatical difference between them: he sees them as switch-reference markers, with *ma* connecting familiar information and *ká* unfamiliar. In particular, he claims that *ká* indicates that topically new information is being introduced.

Carlson says himself that what exactly is meant by 'topic' is hard to delimit; so his account is at best vague. It seems that he sees the obvious syntactic difference between the two co-ordinating conjunctions as irrelevant. What there is in common between his analysis of these conjunctions in terms of switch reference and an account in terms of semantic constraints on relevance is that no connection is made between syntactic form and pragmatic effects. The pragmatic differences in both cases would result from the lexical meaning of the conjunctions themselves.

There is, however, another possibility. The pragmatic differences between the different types of co-ordination might be derivable from their syntactic differences. As Sperber and Wilson (1986a:202–24) argue, utterances which are truth-conditionally equivalent may, none the less, differ in their stylistic effects. Differences in word order, for example, may be exploited to give favoured access to different encyclopaedic entries, yielding different possible contexts and contextual effects. Differences in linguistic processing cost may be exploited in a variety of ways, in line with the general principle that increases in processing cost must be offset by increases (or at least alterations) in contextual effect. It is this line of explanation that I want to pursue.

Compare the following examples:

(28)   Jim and Jill have gone to Africa.
(29)   Jim has gone to Africa and Jill has gone to Africa.

Suppose that if (28) were used, the most natural assumption in the circumstances would be that Jim and Jill had gone to Africa together. This is not, of course, the only possible interpretation of (28), but let us suppose that in the circumstances in which (28) is uttered it is the most natural one, and hence the only one consistent with the principle of relevance. Then, in these circumstances, a speaker who did *not* want to be understood as saying that Jim and Jill had gone to Africa together would have to find another form of utterance than (28). Example (29), a costlier sentential conjunction, is one obvious candidate. It is costlier, yes, but the less costly form of utterance, (28), is ruled out as carrying undesirable contextual effects. This sketch of an account thus goes some way towards explaining the link between the choice of sentential conjunction and implications of unexpectedness or unusualness in the events described. As will be seen in the next section, considerations of processing effort also affect the choice between *rí* and *arí* as NVC conjunctions, and the presence or absence of *a* in VP conjunctions.

8.5   Stylistic effects of conjunction in Sissala

8.5.1   Parallel NVC processing

My hypothesis is, then, that it is the syntax of co-ordination itself which is responsible for the pragmatic effects of co-ordination. In the light of this hypothesis, let us return to example (1):

(1)   Piléké   rí   wɔ́wʊ́lɛ́nɛ́rɛ́ nɛ́   mʊɛ́ hɛ́ baksɛ . . .
       chameleon and spider   SDM went put farms
       'The chameleon and the spider went and made their farms . . . '

The idea is that NP co-ordination will be used when the most natural assumption about how the chameleon and spider set about making their farms is the one the speaker intends. If there is a stereotypical way of making farms, for example, then the implication is that this is the method both chameleon and spider used. In this sense, a common context can be used for processing each of the conjoined NPs.

Notice now that in some conjoined NPs *arí* is used instead of *rí*. It is used either when the interpretation is meant to be 'with' or when the conjunct added is semantically or pragmatically quite different from the first. Consider (30):

(30)   Múlnémi óŋ   ná   nìɛ́   ha-á   nɛ́ barásɛ́ ná   nɛ́
       now   thing DEF people which-IPF gain dam   DEF SDM
       ká: gɛsɛsɛ-nyii   rí   6ıfoole,   arí naŋwʊlɛ
       is   clothes-washing-water and bathing-water and fish
       bıkana.
       a-lot
       'Now, what the people gain from this dam is this: washing water and bathing water and a lot of fish.'

Example (30) could be seen as an answer to the question 'What do the people gain from the dam?' Each conjunct provides a partial answer to this question. However, 'washing water' and 'bathing water' are semantically and pragmatically similar, whereas 'fish' has little in common with the items mentioned in the two preceding conjuncts. The extra effort needed to process *arí* may give a forewarning of this fact.

Or consider (31):

(31)   Kíŋkáná 6ʊ́ aama   rí   kóní   arí ballɛwiɛla
       lion   kills bushbucks and roan-antelopes and animals-small
       ná   náŋá nɛ́   a-á   dí.
       DEF other SDM and-IPF eat.
       'The lion kills the bushbucks and roan antelopes and the other small animals for eating.'

Clearly, there are greater similarities among types of antelopes than among antelopes and other animals. The suggestion is, then, that the phonologically reduced form *rí* is more appropriate for the second conjunct, and the fuller form *arí* for the third.

8.5.2   Parallel VP processing

What is immediately evident when examining the uses of *a* is that it is sometimes used to conjoin particular verbs which could under no circumstances be S-conjoined with *ká* – verbal combinations which create such interpretations as 'benefactive', 'instrumental', 'comparative', 'causative'; and that at other times, it occurs in co-ordinate constructions in discourse which could in the appropriate circumstances be S-conjoined with *ká*. In the latter case, the choice between *a* and *ká* is pragmatically conditioned.

Let us consider first the more 'fixed' constructions which always have either *a* or no co-ordinate conjunction at all. The latter constructions are of the kind which are typical of serial-verb constructions (SVCs) in other languages (see Bamgbose 1966; Sebba 1987; Stahlke 1974). Sissala, unlike other West African languages, has both serial-verb constructions and VP-conjoining with *a*. I will call the serial-verb constructions 'paratactic structures'. My primary concern is not with paratactic structures; however, since they are variants of the conjoined VP structures which I do want to discuss, I shall mention a few relevant insights from the literature on these constructions.

Christaller's (1875) study of Twi contrasts 'essential combinations' and 'accidental combinations'. The former are what I have called 'fixed combinations' of verbs. According to Christaller, in such constructions one verb is principal and the other is an auxiliary verb, yielding an adverb of time or manner. Bamgbose (1982), who uses the terminology 'co-ordinate SVC' for the non-fixed kind and 'modifying SVC' for the fixed kind, is of the opinion that though in the latter type one of the verbs has a different meaning from its use in single-verb constructions, it is still a full verb, as long as it does not differ morphologically from other verbs. I share Bamgbose's view, and since all such verbs in Sissala (except *ka* 'take (it)') undergo normal verb affixing, I will treat these constructions as normal VP co-ordinations when *a* is present, and as non-subordinating paratactic structures when *a* is absent.

Though syntactically there seem to be no real problems involved, the question is how are these constructions to be viewed propositionally? In particular, do they express a single proposition or two co-ordinate propositions? It seems obvious that in many African languages main verbs have the function performed by prepositions and adverbs in European languages. It has, indeed, been observed that these verbs change over time into prepositions and adverbs (Ansre 1966). It therefore seems likely that some of these constructions express only one proposition with adverbial modification. The same is true when the two verbs form idioms, expressing only a single concept.

I shall present the data with *a* in brackets in shorter examples, which have not been taken from particular texts. However, in longer examples I shall mark the presence and absence of *a* as they occurred in my texts. *A* is optional syntactically but not pragmatically, i.e. in some contexts VP co-ordination is pragmatically preferable to parataxis, and in other cases parataxis is preferable to VP co-ordination. While commenting on the interchangeability of VP co-ordination with parataxis, some speakers would say, 'It is all right, but it sounds funny – children speak like this.' Having introduced the data, I will sketch a pragmatic explanation for the presence or absence of *a*.

I have already given some examples of VP co-ordination of the 'accidental' kind. Let us consider two more examples in order to see how they differ from the fixed kind:

(32)   ʊ mʊ́ yɔwɔ (a) yɔwɛ ɓɪɛ.
       she went market (and) bought things
       'She went to the market and bought things.'
(33)   ʊ cɔ́ bɪdíílé (a) dí [e].
       she cooked food (and) ate [e]
       'She cooked food and ate it.'

In both cases the natural interpretation is a temporal one, with the action described in the first conjunct preceding that described in the second. Where *a* is left out, and the utterance requires marginally less processing effort, according to the argument developed above, one would expect the event to happen exactly according to the stereotype or scenario of going to a market, and of cooking and eating food. The addition of *a*, with its marginal increase in processing effort, might alert the hearer to some minor departure from stereotypicality, and hence some slight increase in the relevance of the conjunct introduced.

The next examples are of Christaller's 'essential combination' kind, and the verb 'to give' has a prepositional interpretation such as 'for' or 'to'. *Pá*, for instance, never has this prepositional interpretation other than in these co-ordinate constructions. I shall describe the data using such traditional terms as 'benefactive', 'instrumental', etc., to which I do not ascribe any particular syntactic or semantic function: they are just a convenient shorthand for the sort of interpretation that would be conveyed:

(Benefactive)
(11) Ʋ túmɔ́   (a)   pá   Bʋkέrέ.
      she worked (and) gave Bʋkέrέ
      'She worked for Bʋkέrέ.'
(34) Ʋ búlɔ́   (a)   pá   háálɔ́.
      he spoke (and) gave woman
      'He spoke to the woman.'

(Instrumental)
(26) Ʋ pí   daa   (a)   ŋmɔwɛ   koo.
      he took stick (and) beat   pig
      'He beat the pig with a stick.'

(Comparative)
(35) Ʋ túmɔ́   (a)   kíllέ   Bʋkέrέ.
      he worked (and) surpassed Bʋkέrέ
      'He worked more than Bʋkέrέ.'

(Terminative)
(36) Ʋ túkó   (a)   tenni.
      she pounded (and) finished
      'She finished pounding.'
(37) Ʋ bísέ   nyii   (a)   ta.
      she poured water (and) throw-away
      'She poured the water away.'

The difference between the presence and absence of *a* in these examples can be explained along the lines laid out above, with the paratactic constructions connecting, if anything, a slightly more stereotypical sequence of events. And, of course, the more stereotypical the sequence of events, the more likely it is to be describable in terms of a single (perhaps complex) proposition rather than two independent propositions, each with its own relevance.

That VP co-ordination may have not only a 'mono-propositional' but also a 'mono-conceptual' interpretation can be seen from the following example. It involves the verb *ka*, which could be translated as 'take it'. It is verbal, but has an implicit object, usually co-referential with an object in a preceding conjunct. The verb could be seen as having a causative function, and together with other verbs it conveys the meaning of 'bring'.

(38)   ʊ pí   namɪɛ́ (a)   ka   (a)   ko.
        he took meat (and) take-it (and) come
        'He brought the meat.'

There are also idiomatic co-ordinations which represent only one concept. These expressions are dead metaphors, i.e. the semantic content of the individual words is no longer consciously accessed. The hearers will access a conceptual representation directly when hearing this idiom. Consider (39)–(42):

(39)   ʊ lá   wɪɛ   (a)   di.
        he took matter (and) eat
        'He believed the matter.'
(40)   ʊ lá   ʊ   (a)   ta.
        he took him (and) throw-away
        'He saved him.'
(41)   ʊ pi   ʊ   háálɔ́ wɪɛ́ di rʊ́-ʊ́   bél   ʊ   bio.
        he took his wife's words ate COMP-she watch her child
        'He believed his wife's statement that she watched the child.'
(42)   ʊ bʊl pɔ-ʊ,   rʊ́-ʊ́   la   ʊ   wɪɛ   di.
        he said gave-her, COMP-he take her words eat
        'He said to her that he would believe her.'

The hypothesis that these examples are mono-conceptual is strengthened by the fact that they may either function like higher verbs in propositional-attitude constructions, or be subordinated under a verb of propositional attitude. In (42), for instance, the matrix sentence is made up of a paratactic structure and the subordination includes a VP co-ordination.

While it seems clear that these last examples are idiomatic and have come into the language via metaphor, the exact current status of other constructions is not so clear. My hypothesis is that these so-called 'essential combinations' are idiom chunks too. Verbs like *pa* 'give' and *kɪllɛ* 'surpass' are also 'dead metaphors'. Their conceptual representation is learned and accessed as a unit. There is no evidence, however, that the verbs involved have become prepositions or adverbs.

On the account just developed, it is easy to see why these mono-propositional or mono-conceptual constructions are barred from S co-ordination with *ká*: they cannot be analysed as expressing two different propositions, each making its own contribution to relevance.

In the next section I will discuss in more detail the difference between S co-ordination and VP co-ordination.

8.5.3   S co-ordination versus VP co-ordination

I shall now develop the hypothesis outlined in previous sections by looking at longer stretches of natural text. My main claim is that VP co-ordination is used for relatively more predictable or stereotypical situations, while S co-ordination is used for departure from the interpretation that would be assigned to VP co-ordination on the basis of the principle of relevance, and, more generally, from normal or stereotypical states of affairs.

In (43), from the third conjunct onwards, every conjunct is connected with *a*, except for one which is introduced with *ká*:

(43) ı   kúsέ wɔ́   wuu.
      you cut   them (rice plants) all
      ı   kúsέ
      you cut
      a   hé
      and put
      a   vɔwɛ guumé,
      and bind bunch
      a   hé kúré   mí,
      and put basket in
      a   ka
      and take
      a   ko   jaa,
      and come house
      a   ka
      and take
      a   ko   bil
      and come put
      a   dááné mʋɔɔ,
      and last   a-bit
      ká [e] pí   ŋmɔwɛ,
      and [e] take beat
      a   sıέ máŋsέ
      and now measure
      a   ná έ   ná ı   muì há ɔsέ
      and see manner the your rice how produce
      a   mʋ́ peri.
      and go reach
      'You cut them (rice plants) all. You cut them and bind them into bunches. You put them in a basket and go home. You leave them for a little while and then you beat them. You measure them in order to see how much rice you have produced.'

Syntactically, this discourse consists of two conjoined sentences, each with a cluster of conjoined VPs. The break between the two conjoined Ss coincides with a break in the action after the rice plants have been left for a while. The natural reaction for the hearer is to see the treatment of the rice plants as falling into subroutines, corresponding to two separate schemas in memory, each with its own conditions and consequences. In this case, one might see the difference between VP and S co-ordination as being used to *create* schemas and stereotypes, rather than, as in less procedural discourse, merely exploiting existing schemas.

Because of the length of the discourses I shall present the next example by giving only the English translation and the *a* and *ká* markers.

(44)   How to make TZ (savoury millet porridge).
        If you want to prepare TZ you pound millet,
        a take, enter and wash,
        a take out, let swell.
        You take it, come, grind
        a take, come,
        a sweep rubbish,
        ká boil bathing water,
        a pour out
        ká make, you add sour water.
        So when it boils, you take a light calabash
        a take
        a come, make the flour wet
        a take, pour
        a take ladle, stir,
        a take ladle out,
        ká leave (it).
        (When) it is ready, you look for scraper
        arí ladle
        a take
        a come
        a make (porridge) less (take some out)
        ká so add flour
        a prepare
        a stir.
        It ready, you take out, put TZ calabash in
        a gather
        a go, give TZ-eaters.

This discourse fits the account just presented for (43). In both (43) and (44), *a* occurs with activities which follow each other immediately in time, and which might be regarded as belonging to the same subroutine or subschema. *Ká*, as one would expect on this account, involves rather greater discontinuities.

As we see, not all verbal connections are marked with *a* or *ká*. Those not so marked are highly predictable, and there are more highly predictable actions in (44) than in (43), at least in the eyes of a Sissala, who has access to a scenario for grain preparation. Thus, it is highly predictable that if one takes a stirring stick, one will stir with it; whereas if one takes flour, prepares it and then stirs, the act of stirring is less predictable. This example thus fits the account of the differences between VP co-ordination and parataxis developed in the previous section.

The first *ká* is used when the first phase of TZ making has been completed and the second one starts. The subsequent uses of *ká* fall into the same pattern. My hypothesis is, then, that in this type of procedural text the use of *ká* is a valuable clue to the organisation of the speaker's encyclopaedic memory, and the way she 'chunks' behaviour into routines and subroutines. This example seems to suggest that *ká* and S co-ordination is always used when the activity takes a different 'turn' from the way things went before, where the notion of 'turn' connects with the way information is 'chunked' in memory.

In the following stretches of discourse things are not going at all as expected, and *ká* is used more often. As predicted by the account just outlined, the speaker takes into account the hearer's expectations of how things work under 'normal' circumstances; when things do not go that way, he uses the sentence conjunction *ká*.

When I say that *a* marks more 'expected' actions or states of affairs, this is relative. Of course, none of the activities in (43) and (44) is so predictable that describing them would be irrelevant – particularly to a novice or outsider. But the Sissala speaker has the two types of 'and' available, which he exploits in such a way that he demands special attention from the hearer when he uses *ká* and S co-ordination, for the reasons outlined above.

Example (45) contains extracts from a longer piece of text describing the famine in Burkina Faso.

(45)   a.   When things grew like this all the people said: 'excellent' that this year the crops will grow well.

       b.   This did not last one month
          ká the drought stayed.

       c.   So all the seedlings withered
          ká there was only one here and one there left.

       d.   We had thought that it would be the corn *nɛ* which would save the people.

e.   The name of 'corn' is not even used this year *dé*.
f.   *Ká* when the drought was like this there was no grass for the
     animals to eat.
g.   They were all lean
     ká stayed (to be) skin and bones,
     ká the majority of them died.

Example (45a) describes what the people expected, and the following
utterances describe how events turned out differently. Some of the
conjuncts with *ká* have different subjects and could not have been
replaced by VP co-ordination. However, in (45g) for instance, there is an
implied subject and I suggest that *ká* is preferred to VP co-ordination
because of the element of unexpectedness involved.

Consider a further example, also involving expected and unexpected
states of affairs: (46) is a riddle with its solution.

(46)   a.   A thousand men went farming
            ká did not clear a lot.
       b.   *Ká* one man went farming
            a cleared a lot.
       Solution:
       c.   Many stars appear
            ká they do not have much light.
       d.   *Ká* the moon only appears
            a gives much light.

What is interesting in example (46) is the fact that the many stars giving
little light is conjoined with *ká*, and yet this fact is known to everyone.
The reason for this is to preserve the parallelism to (46a), in which *ká* has
already been used. Here the use of *a* would destroy the analogy. The
contrast between *ká* and *a* may be conditioned by quite subtle and
complex pragmatic factors, as this example shows. Simple analyses in
terms of 'expected' or 'unexpected' events will not always work. What
conditions the choice between *ká* and *a* are considerations of optimal
relevance, i.e. considerations of contextual effect and processing effort.
Generally, unexpected events yield greater contextual effects; the construction of non-stereotypical contexts may involve greater processing
effort. But these are not the only factors affecting contextual effect and
processing effort, and are therefore not the only factors affecting the
choice between sentence and VP co-ordination.

When hearing the first conjunct of (46), the hearer must access certain
assumptions about how much a thousand men could do. The use of *ká*
rather than *a* warns the hearer that the proposition to follow is relevant in

its own right, perhaps because it does not fit this expectation; in (46b) he again uses *ká*, this time for purely syntactic reasons, since a new subject NP is used. The choice of *a* in the fourth line suggests that there is something predictable about the amount that particular man cleared. The result is an impression of paradox, which is only resolved when the two statements are reproduced in the context suggested by the interpretation of (46c–d).

Or consider (47):

(47)   Bala   tɛŋ   to   solosolo, ʊ taŋá ká hʊrahʊra ré,
         monitor-lizard skin is-NEG smooth   it really is rough   TDM
         ká   wɪ   nyʊŋɛ tɛŋ péré.
         and/but NEG frog   skin reach
         'The monitor lizard's skin is not smooth, it is rather rough, but not
         like the frog's skin.'

Here, the use of *ká* might be seen as preventing the hearer from drawing a conclusion he might otherwise have drawn: that the monitor lizard has skin as rough as a frog's.

In example (48), the *ká* has its usual conjoining function, which here results in a 'denial of expectation' interpretation:

(48)   a. Tié   wuu hɪl,
          earth all   dry
          'All the ground was dry',
      b. mɪɛ   paarʊ wuu hil a   vɔwɛ náŋá   mɛ́,
          millet leaves all   dry and stick together at
          'the millet leaves are all dry and stick together',
      c. lɛɛmɪɛ bónní ɓallɛ pɛ́ tíe,
          corn   broken fallen lie ground
          'the corn is broken, has fallen and is lying on the ground',
      d. síwié   paarʊ wuu gunni,
          groundnut leaves all   folded
          'all the groundnut leaves are folded',
      e. ká píɛ́ é dé wɪ   nyʊ́ɛ́   má wuú.
          and yams F F NEG germinated even
          'and the **yams** did not even germinate'.

Every conjunct from (48b) to (48e) provides evidence for (48a), which is not part of the conjunction. Every conjunct provides a partial answer to the same question: 'What were the consequences of the dry ground?' Conjunct (48e) is the most extreme case and is marked with *ká*, with the implication 'this is against your expectations'.

To sum up: what distinguishes the use of S co-ordination with *ká* from

VP co-ordination with *a* is that the conjoined VPs require less processing effort. S co-ordination should be preferred to VP co-ordination only where the use of VP co-ordination would run the risk of misinterpretation, because the interpretation the speaker has in mind is not the one that would be assigned to the VP co-ordination by the criterion of consistency with the principle of relevance. Hence, the intuition that the states of affairs appropriately described by S co-ordination are somehow less typical, usual or predictable than those appropriately describable by VP co-ordination.

In this chapter I have tried to show that the implications of 'unexpectedness' that attach to certain cases of sentential co-ordination in Sissala do not arise from a lexical source, but receive a natural explanation within the framework of relevance theory. At this point someone might object that I have only shown that there *is* an alternative to the lexical explanation – I have not shown that this alternative is to be preferred. Here I would draw the reader's attention to some differences in pragmatic effect which cannot be explained in lexical terms. If *ká* itself creates an effect of unexpectedness, or, more generally, any of the pragmatic effects described in the previous sections, then it should create these effects wherever it appears. However, as pointed out above, these pragmatic effects are, in fact, selectively created: they appear wherever *a* could have been used in preference to *ká*, but not elsewhere (see the discussion of (45) above, for example). It is hard to see how this variation in pragmatic effects could be explained in lexical terms. My results thus tend to confirm what has become increasingly apparent over the years: not all pragmatic effects have semantic causes.[3]

8.6   General conclusion

I have presented this study, on the one hand, as a contribution to the semantic and pragmatic analysis of a particular unstudied language – Sissala; and on the other, as an illustration of the role that relevance theory can play in guiding and constraining such an analysis. I hope that the arguments I have developed have borne out both these claims. In this conclusion, I would like to make a few more general remarks about the broader theoretical implications of my work.

The major claim I made in the first two chapters was that cohesion, coherence and topic are neither necessary nor sufficient for textuality and comprehension, but that relevance relations between text and context are at the heart of comprehension and discourse connectivity. This theoretical insight had an effect on the analysis of the Sissala data in chapters 3 to 8. It could indeed be shown not only that relevance theory can more adequately account for phenomena traditionally dealt with in cohesion, coherence and topic-based frameworks, but also that it accounts for phenomena which hitherto lacked a theoretical explanation altogether. I will review a few of these phenomena in the following paragraphs.

First, I would like to mention the analysis of the particle *ré*. The relevance-theoretic notion of interpretive use proved to play a crucial role in the analysis of this particle. In previous frameworks, *ré* would almost certainly have been analysed as a 'hearsay' particle. I have tried to show how, on a 'hearsay' analysis, an important range of uses of *ré* would have had to be ignored. My study thus suggests that a re-examination of so-called 'hearsay' phenomena in other languages might yield fruitful results. Thus, an important generalisation about a certain phenomenon in Sissala could be recognised and explained within relevance theory, a generalisation which might be exemplified in many other languages.

Secondly, a detailed comparison of the uses of 'also' in English, Sissala and German revealed that the modal and conjunctive uses in Sissala and German and the non-modal uses in English could be explained, taking the relevance-theoretic notion of contextual effect into account. This insight led to the search for other kinds of universal generalisations: I have tried to show how a relevance-based framework suggests a new approach to particle typology. On the one hand, there is a distinction between truth-conditional and non-truth-conditional particles; or in relevance-theoretic terms, between particles that contribute to the propositional content of an utterance, and those that act as semantic constraints on relevance, or guides to processing. I have suggested some criteria for distinguishing these two categories of particle.

On the other hand, within non-truth-conditional particles, one can distinguish inferential and non-inferential varieties, both of which I have examined at some length. One important result has been to show that many inferential particles are geared to achieving particular types of contextual effect – and this fact, I have argued, enables the analyst to bring out a variety of cross-linguistic similarities and differences in particle use.

Other theoretical areas in which I have tried to make a contribution are semantic and stylistic. I have looked in detail at a particle that raises a number of questions about the semantic distinction between ambiguity and vagueness; and I have looked at three different forms of 'and' and their associated stylistic effects.

Though a lot more areas of discourse research than I was able to cover could adequately be dealt with in relevance theory, the areas I did cover point to a new direction in the study of discourse. Once it has been understood that discourse is connected by relevance relations between text and context rather than between parts of text, the notions of 'topic', 'coherence', 'foregrounding' and 'backgrounding' become irrelevant. These notions were theoretical crutches which were embraced because no adequate notions of context and context selection existed. It is inevitable that with a new insight into what discourse connectivity consists of, there will be a shift of theoretical interest. To some degree this shift is to be seen in this study. The obvious areas of theoretical interest in discourse, as I see them and which I have covered, are the distinction between truth-conditional and non-truth-conditional phenomena; the distinction between descriptive and interpretive use; the different ways utterances may have contextual effects; and how linguistic form (words, syntax, etc.) constrains the hearer's processing. By researching these areas it should be possible to come nearer to the goal that most discourse analysts seem to have: to be able to explain the correlation between the structure of discourse and the communicative effects the speaker wants to achieve in the hearer. On a linguistic level, this new approach should lead to greater understanding of the relation between structure and function, and to greater insights into a variety of hitherto puzzling linguistic phenomena – as it did with the Sissala data in this study.

As concerns the task of a field linguist and ethnographer, I hope that the promise of new explanations for a lot of 'puzzling' phenomena in the many still unanalysed languages will spark new interest in research. I hope further that I have shown that by examining particular data within a rich theoretical framework – such as relevance theory – one can not only illuminate the data themselves, but also shed valuable light on theoretical assumptions.

Notes

1   What is discourse?

1 For discussion of the grammaticality/acceptability distinction, see Chomsky (1965, ch. 1).
2 For a discussion of the issues, see Levy-Brühl (1926), Lukes and Hollis (1982), Quine (1959).
3 See Lukes and Hollis (1982) and in particular Sperber (1985).
4 Linguists who have focused their attention on particular cohesive devices which they regard as dominant in guaranteeing textuality or coherence include Reinhart (1983), Givón (1983) for anaphoric structural relations, and Grimes (1975), and Combettes (1983) for thematic relations.
5 As noted earlier (p. 10), I define discourse and text in a broad sense, so that any appropriate exchange is a well-formed text.
6 It is by accident that all sentences in this part of the text have a *dé*.
7 This is not how I use the word 'utterance' though. I apply it solely to linguistic stimuli.

2   Relevance theory and discourse

1 A contextual implication is a special type of logical implication, derived by a restricted set of deductive rules which derive at most a finite set of conclusions from any finite set of premises (see Sperber and Wilson 1986a: 65–108).
2 It might be thought that the distinction between logical and encyclopaedic entries rests on the belief that there are two different kinds of truth: analytic and synthetic truth. However, Sperber and Wilson do not claim that there are two different kinds of truth, but merely that there is a crucial formal and functional distinction between logical and encyclopaedic entries. Encyclopaedic entries are propositional, logical entries are computational. The same information may be representable in either propositional or computational terms, but *both* propositions *and* computations are necessary components of most current computational theories of mind.
3 For other general issues dealing with relevance theory, see Sperber and Wilson (1981, 1982a, 1987) and Wilson and Sperber (1985, 1986, 1987, 1988b).

3   The interpretive-use marker *ré*

1 Hearsay markers have been reported from languages all round the world. They have been found in the Americas, and they seem to be especially common in Australian languages, in languages of Nepal and the Philippines. In African languages, they have been reported to exist as special complementisers in Engenni (Thomas 1978) and Mupun (Frajzyngier 1988).

2 For a shorter version of this chapter, see also Blass (1989c).

3 Examples (12) and (13) contain a use of *ré* not so far encountered: it occurs in final position in (12) and after 'important matter' in (13). In both, *ré* is marked TDM (for typicality discourse marker, see ch. 6). This use has no obvious relation to the COMP and particle uses discussed so far. One of the remaining *ré* markers causes a problem too: we have *ré* following 'think', which is a clear case of 'COMP'; and we have another *ré* following the initial adverbial phrase 'amongst all the animals'. I have not been able to decide whether this is better analysed as a complementiser or a particle.

4 The pronoun is non-referential. These constructions are common in Sissala, since the language has no passive.

5 For further treatment of irony within relevance theory, see Wilson and Sperber (1989).

6 It is possible that *ré* in this case has the function of marking 'non-specific' (see ch. 6). In this case the interpretive use of *ré* would be purely echoic. Further investigation in this area is necessary

4   Constraints on relevance and particle typology

1 Kempson (1975) argues that *therefore* in the scope of logical operators does make contributions to truth conditions.

2 Karttunen and Peters' (1975) analysis of *again* seems to be mistaken (see ch. 6).

3 The terms 'modal' and 'adverbial' are the traditional terms for these phenomena. I do not ascribe to them any particular theoretical content.

4 There are examples in German, like the following, which seem to be counter-examples to my claim:

> A: Man sollte viel mehr für die Umwelt tun.
>   'Much more should be done for ecology.'
> B: Man kann doch nicht alle Autos ohne Katalysator von heute auf morgen aus dem Verkehr ziehen.
>   'It is not possible to ban all cars without catalytic converters overnight.'
> A: Das habe ich **auch** nicht gesagt.
>   'I didn't say that, did I?'

However, although the utterance in which *auch* occurs contradicts the preceding utterance, *auch* is used to confirm something in the context, namely the fact which should have been obvious, that A did not make the claim just imputed to him. Therefore this is not a counter-example to my claims.

5   *Baa*: **truth-conditional or non-truth-conditional particle?**

1 The negative in Sissala may optionally be indicated with SOV word order alone (see Blass 1980).
2 Of course, only the strictly temporal interpretation is possible in English.
3 For a similar discussion of *baa*, see Blass (1989a), and for a similar discussion of other particles within relevance theory, see Blakemore (1988a), Gutt (1988) and Smith and Smith (1988).

6   **Defining in Sissala**

1 Kempson and Cormack (1980) argue that there is vagueness between the specific and non-specific interpretation of the English indefinite marker rather than ambiguity.

     The formal realisations of *ré* and *né* are due to the same phonological rules as the interpretive-use marker (see ch. 3, section 3.3.1).
2 Welmers (1973:309–10) writes about similar phenomena in Fanti and Twi. According to him, the former makes a difference between 'identity with something' marked with *ni* and description of something, which is marked with *yè*. The latter has what Welmer calls 'verbs', *bù* for identification and *di* for description. Welmers uses those examples in the context of 'it is identifiable as fire', which would be with *bù*, and 'it is describable as fire', which would be with *di*.
3 It is also possible that the use of right dislocation was merely to make sure that the referent of *they* had been correctly established as 'people who had caught them'. In that case it would be a repair. I was not able to check on the speaker's intentions.
4 This fits in with remarks above about the use of *this* in colloquial English as a specific indefinite.

7   **Meanings and domains of universal quantification**

1 The uses of *wuu* in (15) and (16) provide support for a quantificational analysis in (14), which might also be seen as adverbial, meaning 'completely'. However, there are no other examples supporting this analysis.

8   **Co-ordination and stylistic effects**

1 The adjective in this case is what I called 'ideophone' in chapter 6. However, ideophone is not a grammatical notion and can apply in Sissala to adverbials and adjectivals. Only adjectivals can coordinate with *rí*. I have therefore decided to use 'adjective' here.
2 It is, however, possible to have all conjuncts except the last marked with perfective aspect and the last marked with imperfective aspect, in which case the last conjunct has a purposive interpretation.
3 For a similar treatment of Sissala 'and', see also Blass (1989b).

References

Allan, K. 1986. *Linguistic meaning, vols. I and II.* London and New York: Routledge and Kegan Paul.

Altmann, H. 1976. *Die Gradpartikeln im Deutschen. Untersuchungen zu ihrer Syntax, Semantik und Pragmatik.* Tübingen: Niemeyer.

Anderson, R. C. 1977. 'The notion of schemata in the educational enterprise', in C. Anderson, R. J. Spiro and W. E. Montague (eds.), *Schooling and the acquisition of knowledge.* Hillsdale, N.J.: Lawrence Erlbaum.

Anderson, R. C., R. E. Reynolds, D. L. Schallert and E. T. Goetz 1977. 'Frameworks for comprehending discourse', *American Educational Research Journal* 14: 367–81.

Ansre, G. 1966. 'The verbid – a caveat to "serial verbs"', *Journal of West African Languages* 3 (1):29–32.

Bach, K., and R. Harnish 1979. *Linguistic communication and speech acts.* Cambridge, Mass.: MIT Press.

Ballard, L. 1974. 'Telling it like it was, Part 1:4, "hearsay particle" of the Philippine languages'. *Notes on Translation* 51:28. Dallas: SIL.

Bamgbose, A. 1966. *A grammar of Yoruba,* West African Language Monographs 5. Cambridge: Cambridge University Press.

1982. 'Issues in the analysis of serial verbal constructions', *Journal of West African Languages* 12 (2):3–22.

Barnes, J. 1984. 'Evidentials in the Tuyuca verb', *International Journal of American Linguistics* 50:255–71.

Beaugrande, R. de 1980. *Text, discourse, and process. Towards a multidisciplinary science of texts,* London and New York: Longman.

Bellert, I. 1974. 'Über eine Bedingung für die Kohärenz von Texten', in W. Kallmeyer, W. Klein, R. Meyer-Hermann, K. Netzer and H. J. Siebert (eds.), *Lektürekolleg zur Textlinguistik, Band II: Reader,* Frankfurt: Athenäum Fischer.

Bendor-Samuel, J. (ed.), 1989. *The Niger-Congo languages.* Lanham/London: University Press of America.

Blakemore, D. 1987. *Semantic constraints on relevance,* Oxford: Basil Blackwell.

1988a. '"So" as a constraint on relevance', in Kempson (1988), 183–95.

1988b. 'The organization of discourse', in Newmeyer (1988), vol. IV: *Language: The socio-cultural context,* 229–50.

Blass, R. (ed.), 1975. *Sisaala–English, English–Sisaala dictionary,* Ghana: Institute of Linguistics.

1980. 'The Sissala negative in the light of universal predictions', unpublished MA thesis, University of London.

1986. 'Cohesion, coherence and relevance', *Notes on Linguistics* 34:41–64. Dallas: SIL.

1988. 'Discourse connectivity and constraints on relevance in Sissala', unpublished Ph.D thesis, University of London.

1989a. '*Baa*: truth-conditional or non-truth-conditional particle?' in Weydt (1989), 416–27.

1989b. 'Pragmatic effects of co-ordination: the case of "and" in Sissala', *UCL Working papers in linguistics*, 32–51, London: University College London.

1989c. 'Grammaticalisation of interpretive use: the case of *ré* in Sissala', *Lingua* 79: 299–326.

Bloomfield, L. 1933. *Language*, New York: Holt, and (1935), London: Allen and Unwin.

Bransford, J. D. and M. K. Johnson 1973. 'Considerations of some problems of comprehension', in W. G. Chase (ed.), *Visual information processing*, New York: Academic Press.

Brown, G. and G. Yule 1983. *Discourse analysis*, Cambridge: Cambridge University Press.

Callow, K. 1974. *Discourse considerations in translating the word of God*, Grand Rapids, Mich.: Zondervan Publishing House.

Carlson, R. 1987. 'Narrative connectives in Sùpyìré', in R. S. Tomlin (ed.), *Typological studies in language*, vol. IX, *Coherence and grounding in discourse*, 1–19, Amsterdam: John Benjamins.

Carston, R. 1984. 'Semantic and pragmatic analysis of *and*', paper read at the spring meeting of the Linguistics Association of Great Britain.

1988a. 'Implicature, explicature and truth-theoretic semantics', in Kempson (1988).

1988b. 'Language and cognition', in Newmeyer (1988), vol. III, *Language: Psychological and biological aspects*, 38–68.

Chafe, E. and J. Nichols (eds.), 1986. *Evidentiality*, Norwood: Ablex.

Charolles, M. 1983. 'Coherence as a principle in the interpretation of discourse', *Text* 3 (1): 71–97.

Chomsky, N. 1965. *Aspects of the theory of syntax*, Cambridge, Mass.: MIT Press.

1981. *Lectures on government and binding*, Dordrecht: Foris.

Christaller, Rev. J. G. 1875. *A grammar of the Asante and Fante Language called Tshi*, Basel: Basel Evangelical Missionary Society. Republished 1965, Ridgewood: Gregg.

Clark, H. H. 1977. 'Bridging', in P. Johnson-Laird and P. Wason (eds.), *Thinking: readings in cognitive science*, Cambridge: Cambridge University Press.

Clark, H. H. and E. V. Clark 1977. *Psychology and language*, New York: Harcourt Brace Jovanovich.

Clark, H. H. and C. Marshall 1981. 'Definite reference and mutual knowledge', in A. Joshi, B. Webber and I. Sag (eds.), *Elements of discourse understanding*, Cambridge: Cambridge University Press.

Combettes, B. 1983. *Pour une grammaire textuelle. La Progression thématique*, Brussels.

Crozier, D. H. 1984. 'A study in the discourse grammar of Cishingini', unpublished Ph.D. thesis, University of Ibadan.

Dahl, Ö. 1975. 'On generics', in L. Keenan (ed.), *Cambridge colloquium on formal semantics of natural language*, 99–111, Cambridge: Cambridge University Press.

Derbyshire, D. C. 1979. *Hixkaryana*, Lingua Descriptive Series, 1, Amsterdam: North Holland.

Doherty, M. 1973. '*Noch* and *schon* and their presuppositions', in F. Kiefer and W. Ruwet (eds.), *Generative Grammar in Europe*, 154–77, Dordrecht: Reidel.

Donaldson, T. 1980. *Ngiyambaa: the language of the Wangaaybuwan*, Cambridge: Cambridge University Press.

Donnellan, K. S. 1966. 'Reference and definite description', *Philosophical Review* 77:203–15.

Dowty, D. R. 1979. *Word meaning and Montague Grammar*, Dordrecht, Boston, London: Reidel.

Dowty, D. R., R. E. Wall and S. Peters 1981. *Introduction to Montague Semantics*, Dordrecht: Reidel.

Firth, J. R. 1957. *Papers in linguistics 1934–1951*, London: Oxford University Press.

Fodor, J. A. 1983. *The modularity of mind*, Cambridge, Mass.: MIT Press.

Frajzyngier, Z. 1988. 'The de dicto domain in language', paper presented at the Symposium on Grammaticalization: Eugene, Oregon, May 1988.

Franck, D. 1980. *Grammatik und Konversation*, Königstein: Scriptor.

Funke, E. 1928. 'Die Isala-Sprache im Westsudan. Kurzer Abriß ihrer Grammatik', *Mitteilungen des Seminars für orientalische Sprachen*, issues 23, 24, 25, section 3.

Gazdar, G. 1979. *Pragmatics, implicature, presupposition, and logical form*, London, New York: Academic Press.

Givón, T. 1976. 'Topic, pronoun and grammatical agreement', in C. N. Li (ed.), *Subject and topic*, 149–88, New York: Academic Press.

(ed.) 1979. *Syntax and semantics*, vol. 12: *Discourse and syntax*, New York: Academic Press.

1982. 'Evidentiality and epistemic space', *Studies in Language 6* (24):24.

(ed.) 1983. *Topic continuity in discourse. A quantitative cross-language study*, Amsterdam and Philadelphia: John Benjamins.

Greenberg, J. H. 1966. 'Some universals of grammar with particular reference to the order of meaningful elements', in J. H. Greenberg (ed.), *Universals of language*, 73–113, Cambridge, Mass.: MIT Press.

Grice, H. P. 1957. 'Meaning', *Philosophical Review*, 66: 377–88.

1967. 'Logic and conversation', unpublished William James lecture, Harvard University.

1975. 'Logic and conversation', in P. Cole and J. L. Morgan (eds.), *Syntax and semantics*, vol. III: 41–58, *Speech acts*, New York: Academic Press.

1978. 'Further notes on Logic and conversation', in P. Cole and J. Morgan (eds.), *Syntax and semantics*, vol. 9: *Pragmatics*, 113–25, New York: Academic Press.

Grimes, J. E. 1975. *The thread of discourse*, Janua Linguarum Series Minor 207, The Hague: Mouton.

(ed.) 1978. *Papers on discourse*. Dallas: SIL.

Gutt, E.-A. 1988. 'Towards an analysis of pragmatic connectives in Silt'i', in *Proceedings of the eighth International Conference of Ethiopian Studies, Addis Ababa University*, vol. I, 665–78, Hundingdon: ELM.

Halliday, M. A. K. 1984. 'Language as code and language behaviour: a systemic-functional interpretation of the nature of ontogenesis of dialogue', in R. P. Fawcett, M. A. K. Halliday, M. Lamb and A. Makkai, *The semiotics of culture and language*, vol. I, London and Dover, N.H.: Frances Pinter.

Halliday, M. A. K. and R. Hasan 1976. *Cohesion in English*, London: Longman.

Harris, Z. 1952. 'Discourse analysis' *Language* 28: 1–30 and 474–94.

Haviland, J. B. 1987. *Fighting words: evidential particles, affect and argument*, Berkeley Linguistics Society, 13, Berkeley, Calif.: Berkeley Linguistics Society.

Hawkins, J. A. 1978. *Definiteness and indefiniteness: A study in reference and grammaticality prediction*, London: Croom Helm.

Hewitt, B. G. 1979. *Abkhaz*, Lingua Descriptive Series, 2, Amsterdam: North Holland.

Hobbs, J. R. 1978. 'Why is discourse coherent?' Technical Note 176, SRI Project 5844, 7510, 7910.

1979. 'Coherence and coreference', *Cognitive Science* 3: 67–90.

Hoepelman, C. and C. Rohrer 1981. 'Remarks on *noch* and *schon* in German', in P. J. Tedeschi and A. Zaenen (eds.), *Syntax and semantics*, vol. XIV *Tense and aspect*. New York, London: Academic Press.

Höhlig, M. 1978. 'Speaker orientation in Syuwa (Kagate)', in Grimes (1978), 19–24.

Hopper, P. J. 1979. 'Aspect and foregrounding in discourse', in Givón (1979), 213–41.

Hymes, D. 1964. 'Toward ethnographies of communicative events' in P. P. Giglioli (ed.), *Language and social context*, Harmondsworth: Penguin.

Johnson-Laird, P. N. 1981. 'Comprehension as the construction of mental models', in *The psychological mechanisms of language*, Philosophical Transactions of the Royal Society of London, London, The Royal Society and The British Academy.

1983. *Mental models*, Cambridge: Cambridge University Press.

Karttunen, F. and L. Karttunen 1977. '*Even* questions', in *NELS 7: Proceedings of the seventh annual meeting of the North Eastern Linguistic Society*, 115–34.

Karttunen, L. 1974. 'Presupposition and linguistic context', *Theoretical Linguistics* 1: 181–94.

Karttunen, L. and S. Peters 1975. 'Conventional implicature in Montague

Grammar', in *Proceedings of the first annual meeting of the Berkeley Linguistics Society*, 266–78, Berkeley Linguistics Society 1, Berkeley, Calif.: Berkeley Linguistics Society.

1979. 'Conventional implicature', in Ch. Oh and D. A. Dinnen (eds.), *Syntax and semantics*, vol. 11: *Presuppositions*, 1–56, New York: Academic Press.

Kempson, R. M. 1975. *Presupposition and the delimitation of semantics*, Cambridge: Cambridge University Press.

(ed.) 1988. *Mental representation: the language reality interface*, Cambridge: Cambridge University Press.

Kempson, R. M. and A. Cormack 1980. 'Quantification and ambiguity', *Linguistics and Philosophy* 4: 259–309.

König, E. 1977. 'Temporal and non-temporal uses of *noch* and *schon*', *Linguistics and Philosophy* 1: 173–98.

1981. 'The meaning of scalar particles in German', in H. J. Eikmeyer and H. Rieser (eds.), *Research in texttheory, words, worlds and contexts*, 107–32, Berlin: de Gruyter.

Laughren, M. 1981. 'Propositional particles in Walpiri', in S. Swartz (ed.), *Papers in Walpiri grammar, in memory of Lothar Jagst*, Darwin: SIL-Australia.

Levinsohn, S. H. 1975. 'Functional perspectives in Inga', *Journal of Linguistics* 11:1–37.

Levy-Brühl, L. 1926. *How natives think: Les fonctions mentales dans les sociétés inférieures*, London: George Allen and Unwin.

Longacre, R. E. 1976. '"Mystery" particles and Affixes', *Chicago Linguistics Society*. 12:468–75.

1983. *The grammar of discourse*, Dallas: SIL.

Lowe, I. 1972. 'On the relation of the formal and sememic matrices with illustrations from Nambiquara', *Foundations of Language* 8:360–90.

Lukes, S. and M. Hollis (eds.), 1982. *Rationality and relativism*, Oxford: Blackwell.

Lundquist, L. 1986a. 'Marqueurs d'orientation et programme argumentatif', unpublished ms.

1986b. 'Argumentative text structure, a procedural model', unpublished ms.

Lyons, J. 1975. 'Deixis as the source of reference', in E. L. Keenan (ed.), *Formal semantics of natural language*, 61–83, Cambridge: Cambridge University Press.

1977. *Semantics*, 2 vols., Cambridge: Cambridge University Press.

1981. *Language, meaning and context*, London: Fontana.

Maclaran, R. 1982. 'The semantics and pragmatics of the English demonstratives', unpublished Ph.D. thesis, University of Cornell.

Manessy, G. 1969a. *Les Langues Gurunsi*, vol. I, Bibliothèque de la SELAF 12, Paris: SELAF.

1969b. *Les Langues Gurunsi*, vol. II, Bibliothèque de la SELAF 13, Paris: SELAF.

1979. *Contribution à la classification généalogique des langues voltaïques*, Langues et civilisations à tradition orale, 37. Paris: SELAF.

Minsky, M. 1975. 'A framework for representing knowledge', in P. H. Winston, *The psychology of computer vision*, New York: McGraw-Hill.

Morton, A. 1986. 'Domains of discourse and common-sense metaphysics', in Travis (1986), 105–24.

Naden, A. 1989. 'Gur', in Bendor-Samuel (1989), 141–68.

Newmeyer, F. J. (ed.) 1988. *Linguistics: The Cambridge survey*, 4 vols., Cambridge: Cambridge University Press.

Nunberg, G. D. 1977. 'The pragmatics of reference', unpublished doctoral dissertation, City University of New York.

Palmer, F. R. 1976. *Semantics, a new outline*, Cambridge: Cambridge University Press.

1986. *Mood and modality*, Cambridge: Cambridge University Press.

Pike, K. L. 1967. *Language in relation to a unified theory of the structure of human behaviour*, The Hague: Mouton.

Pike, K. L. and E. G. Pike 1977. *Grammatical analysis*, Dallas: SIL.

1983. *Text and tagmeme*, London: Frances Pinter.

Quine, W. V. 1959. 'Meaning and translation', reprinted in J. A. Fodor and J. J. Katz (eds.), *The structure of language: Readings in the philosophy of language*, 461–78, Englewood Cliffs, N.J.: Prentice-Hall, 1964.

1960. *Word and object*, Cambridge, Mass.: MIT Press.

Reinhart, T. 1983. *Anaphora and semantic interpretation*, Chicago: University of Chicago Press.

Rombouts, J. 1979. 'Dutch *nog* and *al* as degree particles', in W. Vandeweghe and M. Van de Velde (eds.), *Linguistische Arbeiten, Bedeutung, Sprechakte und Texte*, Tübingen: Niemeyer.

Rothkegel, A. 1979. '*Wieder* und komplexe Verbbedeutungen', in Weydt (1979), 299–308.

Rowland, R. 1965. *Collected field reports on the phonology of Sisala*, University of Ghana: Institute of African Studies.

Rumelhart, D. E. and D. A. Norman 1978. 'Accretion, tuning and restructuring: Three models of learning', in J. W. Cotton and R. L. Klatzky (eds.), *Semantic factors in cognition*, Hillsdale, N.J.: Lawrence Erlbaum.

Sacks, H. 1972. 'An initial investigation of the usability of conversational data for doing sociology', in D. Sudnow (ed.), *Studies in social interaction*, New York: The Free Press.

Samet, J. and R. Schank 1984. 'Coherence and connectivity', *Linguistics and Philosophy* 7: 57–82.

Schank, R. C. and R. Abelson 1977. *Scripts, plans, goals and understanding*, Hillsdale, N.J.: Lawrence Erlbaum.

Searle, J. 1969. *Speech acts*, Cambridge: Cambridge University Press.

Sebba, M. 1987. *The syntax of serial verbs*, Creole Language Library, 2, Amsterdam: John Benjamins.

Seuren, P. A. M. 1985. *Discourse semantics*, Oxford: Basil Blackwell.

Slobin, D. 1979. *Psycholinguistics*, Glenview, Ill.: Scott, Foreman.

Slobin, D. and A. Aksu 1982. 'Tense, aspect and modality in the use of the Turkish evidential', in P. J. Hopper (ed.), *Tense–aspect: Between semantics and pragmatics*, 185–200, Amsterdam: John Benjamins.

Smith, N. V. 1975. 'On generics', *Transactions of the Philosophical Society*, 27–48.

(ed.) 1982. *Mutual knowledge*, London: Academic Press.

Smith, N. V. and A. Smith 1988. 'A relevance-theoretic account of conditionals', in L. Hyman and Ch. Li (eds.), *Language, speech and mind. Studies in honour of Victory A. Fromkin*, London: Routledge.

Sperber, D. 1985. *On anthropological knowledge*, Cambridge: Cambridge University Press.

Sperber, D. and D. Wilson 1982a. 'Pragmatics', *Cognition* 10:4.

1982b. 'Mutual knowledge and relevance in theories of comprehension', in Smith (1982), 61–131.

1986a. *Relevance: Communication and cognition*, Oxford and Harvard: Basil Blackwell.

1986b. 'Loose talk', *Proceedings of the Aristotelian Society 1985/6*, 86:153–71.

1987. 'Précis of *Relevance: Communication and cognition*', *Behavioural and Brain Sciences*, 10: 697–754.

Stahlke, H. F. W. 1974. 'Serial verbs', *Studies in African Linguistics* 1 (1): 60–99.

Stalnaker, R. 1974. 'Pragmatic presupposition', in M. Munitz and P. Unger (eds.), *Semantics and philosophy: Studies in contemporary philosophy* 197–293, New York: New York University Press.

1975. 'Presuppositions', in D. Hockney, W. Harper and B. Freed (eds.), *Contemporary research in philosophical logic and linguistic semantics*, Dordrecht: Reidel.

Thavenius, C. 1983. *Referential pronouns in English conversation*, Lund: Liber.

Thomas, E. 1978. *A grammatical description of the Engenni language*, Dallas: SIL.

Thorne, J. P. 1972. 'On the notion "definite"', *Foundations of Language* 8:562–8.

1974. 'Notes on "Notes on 'On the notion "definite"'"', *Foundations of Language* 11:111–14.

Travis, C. (ed.) 1986. *Meaning and interpretation*, Oxford: Basil Blackwell.

Van de Velde, R. G. 1984. 'Prolegomena to inferential discourse processing', *Pragmatics and Beyond*, 5 (2).

Van Dijk, T. A. 1977. *Text and context*, London and New York: Longman.

Vendler, Z. 1967. *Linguistics in philosophy*, Ithaca: Cornell University Press.

Welmers, W. E. 1973. *African language structures*, Berkeley, Los Angeles and London: University of California Press.

Werth, P. (ed.) 1981. *Conversation and discourse*, London: Croom Helm.

1984. *Focus, coherence and emphasis*, London: Croom Helm.

Weydt, H. (ed.) 1977. *Aspekte der Modalpartikeln*, Tübingen: Niemeyer.

(ed.) 1979. *Die Partikeln der deutschen Sprache*, Berlin and New York: Walter de Gruyter.

1983. *Partikeln und Interaktion*, Tübingen: Niemeyer.

(ed.) 1989. *Sprechen mit Partikeln*, Berlin: de Gruyter.

Willet, T. 1988. 'A cross-linguistic survey of the grammaticalisation of evidentiality', *Studies in Language* 12:51–97.

Wilson, D. 1975. *Presupposition and non-truth-conditional semantics*, London and New York: Academic Press.

References 271

Wilson, D. and D. Sperber 1979. 'Ordered entailments: an alternative to presuppositional theories', in C. K. Oh and D. A. Dinneen (eds.), *Syntax and semantics*, vol. XI *Presupposition*, New York and London: Academic Press.

1981. 'On Grice's theory of conversation', in Werth (1981), 155–78.

1985. 'An outline of relevance theory', in H. O. Alves (ed.), *Encontro de linguistas actas, unidade cientifico-pedagógica de letras e artes*, Minho, Portugal: Universidade do Minho, 21–41; also in *Notes on Linguistics* 39: 5–24, Dallas: SIL.

1986. 'Inference and implicature', in Travis (1986), 45–75.

1988a. 'Representation and relevance', in Kempson (1988), 133–53.

1988b. 'Mood and the analysis of non-declarative sentences', in J. Dancy, J. Moravcsik and C. Taylor (eds.), *Language, duty and value*, Stanford: Stanford University Press.

1989. 'On verbal irony', in *UCL Working Papers in Linguistics*, vol. 1, London: University College London.

Index